COMMUNICATING IN MULTINATIONAL ORGANIZATIONS

INTERNATIONAL AND INTERCULTURAL COMMUNICATION ANNUAL

Volume XVIII   **1994**

Co-Editors

Richard L. Wiseman
California State University, Fullerton

Robert Shuter
Marquette University

Editorial Assistants

Judith A. Sanders
California State Polytechnic University, Pomona

Tasha Van Horn
California State University, Fullerton

Consulting Editors for Volume XVIII

Rosita Albert
University of Minnesota

Benjamin Broome
George Mason University

Patrice M. Buzzanell
Michigan State University

Fred L. Casmir
Pepperdine University

Povl Henningson
Århus School of International Business, Denmark

L. Brooks Hill
Trinity University

Young Yun Kim
University of Oklahoma

Robert McPhee
University of Wisconsin at Milwaukee

Tsukasa Nishida
Nihon University, Japan

William Starosta
Howard University

Lea Stewart
Rutgers University

June O. Yum
Towson State University

INTERNATIONAL AND INTERCULTURAL COMMUNICATION ANNUAL
VOLUME XVIII   1994

COMMUNICATING IN MULTINATIONAL ORGANIZATIONS

edited by

Richard L. WISEMAN
Robert SHUTER

**Published in Cooperation with
the Speech Communication Association
International and Intercultural Communication Division**

SAGE Publications
International Educational and Professional Publisher
Thousand Oaks   London   New Delhi

For information address:

SAGE Publications, Inc.
2455 Teller Road
Thousand Oaks, California 91320
E-mail: order@sagepub.com

SAGE Publications Ltd.
6 Bonhill Street
London EC2A 4PU
United Kingdom

SAGE Publications India Pvt. Ltd.
M-32 Market
Greater Kailash I
New Delhi 110 048 India

Printed in the United States of America

Library of Congress Cataloging-in-Publication Data

ISBN 0-8039-5538-3
ISBN 0-8039-5539-1 (pbk.)
ISSN 0270-6075

97 98 99 00 01 02 03 04 10 9 8 7 6 5 4 3 2

Sage Production Editor: Astrid Virding

Contents

Preface   vii

PART I: THEORETICAL AND RESEARCH FOUNDATIONS

1. Communication in Multinational Organizations: 3
   Conceptual, Theoretical, and Practical Issues
   Robert Shuter and Richard L. Wiseman

2. Intercultural Organizational Communication Research   12
   in Multinational Organizations
   JC. Bruno Teboul, Ling Chen,
   and Lynn M. Fritz

3. Minimizing Threats to the Validity of Cross-Cultural   30
   Organizational Research
   Jeffrey C. Ady

**PART II: CULTURAL BASES FOR COMMUNICATION IN
MULTINATIONAL ORGANIZATIONS**

4. Communication in Japanese Multinational   45
   Organizations
   Alan Goldman

5. Communication in Latin American Multinational   75
   Organizations
   Lecia Archer and Kristine L. Fitch

6. Communication in Multinational Organizations in the   94
   United States and Western Europe
   Donald P. Cushman and Sarah Sanderson King

**PART III: DIVERSITY AND ADJUSTMENT IN
MULTINATIONAL ORGANIZATIONS**

7. Intercultural Challenges and Personal Adjustments: 117
    A Qualitative Analysis of the Experiences of
    American and Japanese Co-Workers
    Young Yun Kim and Sheryl Paulk

8. Co-Cultural Communication Within the Organization   141
    Devorah A. Lieberman and Ellene Gurtov

9. Cultural Diversity and Intercultural Training in   153
    Multinational Organizations
    Rosita Daskal Albert

References   166

Index   187

About the Contributors   191

Preface

This is the eighteenth volume of the **International and Intercultural Communication Annual.** This series is sponsored by the Speech Communication Association's International and Intercultural Communication Division. The series of theme-based publications aims at promoting better understanding of communication processes in international and intercultural contexts. The guiding principle in preparing this volume was to bring together current theoretical and research studies focusing on communication in multinational organizations. More specifically, *Communication in the Multinational Organization* presents emic and etic approaches, theory and empiricism, to provide a basis for an international exploration and unique insights into intercultural organizational communication within and among organizations in Latin America, Asia, Western Europe, and the United States. Recommendations for topics and research methods of future studies are made.

The volume is developed in three parts. Part I presents theoretical and research foundations for the investigation of intercultural organizational communication. Metatheoretical, theoretical, and empirical bases for research are explored. Decisions regarding conceptualization, operationalization, research design, and sampling are examined. Part II probes the cultural bases for communication in multinational organizations by contrasting Latin American, Asian, Western European, and North American styles of communicating. Part III details issues regarding cultural diversity, intercultural training, and adjustment in the workforce. The volume should be of assistance to scholars, trainers, and practitioners involved with organizations crossing cultural or national boundaries.

We would like to note that the order of editorship is not an indication of editorial contribution; both editors collaborated equally in the creation, conceptualization, and execution of this volume. Both of us contributed considerable time, resources, and energy in bringing this project to fruition. We hope the quality of the volume reflects our extensive efforts.

Many people were involved in the completion of the volume. First, we want to extend our appreciation to all of the authors who donated their time and energy to this volume. Without their creative thinking, articulate expression, and long hours of work, this volume would not exist. Second, we want to thank Judith Sanders and Tasha Van Horn, the editorial assistants, for their keen eye for composition, logic, and coherence, and to all of the editorial board members for generously offering their time and expertise in reviewing manuscripts. Last but not least, we wish to thank our families for their patience, sacrifice, and emotional support.

Richard L. Wiseman
California State University, Fullerton
Robert Shuter
Marquette University

I

THEORETICAL AND RESEARCH FOUNDATIONS

1

Communication in Multinational Organizations

Conceptual, Theoretical, and Practical Issues

ROBERT SHUTER • *Marquette University, Milwaukee*
RICHARD L. WISEMAN • *California State University, Fullerton*

Multinational organizations (MNOs) are increasingly dominating the world economy. U.S. companies expanded their markets between 1980 and 1992 by opening foreign subsidiaries in ever-increasing numbers. European and East Asian companies extended their reach during the last two decades with subsidiaries across the globe. Joint ventures have multiplied as well, with European, Japanese, and U.S. MNOs joining forces to develop and deliver products on a worldwide basis.

As multinational companies have globalized their operations, organizational communication has become more complex. Not only are organizations struggling to adapt their communication to a world customer base, but communication within and between multinational organizations is also confounded by cultural issues. In this chapter, we provide an overview of the literature on communication in MNOs, offer a communication perspective for conducting research in the multinational setting, and preview the contributions made in this volume.

COMMUNICATION IN MULTINATIONAL ORGANIZATIONS

Although the body of literature on MNOs is growing, little of this research has focused on communication or, especially, intercultural organizational communication (Shuter, 1989). In contrast, research abounds on managing across cultures (Adler, 1983; Hofstede, 1980), training in multinational organizations (Tung, 1987), career development (Black & Mendenhall, 1990), culture shock (Furnham & Bochner, 1986), negotiating across cultures (Sullivan, 1981), and leadership style in business settings (Smith & Petersen, 1988). Limited research has been conducted by business scholars on interpersonal and small group factors in MNOs, including initial interaction, conflict communication, and nonverbal messages (Sullivan, 1981; Usunier, 1991). Although communication researchers have examined these factors interculturally, few of these investigations have been conducted in MNOs (Friday, 1989).

Two major thrusts can be identified in the research and theory on MNOs: an approach stressing organizational universals, and an approach focusing on national cultural differences. The organizational-universals literature posits organizational principles and behaviors that are endemic to organizations regardless of culture. For example, Hickson, Hinings, McMillan, and Schwitter (1974) argue that as organizations become larger, they decentralize controls, develop more formal procedures, and become more specialized. Similarly Doktor, Lie, and Pillon (1991) use systems theory to analyze international management and offer a supranational organizational framework that can be applied globally, eliminating the need for regional adaptations.

The Aston studies, a comprehensive investigation of organizational structure and behavior worldwide, frequently are cited as the principal evidence for organizational universals (Seror, 1988). Interestingly, Donaldson (1986) criticizes the Aston studies by suggesting that their conclusions are limited to Western countries. For example, analyses of Hong Kong, Japanese, British, and U.S. firms of comparable size uncovered dissimilar organizational structures and behaviors (Lincoln & Kalleberg, 1990; Redding & Pugh, 1986).

The research on organizational universals has suggested that certain leadership traits are effective worldwide (Sarros, 1992; Wittenberg-Cox, 1991). These traits include flexibility, sense of humor, patience, resourcefulness, and positive regard for others (Thornton, 1990). The research on intercultural communication effectiveness, though not specifically aimed at organizational success, also identifies similar traits that are presumed to be effective worldwide (Abe & Wiseman, 1983; Ruben, 1977).

Researchers have identified leadership principles that are thought to be generalizable across the globe. For example, Howe (1971) suggests that leadership style works best when it facilitates a subordinate's progress toward a goal, whereas Vroom and Yetton (1973) argue that leadership style must be consistent with the types of decisions being made. Hersey and Blanchard (1982) report that leadership style must be adapted to the subordinate's maturity, and Fiedler (1967) offers a contingency theory of leadership based on several group factors as well as task complexity.

The literature on organizational universals also identifies factors related to expatriate success (Bird & Dunbar, 1991), principles for improving communication between MNOs and their subsidiaries (Zeira & Shenkar, 1990), and critical components of effective global marketing in public relations campaigns (Garfein, 1989). Despite the extensive literature on organizational universals, there is compelling research that national culture has a significant influence on organizational behavior.

The literature on the influences of national culture on organizational behavior can be divided into two major areas: etic and emic approaches to organizations. The *etic approach* assumes that certain national cultures share common values and can be grouped into value classifications (Hofstede, 1980). In contrast, the *emic approach* does not attempt to classify cultures on the basis of values; rather, it draws conclusions about organizational dynamics within a specific country. Most research is of an etic nature and focuses largely on organizational behavior, rather than on communication.

In the etic literature, Hofstede (1980) concludes that societies can be classified on the basis of four value dimensions: individualism-collectivism, power distance, uncertainty avoidance, and masculinity-femininity. Using his value studies, researchers have conducted cross-national investigations on various organizational dynamics to compare and contrast cultural types, such as collectivistic versus individualistic societies. For example, Smith (1992) offers a cogent analysis of the many ways national culture is expressed organizationally. Using Hofstede's value research as a springboard, Smith and Tayeb (1988) demonstrate how persons from collectivistic cultures—notably Japan, Taiwan, India, and Iran—tend to gravitate to a single effective leadership style, as opposed to persons from individualistic cultures, who find a variety of leadership styles effective. Zhurvlev and Shorokhova (1984) examine selected individualistic societies in Europe and the former Soviet Union and find that effective leaders adapt their styles to situational demands. Stewart (1985) examines organizational decision making in several countries and notes that decision-making style is a function of cultural values, with a technical and logical style employed in individualistic cultures such as the U.S. and Britain, and a social-collective style employed in group-oriented cultures such as Japan. Likewise, Bass, Burger, Doktor, and Barrett (1979) study the effects of cultural values on decision making and managerial communication in 12 countries. Finally, Adler's (1983, 1991) research also demonstrates the linkage between cultural values and organizational behavior.

The emic approach to cross-cultural organizational studies has become increasingly popular in recent years, with guides being published on how to do business in certain countries (Axtell, 1989; Copeland & Griggs, 1985), as well as more scholarly investigations (Barsoux & Lawrence, 1991; Eze, 1984). Most of this research focuses on management behavior, with few communication studies on other aspects of organizational life (Adler, 1991).

After conducting a computer search of 800 business journals, Shuter (1992) found that since 1989, the most-researched countries outside the U.S. on management behavior and communication are Japan (66 studies) and the People's Republic of China (22 studies). Interestingly, few published studies were located since 1989 on management behavior and communication in the remaining countries of the world. For example, only five studies were found on French managers, nine on German managers, and no reported studies on Danish, Swiss, or Spanish managers. In fact, only 26 investigations on management behavior and communication were located for 17 countries in Europe, Asia, Africa, and Latin America, when Japan and China were excluded from the computer search.

Despite the limited number of studies using the emic approach, many of them have heuristic value in understanding organizational behavior. For example, the bulk of Middle Eastern organizational studies focuses on three areas: (a) Middle Eastern work values, (b) Arabic management style, and (c) motivational issues in Middle Eastern organizations. Yasin and Stahl (1990) find Arab managers emphasizing affiliation and achievement, rather than power, in managing people. Consistent with this finding, Abboushi (1990) identifies job involvement and organizational affiliation as key work values of Palestinian Arabs. However, Atiyahi's (1992) extensive review of Arabic organization and management research finds conflicting views of Arab managers as authoritarian and consultative, which Atiyahi argues cannot be explained by culture alone.

The research on European organizations and management is also heuristic, but inconclusive due to its limited and fragmented nature. For example, French management and organizations frequently are described as hierarchical and benevolent dictatorial (Barsoux & Lawrence, 1991; Siegle, 1993). In contrast, German management sometimes is viewed as participative (Siegle, 1993) and occasionally is described as overly controlling (Grunwald & Bernthal, 1983). Swedish organizations consistently are found to be among the least hierarchical and most participative in Europe (Shuter, 1985b). Unfortunately, little of the research on European organizations focuses on communication. Notable exceptions are Friday's (1989) research on German discussion behaviors in the workplace, Barsoux and Lawrence's (1991) examination of French managers' argumentation patterns, and Shuter's (1985a) review of European interpersonal practices in the workplace.

Country- and region-specific research is abundant on East Asian organizations, particularly Japan and the People's Republic of China, with only a few investigations of management practices in other Asian countries (Swierczak, 1991). The rich data on Japanese management and communication practices are exemplary because they provide a detailed examination of the Japanese system, including the development of intracultural management theory (Misumi & Peterson, 1985).

Finally, management and organizational research in Latin America and Africa is scarce, with most research available on Mexico (Ayman & Chemers, 1991; Chemers & Ayman, 1985; Page & Wiseman, 1993), Brazil (Rossi & Todd-Mancillas, 1987), and Nigeria (Eze, 1984). The dearth of investigations on organizational behavior and communication in these regions makes it very difficult to draw valid conclusions about organizational life in Latin America and Africa.

IN SEARCH OF A COMMUNICATION PERSPECTIVE

Because the bulk of the research on MNOs has been conducted by business scholars and social psychologists, it is not surprising that the literature on both organizational universals and national cultural influences infrequently focuses on communication issues. What is missing from much of this research is an examination of communication factors that are linked historically to the fields of intercultural or organizational communication. Moreover, it is difficult to locate a dedicated line of research on an organizational communication factor across multiple national cultures. As a result, we know little about *communication* in MNOs, and even less about multinational communication in specific countries and world regions.

Research providing a communication perspective is essential because communication shapes the form and functioning of MNOs. For an organization to be effective multinationally, it must develop effective internal and external communication. As organizational communication becomes intercultural, another dimension is added to the analysis necessary to understand MNOs. Shuter (1984, 1985b, 1990b) hypothesized that *intercultural organizational communication* (IOC) is the interface between national culture and organizational communication. More specifically, IOC occurs in the organizational setting and reflects the national culture (the country in which an organization and its employees reside). For example, to fully understand German employees and German corporate culture, an IOC perspective requires a close examination of the relationship between German culture and German organizational communication. In an extension of this reasoning, Shuter (1989) offers a framework for studying IOC identifying specific communicative factors affected by national culture: (a) organizational structure and communication (e.g., departmental communication), (b) role performance in an organizational culture (e.g., management style), (c) international human resource communication (e.g., expatriate and repatriate communication), (d) communication between corporate headquarters and foreign subsidiaries, and (e) marketing communication.

In search of a communication perspective, researchers interested in MNOs need to focus their attention on organizational questions that deal fundamentally with the transfer and reception of information within and between organizations in the same or different national cultures. This perspective raises several basic communication questions that have yet to be answered or, in most instances, addressed by multinational researchers.

1. What is the linkage between national culture, corporate culture, and organizational communication?
2. How does national culture influence the communication between organizations in different countries?
3. How does national culture influence communication within and between organizations in the same country or world region?
4. How do ethnicity and race influence the transmission and reception of information within and between organizations in the same national culture?

Although the extant literature is clearly insufficient to provide definitive answers to any of these questions, this volume both reviews the existing literature relevant to each question and provides a framework to shape our research in search of more definitive answers.

INTERCULTURAL ORGANIZATIONAL COMMUNICATION: PERSPECTIVES OF THIS VOLUME

Carping about the paucity of comprehensive research on communicating in MNOs is not sufficient for an increasingly interdependent world where multinational corporations are becoming even more pervasive and powerful. What is needed are books, such as this volume, that examine MNOs from a communication perspective. This volume is a groundbreaking effort for several reasons. For example, it examines the relationship between national culture, corporate culture, and communication behavior. Teboul, Chen, and Fritz's analysis (Chap. 2) is noteworthy for its conceptual thoroughness and its articulation of hypotheses that link national culture and organizational communication. Teboul et al. provide a framework for examining the first three of our questions. Using Hofstede's values, they identify a number of hypotheses about the relationship between MNO structuring processes (formalization, complexity, centralization) and communication. They further suggest that a thorough understanding of communication in MNOs must consider informal communication networks, organizational assimilation, and new communication technologies. Their hypotheses and research questions can structure our search for the links between organizational communication, national culture, organizational culture, crossnational communication, and intraregional communication.

Research in each new context brings both promises and pitfalls. Ady (Chap. 3) provides us with cautions in our search for answers to our questions by articulating ways to reduce validity errors in cross-cultural and intercultural organizational communication research. He argues for a careful conceptualization and definition of culture, as well as the identification of pancultural variables that exhibit less cross-cultural variance than culture-specific variables. He provides the foundation for avoiding confounding variables in intercultural organizational communication and examines the problem of measure equivalence across cultures. Thus Chapters 2 and 3 serve as conceptual springboards for delving into country- and region-specific investigations of MNO communication, as well as intercultural communication within and among MNOs.

How does national culture influence communication between organizations in different countries? Kim and Paulk (Chap. 7) provide insight into that question by a richly detailed ethnographic examination of the communication of Japanese and U.S. co-workers in a Japanese multinational organization located within the United States. Their analysis examines the difficulties that arise in intercultural organizational communication and identifies cognitive, affective, and behavioral strategies that workers found most helpful in overcoming such problems. They provide specific, real-life examples of the ideas of accommodation and divergence in the speech accommodation theory (Giles, Mulac, Bradac, & Johnson, 1987) and adaptation (Kim, 1988) fundamental to intercultural communication competence. Beyond identifying problems in intercultural organizational communication, Albert (Chap. 9) examines the need for worker training and methods to minimize such problems.

The relationship between national culture and communication within and among MNOs is explored in several ways in this volume. The inclusion of chapters on communication in European, Latin American, and East Asian organizations is one of the volume's distinctive features. Goldman (Chap. 4) argues for the need for emic approaches to understanding the Japanese organization. He helps provide this awareness by elucidating the philosophic principles infused in communication in Japanese organizations. Archer and Fitch's research (Chap. 5) may be one of the first attempts to identify communication themes endemic to Latin America and then to trace their impact on organizational life. Again, they stress the need for an emic understanding of Latin American organizations and provide us with the frame to derive that knowledge. Finally, Cushman and King (Chap. 6), writing on Western Europe, present a descriptive comparison of organizational structure and communication in European versus American corporations. By identifying the communication characteristics of extremely successful model organizations in the United States and Western Europe, they detail the influence of national culture on organizational communication.

The role of ethnicity and race within and between organizations in the same national culture is examined in Chapters 8 and 9. Persons in MNOs not only communicate across national borders but also are generally employees from different ethnic groups and races who may share the same national culture. In the United States, the organizational mix of ethnic groups and races is referred to as *cultural diversity*. Cox and Nkomo (1990) provide one of the most compelling analyses of cultural diversity research to date. They argue in their meta-analysis of studies published in 20 major business journals between 1964 and 1989 that race and ethnicity are infrequently the subject of organizational studies and that the "recent trend is for less rather than more research" (p. 419). Shuter (1990a) notes similar trends in major communication journals and surprisingly few studies on race and ethnicity between 1980 and 1989. However, Liebermann and Gurtov (Chap. 8) offer a model of cultural diversity and communication in organizations. They provide both a strong argument for the need to increase such research and the framework to guide study on communication in multicultural settings. Examining the need to minimize such difficulties, and providing a structure to do so, Albert (Chap. 9) explores training insights for culturally diverse organizations. The research of Kim and Paulk (Chap. 7) also explores the impact of ethnicity within the MNO.

As organizations globalize, so does our need to explore intercultural communication. This volume, through both emic and etic approaches, theory and empiricism, provides a basis for our international exploration and provides unique insights into intercultural organizational communication within and among organizations in Latin America, Asia, Western Europe, and the United States. With greater insight and understanding of the communication in MNOs, we can promote cultural synergy in the workforce (Moran & Harris, 1982) and reap the benefits of greater productivity, higher morale, and better relationships among the members of the multinational organization.

2

Intercultural Organizational Communication Research in Multinational Organizations

JC. BRUNO TEBOUL • *DePaul University, Chicago*
LING CHEN • *University of Oklahoma, Norman*
LYNN M. FRITZ • *Antolino & Associates, Inc.*

The multinational organization (MNO) is an ascendant organizational form in today's global business environment. This trend is readily apparent in the consistent increases in both U.S. direct investment abroad and foreign direct investment in the United States during the last decade. According to the U.S. Bureau of Economic Analysis, U.S. investment abroad increased from $215 billion in 1980 to $373 billion in 1989. Foreign direct investment in the United States increased even more dramatically: from $83 billion in 1980 to a preliminary figure of $401 billion in 1989 (U.S. Bureau of the Census, 1991). Further, the total number of multinational corporations operating in the United States was estimated recently to be 3,500 (Harris & Moran, 1991).

Given the internationalization of business, one would expect an abundant amount of programmatic research to be devoted to understanding how "firms that own and control activities in more than one country" function (Rosenzweig & Singh, 1991, p. 340). Although it is true that MNOs have been given a good deal of attention over the years, extant scholarship on this type of organization comes to us mainly from the fields of economics and business management. One of the greatest contributions these areas of inquiry make to our understanding of MNOs lies in their documentation of the economic and financial aspects of MNO operations. Here, they render evident the extent to which the environmental complexity (Huber & Daft, 1987) that an MNO faces serves to distinguish it from a national or domestic counterpart. Numerous researchers have documented the many types of environmental factors that multinational corporations face. Economic factors include multiple denominations of value (Sundaram & Black, 1992), inflation (Bechtold, 1984; Choi & Czechowicz, 1983), fluctuating exchange rates (Vineberg, 1985), market fluctuations (White & Poynter, 1984), unemployment and host country level of development (White & Poynter, 1984), tax policies and treaties (Borsack, 1987; Forbes, 1984; Leak & Smith, 1984; Meyer, 1986), host country energy policies (Jeannet, 1985), financial and technology flow regulations (Poynter, 1986), quality and safety regulations (Sethi, 1987), antitrust laws (Jones, 1984), and export licenses imposed by the parent country of the MNO (Stebbings, 1987). Besides confronting diverse economic environments, multinational corporations must adjust to the sociopolitical milieu of the countries in which their subsidiaries operate—for example, multiple sources of external authority (Sundaram & Black, 1992), differing ideological and political systems, varying political power relationships (Fayerweather, 1982; Leitko & Kowalewski, 1985), sociopolitical instability (Buckley, 1987), and forms of government labor regulation (Gates & Egelhoff, 1986; Laidlaw, 1977; Toyne, 1976).

Business management researchers have not stopped at identifying environmental factors that distinguish MNOs from their domestic counterparts. Those scholars also have examined how environmental complexity influences internal MNO practices and processes. For example, Sundaram and Black (1992) argue that multiple sources of external authority and multiple denominations of value influence "four aspects of MN[O] internal organization: modes of entry abroad, configuration of activities, coordination of control, and competitive strategy" (p. 729). Considerable attention has been given especially to how MNOs control and coordinate the operations of their foreign subsidiaries and, as a corollary, the forms of communication to achieve this purpose (Cray, 1984; Doz & Prahalad, 1981; Edstrom & Galbraith, 1977; Gates & Egelhoff, 1986; Hedlund, 1981; Jaeger, 1983; Schollhammer, 1971). As a result, various typologies of MNOs have emerged.

One popular typology categorizes multinational enterprises according to the headquarter's orientation toward subsidiaries (Heenan, 1975; Heenan & Perlmutter, 1979; Perlmutter, 1969). Four MNO types are identified: ethnocentric, polycentric, regiocentric, and geocentric. In *ethnocentric* organizations, authority is located at headquarters, and people from other cultures are not trusted. *Polycentric organizations* recognize differences between cultures, and local nationals hold key positions in the subsidiary. A regional basis for staffing and personnel development is issued by *regiocentric* organizations with a regional headquarters, whereas *geocentric* organizations "attempt to integrate diverse regions into a global system of decision-making" (Triandis & Albert, 1987, p. 275). By definition, ethnocentric organizations are dominated by the home culture of the parent company, whereas in polycentric and regiocentric organizations, foreign subsidiaries are heavily influenced by the culture of their respective host nations. Geocentric organizations are not dominated by any particular culture, but rather exhibit a kind of cultural synergy (Adler, 1980). The difference between the polycentric and regiocentric MNO is that the former grants independence to its subsidiary with respect to local management—as long as it turns a profit—whereas the latter exhibits interdependence between the regional headquarters and the subsidiary, as well as among subsidiaries themselves.

Unfortunately, little can be said about these MNO types beyond what already has been articulated here; one variable that can aid in identifying concrete differences in organizational communication within these types of multinational organizations is culture.

MNOs AND THEIR CULTURAL ENVIRONMENTS

Although many MNO management theorists have recognized that culture is a critical variable affecting the MNO's internal operations (Mascarenhas, 1982; Rosenzweig & Singh, 1991), few have studied systematically its impact on organizational processes and practices. Little attention appears to have been given over the years to cross-cultural or intercultural issues in MNO operations. According to Adler (1983), less than 5% of all articles in 19 management, 3 applied psychology, and 2 international journals from 1971 to 1980 was devoted to cross-cultural issues, or "the study of the behavior of people in organizations located in cultures and nations around the world" (p. 226). Less than 1% reflected intercultural concerns—that is, the "interaction between [among] organization members from two or more countries" (Adler, 1983, p. 227).

This trend is also evident in the field of communication. Few communication scholars have investigated intercultural communication in the MNO. From 1978 to 1991, *Communication Abstracts* reviewed only 11 articles on "multinational corporations," 3 on "multinational enterprises," 10 on "transnational enterprises," and 8 on "transnational corporations." None of these articles focused on intercultural organizational communication in the MNO (Shuter, 1989). This finding is surprising, given the field's increasing sensitivity to the culture construct (Smircich & Calas, 1987) and the obvious implications of cultural issues for MNOs. One explanation for this lack of research is that MNOs may be more difficult to access. Distance, language, and managerial policy all pose major obstacles to the study of communication in the MNO. Although these obstacles are formidable, the preponderance of this organizational form mandates that they be overcome.

Although there appears to be little MNO context-specific intercultural management or organizational communication research conducted to date, there is much room for speculation about how culture might affect communication in the multinational organization. Such speculation is based on a number of cultural variables linked to communication practices and processes (Triandis & Albert, 1987). These cultural variables include contextuality (Hall, 1976), power distance, individualism/collectivism, and uncertainty avoidance (Hofstede, 1980, 1991). The implications of these cultural dimensions for communication are extrapolated easily. For example, one might expect individuals of a low-context culture to rely more heavily on explicit communication than those from a high-context culture (Triandis & Albert, 1987).

The purpose of this chapter is to set a tentative agenda for intercultural organizational communication research in MNOs. To achieve this aim, cultural variables are posited to influence communication in the MNO. Research findings from one traditional (formal organizational structure) and three emerging (informal networks, organizational assimilation, and new communication technologies) areas of organizational communication research are reviewed (Fulk & Boyd, 1991; Putnam & Cheney, 1983) and applied in light of the dimensions of cultural variability. Finally, in an attempt to identify substantive organizational differences between MNO types (Heenan & Perlmutter, 1979), hypotheses are advanced regarding how MNO structure mediates the influence of culture on organizational communication.

STRUCTURING PROCESSES
IN THE MNO AND COMMUNICATION

Many researchers who have studied communication in MNOs have regarded it as a tool for the control and coordination of MNO operations (both at home and overseas). Although few investigations have examined the relationship between MNO structural *properties* (organizational size, subunit size, level in the hierarchy, and span of control) and communication, a number of studies have examined the relationship between MNO structuring *processes* (formalization, vertical and horizontal complexity, and centralization) and communication (Dalton, Todor, Spendolini, Fielding, & Porter, 1980).

MNO Formalization

Formalization has been defined in terms of employee perceptions of job specificity and familiarity with job description (Hage, Aiken, &

Marrett, 1971). This structuring process is inversely related to overall unscheduled communication in organizations. Given that organizations facing a high degree of environmental uncertainty tend to cope by using less formal coordination and control mechanisms in structuring their operations (Burns & Stalker, 1961; Lawrence & Lorsch, 1967), one might expect MNOs to control and coordinate their operations in a relatively informal manner. Some support for this claim is Hedlund's (1981) discovery that foreign subsidiaries operating in lesser developed nations (LDNs) relied more on informal than formal coordination mechanisms. Environmental uncertainty is likely to be greater in LDNs because of the increased potential for sociopolitical and economic instability.

This relationship between formalization and communication might be complicated by the degree of uncertainty avoidance present in both the national culture of the MNO and the MNO foreign subsidiary host country. Hofstede (1991) argued that "in uncertainty avoiding societies there are many formal laws and/or informal rules controlling the rights and duties of employers and employees [and] many internal rules and regulations controlling work process" (p. 120). Three hypotheses are posited for these interrelationships:

Hypothesis 1: MNOs from high-uncertainty-avoidance cultures are likely to structure their operations at home in a more formalized manner than their low uncertainty-avoidance counterparts.
Hypothesis 2: High uncertainty-avoidance ethnocentric MNOs formalize the operations of their foreign subsidiaries.
Hypothesis 3: Foreign subsidiaries operating in high-uncertainty-avoidance cultures formalize operations when MNO headquarters are polycentric.

MNO Vertical Complexity

The *vertical complexity* of an MNO refers to the number of hierarchical levels between the MNO headquarters and the foreign subsidiary. Brooke and Remmers (1970) found increases in the number of hierarchical levels between the foreign subsidiary and the home office to be inversely related to home office understanding of foreign subsidiary affairs. Brandt and Hulbert (1976) discovered no differences between U.S. and European MNO home office understanding of foreign subsidiary operations, even when the former was more vertically complex than the latter. These results confound, but do not necessarily contradict, Brooke and Remmers's findings. It is quite possible that understanding decreases only after a critical level of vertical complexity between headquarters and foreign subsidiary is reached. If, in the Brandt and Hulbert study, the vertical complexity of the U.S. MNOs did not reach this critical level, then their findings would be quite consistent with those posited by Brooke and Remmers (1970). Nor are such results inconsistent with the notion that increased organizational vertical complexity implies greater coordination needs and, consequently, communication requirements for the organization (Bacharach & Aiken, 1977).

MNO Horizontal Complexity

The MNO's *horizontal complexity* refers to the number of foreign subsidiaries in an MNO. Both Brandt and Hulbert (1976) and Hulbert and Brandt (1980) found that both impersonal (e.g., memos, reports) and personal forms of communication (e.g., visits, meetings) between MNO headquarters and the foreign subsidiary increase in relation to the total number of subsidiaries the MNO has to manage. In a sense, MNOs need to devote more of their energy to control and coordination as they expand. This finding is consistent with Hage et al.'s (1971) finding indicating a positive correlation between horizontal complexity (defined in terms of the number of functional specialties) and "the average number of scheduled organization wide committee meetings attended, frequency of department heads' unscheduled communication with other department heads" (Jablin, 1987a, p. 402), employee trans-unit interaction, and overall unscheduled communication in U.S. organizations. Other research suggests that these results may not be consistent across all forms of communication. Bacharach and Aiken (1977), who defined horizontal complexity in terms of the number of different departments within an organization, found horizontal complexity to be inversely related to frequency of subordinates' upward, lateral, and total communication. Jablin (1987a) pointed out that organizational size may be a moderating variable worth pursuing in this line of research.

MNO Centralization

Centralization has been found to be inversely related to frequency of communication in U.S. organizations (Berger & Cummings, 1979). Hage et al. (1971), for instance, found decentralization to be positively related to both average number of, and frequency of attendance at, organization-wide committee meetings; frequency of attendance at department meetings; and frequency of unscheduled interaction with individuals of same and higher status in different departments. Finally, Bacharach and Aiken (1977) found a positive relationship between decentralization and subordinates' upward, downward, lateral, and total oral communication, as well as department heads' upward, lateral, and total communication.

MNO-specific research examining the relationship between centralization and communication is more limited. Jaeger (1983) established that MNOs that grant their foreign subsidiaries greater autonomy tend to rely more on face-to-face communication than on company impersonal and formalized communication channels (e.g., manuals, reports) for coordination and control. Given that the Heenan and Perlmutter (1979) MNO typology also addresses the extent to which an MNO grants autonomy to its foreign subsidiaries, a hypothesis is suggested:

Hypothesis 4: Personalized and informal control and coordination mechanisms are more likely to be found in polycentric, regiocentric, and geocentric MNOs than in ethnocentric MNOs.

Engelhoff (1984) studied centralization in the MNO and found that countries typically differ in the amount of autonomy their MNOs grant foreign subsidiaries. European MNOs are typically less centralized than their U.S. counterparts. From only one study, any conclusions regarding the relation between culture and level of centralization would be premature. For example, a study by Chan (1980) appears to indicate that the amount of autonomy an MNO grants its foreign subsidiaries may be more a product of company policy than MNO national culture. In a related finding, Kujawa (1983) found that Japanese MNOs' degree of centralization depends on specific strategic and competitive considerations, not on nationality. Also, certain MNOs may choose to maintain more centralized control over some strategic subsystems, while being less concerned with others (Chan, 1980). This finding is important; centralization in an organization is not often studied at a subsystemic level. It suggests that communication patterns may vary even within the MNO's subsystems.

Although these studies appear to point to little or no relationship between centralization and culture, Hofstede (1991) firmly believes such a relationship exists. He wrote:

In the large power distance situation superiors and subordinates consider each other as existentially unequal; the hierarchical system is felt to be based on this existential equality. Organizations centralize power as much as possible in a few hands. Subordinates are expected to be told what to do. There are a lot of supervisory personnel, structured into tall hierarchies of people reporting to each other. (p. 35)

These contradictory positions warrant that the following research question be answered:

Research Question 1: To what extent do MNOs from large-power-distance cultures centralize their overseas operations?

Answers to the above question might help establish the relative weight of MNO strategy, policy, or orientation (type) and culture in determining the MNO's tendency to centralize control and coordination of its operations.

Communication research on MNOs has focused almost exclusively on the three structuring processes described above. Researchers have ignored many other organizational communication topics of particular relevance to MNOs and their foreign subsidiaries. Of the emerging organizational communication research foci identified by Putnam and Cheney (1983) and Fulk and Boyd (1991), three seem most pertinent to MNO/foreign subsidiary research: (a) informal communication networks, (b) organizational assimilation, and (c) new communication technologies. Again, extant research for each topic is reviewed in light of the dimensions of cultural variability.

INFORMAL COMMUNICATION NETWORKS
IN THE MNO FOREIGN SUBSIDIARY

Little research examining the effects of formal MNO structuring processes on communication currently exists. Even less is known about informal communication structures/networks in the MNO. This finding is surprising, considering the abundant research that organizational communication researchers have conducted on informal networks.

It is expected that informal communication networks of MNOs, especially within foreign subsidiaries, differ from those of domestic/single-culture organizations. For one, the degree of cultural homogeneity of organizational members varies greatly between the two. If the assumption that people tend to prefer to socialize with others of similar linguistic and cultural backgrounds is correct, then it is quite possible for MNO foreign subsidiaries to be characterized by a number of culturally based "parallel informal networks" (PINs): one for members of the subsidiary host country, another for expatriate employees, and yet a third in which members of both cultures/nations communicate informally. The following hypotheses thus are put forward for future testing:

Hypothesis 5: A greater number of parallel informal networks are in the MNO foreign subsidiary than in the single culture organization.

Hypothesis 6: Multicultural parallel informal networks are more widespread and influential in the foreign subsidiaries of regiocentric and geocentric MNOs than in those of ethnocentric or polycentric MNOs.

Hypothesis 7: Single-culture parallel informal networks are more prevalent in the foreign subsidiaries of ethnocentric and polycentric MNOs than in those of regiocentric and geocentric MNOs.

Hypothesis 8: In ethnocentric MNOs, the dominant single-culture parallel informal network is likely to be that of the parent company. In polycentric MNOs, the dominant single-culture parallel informal network is likely to be that of the host culture.

The notion that parallel informal networks might exist in culturally diverse organizations has implications for network role research. For instance, it might be possible to predict which employees in the foreign subsidiary will hold given roles in the organization's PINs. For example, a bilingual or even bicultural person—one adept at understanding the values of diverse cultures—might be perceived as approachable by organizational members of different cultures and be valued for possessing intercultural communication abilities. Such a person might establish broad connections within the organization and serve as a liaison in a multicultural PIN. In turn, familiarity with both the language and the culture of the host country, as well as that of the parent company, may be a prerequisite for a boundary spanner. Stated in terms of research hypotheses:

Hypothesis 9: Interculturally competent or versatile employees are more likely than others to emerge as bridges or liaisons in the multicultural PIN of the MNO foreign subsidiary.

Hypothesis 10: Interculturally competent or versatile employees are more likely than others to be selected as boundary spanners in MNO foreign subsidiaries.

Hypothesis 11: The most influential PINs in the foreign subsidiaries of ethnocentric MNOs are less likely to include employees of both cultures than those in geocentric organizations.

The determination of network roles should be related also to whether in dominant cultures in the foreign subsidiary of the MNO, the emphasis is on people, ideas, or actions (Glenn, 1981; Triandis & Albert, 1987). In cultures emphasizing people, those most adept at maintaining interpersonal relationships may emerge as network liaisons or bridges. In contrast, in cultures emphasizing ideas or actions, those most instrumental in idea development and goal attainment in the organization might become liaisons or bridges. These issues certainly are complicated by the presence of multiple cultures within an organization. Other cultural dimensions also might influence the composition of networks in MNOs. Hofstede's dimensions of power distance and uncertainty avoidance are probable determinants. Some cultures, such as the United States, are characterized by small power distance (low regard for hierarchically determined power relations), whereas others, such as Japan, display large power distance. In the United States, symmetrical relations and minimal status differences are emphasized, while in Japan, hierarchies are stressed (Condon, 1978). Given that hierarchies will exist in all types of organization, we hypothesize:

> Hypothesis 12: Single-culture PINs in low-power-distance ethnocentric and polycentric MNO foreign subsidiaries span more organizational levels than their high-power-distance ethnocentric and polycentric counterparts.

Similarly, one might expect employees from strong uncertainty-avoidance cultures to have a great need to keep informed when faced with uncertain situations. Thus, we posit:

> Hypothesis 13: Single-culture PINs in strong uncertainty-avoidance ethnocentric and polycentric MNO foreign subsidiaries are more active than their weak uncertainty-avoidance ethnocentric and polycentric counterparts.

Because we cannot be sure of how employees' diverse cultural orientations influence MNO foreign subsidiary network composition, we ask:

> Research Question 2: Do multicultural PINs in regiocentric and geocentric MNOs develop when network members fail to share similar cultural orientations (e.g., low vs. high power distance; weak vs. strong uncertainty avoidance)?

An answer to this last question might shed some light on the origin of strained intercultural relations in organizations.

Research on information distortion in informal networks of MNO foreign subsidiaries is warranted by the fact that as many as five out of every six messages in the organization appear to be transmitted through the organization's informal network (Hellweg, 1987). Cultural and language diversity may play a significant part in the distorting of messages through transmission. For example, although research has found that informal grapevines carry more accurate than inaccurate information (Davis, 1972; Hellweg, 1987) and are expedient channels for message diffusion (Walton, 1961), this may not always be the case in the MNO foreign subsidiary. Given the linguistic and cultural diversity of members of multicultural PINs and the greater likelihood of distortion in those networks, we hypothesize:

Hypothesis 14: Relatively more inaccurate information will be transmitted through multicultural than through unicultural PINs.

Hypothesis 15: Information will travel more slowly in multicultural than in unicultural PINs.

Meanwhile, the tools to study informal communication networks in MNOs or their subsidiaries already exist (Rice & Richards, 1985). NEGOPY is one technique that might prove particularly useful in this realm. Dallinger (1987), for example, used NEGOPY to measure gender differences in task and social communication networks in organizations. More recently, Albrecht and Hall (1991) used this instrument to study the communication patterns of elites and outsiders in innovation networks. The NEGOPY research could be used to identify parallel informal networks in culturally diverse organizations.

EMPLOYEE ASSIMILATION IN THE MNO

Organizational assimilation is viewed as the process by which "an individual becomes integrated into the 'reality' or culture of an organization" (Jablin, 1987b, p. 693). For most assimilation researchers, the process consists of attempts on the part of the organization to change (or socialize) the individual and for the individual then to change/shape (or individualize) the organization. *Socialization* often is conceptualized as a process with three distinct stages (Van Maanen, 1976): (a) anticipatory socialization (prior to entry), (b) encounter (at and shortly after entry), and (c) metamorphosis (postadaptation).

One limitation of this line of research appears to be its lack of sensitivity to potential cultural differences in organizational assimilation processes. Currently, little is known concerning how individuals around the world are socialized into organizations. This research rarely acknowledges that people who work for organizations in other countries, or for organizations designed and managed by people of different cultures, might experience the encounter stage of socialization in different ways, have different information needs during this socialization stage, and resort to different information-seeking strategies to reduce shock or uncertainty. Knowledge regarding how individuals of diverse cultures differ concerning the strategies they use to attempt metamorphosis or individualization in organizations also is lacking. Furthermore, even less is known about how individuals of one culture are assimilated into organizations operating where another culture predominates. One exception to this lack of research is Lee and Larwood's (1983) study examining the effects of socialization on individuals in the MNO foreign subsidiary, where it was found that the work attitudes of American expatriates employed by U.S. MNOs operating in Korea were closer to work attitudes held by Koreans than to work attitudes of their American counterparts in the United States

To study organizational assimilation in MNOs, we need first to examine how different cultures socialize organizational new hires. The cross-cultural communication literature provides a basis for comparative research, and clues regarding issues relevant to the study of employee assimilation in MNO foreign subsidiaries. From what is known about cultural variabilities, we can hypothesize, for example, the likely influence of Hofstede's (1991) cultural dimensions on organizational assimilation. In a collectivistic culture (e.g., Japan), where the goals of the group or collectivity outweigh those of the individual, collective socialization is more likely to occur than individualized socialization. Any socialization strategy that is oriented toward imparting a group orientation is more likely to be used in collective-culture organizations. The question of how employees of individualistic cultures fare when socialized into collective-culture organizations (and vice versa) is one that remains to be addressed. This is a particularly relevant issue, given the prevalence of Japanese-managed firms currently operating in the United States (Kujawa, 1983). If, in turn, cultural influence is mediated by MNO type, we can expect MNOs of the same culture to vary in organizational assimilation practices (due to differences in headquarters-to-subsidiary orientations). Consequently, we summarize the preceding argument in the following research questions and hypothesis:

Research Question 3: How do people in different cultures experience organizational socialization and individualization?

Hypothesis 16: In collectivistic cultures, collective organizational socialization is preferred over individualized organizational socialization.

Research Question 4: Does MNO type mediate the influence of collectivistic versus individualistic cultural orientations on socialization practices and processes?

Power distance (Hofstede, 1991) also might have some bearing on socialization processes in the MNO. For instance, more information (e.g., relational, appraisal, referent; Miller, 1989) might be sought and obtained by newcomers through vertical channels than through horizontal ones in domestic organizations operating in high-power-distance cultures (cultures emphasizing hierarchical orders where everyone has a place associated with certain obligations and duties that need no further justification). The inverse might be expected in low-power-distance cultures. One also might expect less individualization/role-making attempts from high-power-distance organizational members than from their low-power-distance counterparts in domestic organizations. These relationships are likely to be moderated by the relative predominance of either the parent or the host culture in the foreign subsidiary (Heenan & Perlmutter, 1979). Therefore, we posit:

Hypothesis 17: Organizational newcomers from high-power-distance cultures are more likely than their low-power-distance counterparts to seek information through the organization's hierarchical channels.

Hypothesis 18: Organizational newcomers from low-power-distance cultures are more likely than their high-power-distance counterparts to seek information from horizontal channels.

Hypothesis 19: Employees from low-power-distance cultures are more likely to engage in individualization attempts than are their high-power-distance counterparts.

Research Question 5: Does MNO type mediate the influence of power distance on information-seeking and individualization/role-making behavior?

Hofstede's (1991) dimension of uncertainty avoidance, indicating the degree to which members of a culture feel uncomfortable with uncertainty, may have an impact on the relationship between uncertainty during organizational encounter and information seeking. One might speculate that new hires from strong uncertainty-avoidance cultures engage more readily in information seeking during organizational encounters than do newcomers from cultures that exhibit weak uncertainty avoidance. Work by Gudykunst and Nishida (1984) on uncertainty-reduction theory reveals the form that such information seeking might take. They compared Japanese and U.S. managers' communication and found that U.S. managers self-disclose and interrogate more than their

Japanese counterparts during uncertain situations. This argument is factored into the following hypothesis:

Hypothesis 20: When faced with uncertainty, new hires from high-uncertainty-avoidance cultures are more likely to seek information and will do so more overtly than their low-uncertainty-avoidance counterparts.

Finally, intercultural researchers have tried to determine how contextuality can serve to differentiate the communication behaviors of individuals of different cultures (Hall, 1976). High-context cultures rely more on indirect or contextual cues, rather than explicit ones, during communication. One might speculate that high-context cultures rely less on ambient and more on oral/discretionary forms of communication to socialize employees (Jablin, 1987b). It is unknown whether MNOs are sensitive to this possibility and adjust their socialization strategies in accordance with the contextuality of their foreign subsidiary employees. We therefore advance:

Hypothesis 21: High-context-culture organizations rely less on ambient and more on oral/discretionary forms of communication to socialize their employees than do their low-context-culture counterparts.

We believe that comparative organizational assimilation research, though still in its infancy, promises to be a fruitful area of inquiry. Little is known about how socialization and individualization differ across cultures. Even less is known about intercultural *organizational* assimilation (how individuals of one culture are assimilated into organizations of another). The foreign subsidiary of the MNO is one place where answers to a few of these speculations and questions may be found.

NEW COMMUNICATION TECHNOLOGIES IN THE MNO

Research on the use of new communication technologies in MNOs is another area worth exploring. Teleconferencing—computer, audio, and video—seems to be a particularly consequential form of communication technology for MNOs. Unfortunately, it appears that teleconferencing system designers have ignored the cultural diversity of their potential users (Acker & McCain, 1990). Studies on the relationship between culture and media/technology use in organizations can only lead to the design and adoption of better, user-oriented teleconferencing systems.

Research indicates that computer, audio, and video teleconferencing typically serves certain functions better than others. Philips (1983) indicated that the computer conference is usually best suited for certain types of communication (e.g., those requiring a written record). Tasks not requiring synchronous interaction (e.g., memos requesting reports, files, information) especially might benefit from this medium. Although this teleconference mode has been found to provoke more thoughtful communication, it also has been found to privilege those particularly articulate in written communication (Philips, 1983). This advantage could be problematic in a multinational organization where some groups of employees, particularly in a foreign subsidiary, are more likely to be articulate in the written expression of an "official" language than others. In addition, a number of human factors need to be assessed in the design of the human-machine interface (e.g., menu selection formats, screen layout, display rates, error messages) in terms of their application across cultures. For example, do Portuguese employees at the foreign subsidiary of a U.S. MNO continue to use an AZERT or HCESAR keyboard, if writing in English, or do they switch over to a QWERTY system? Evidence indicates that cultures differ in their interface preferences, depending on their general cultural styles (e.g., reflection or action-oriented; Schneiderman, 1987). On the one hand, if adjustment controls cannot be incorporated into the computer conference system, then this teleconference mode may be inappropriate. On the other hand, if such cultural factors go unattended, then this system cannot be considered to be truly user-oriented in the MNO context. It therefore becomes imperative that the following research questions be addressed:

Research Question 6: Does computer conferencing privilege MNO employees particularly articulate in the written expression of an "official" organizational language over others more fluent in a secondary language?

Research Question 7: How prevalent and effective is computer conferencing in controlling and coordinating MNO foreign subsidiary operations, and what other functions does this form of teleconferencing serve in the MNO?

Research Question 8: Do different cultures vary in their computer interface preferences and, if so, can adjustments be incorporated into the computer conference system to account for differences in user-interface preferences?

Facsimile (fax), though not a computer conference "mode," is one computer-mediated technology that may be suited particularly to interorganizational and international use. *Fax* is defined as "any system by which printed or pictorial matter is transmitted electronically from one place to another and a reasonably faithful copy permanently recorded at the receiving end in any one of several forms" (Costigan, 1971, p. 2).

Several unique features of a fax make it amenable to interorganizational applications: (a) Fax is based on the universal telephone system, which has a well-developed address system (Wilkes, 1990), (b) fax is not subject to the internetworking difficulties of electronic mail (Wilkes, 1990), (c) fax, like other electronic media, allows communication between geographically dispersed locations (Culnan & Markus, 1987), (d) fax allows two-way interaction either at the same time (synchronously) or at different times (asynchronously) (Culnan & Markus, 1987), and (e) fax is compatible with normal office routines and is operated easily by office personnel; it does not require knowledge of computers (Wilkes, 1990).

Despite the great impact and future potential impact of fax technology, the effects of fax technology on organizational communication within MNOs are not understood. The use of fax probably mediates the effects of power distance on communication. Research indicates that computer-mediated communication technologies increase equality of participation in interaction (Hiltz & Turoff, 1978; Kiesler, Siegel, & McGuire, 1984; Krueger, 1976; Uhlig, Farber, & Bair, 1979) and increase existing, as well as establish new, communication linkages (Crawford, 1982; Foster & Flynn, 1984; Rice, 1984; Sproull & Kiesler, 1986). Because using fax requires no knowledge of computers and is operated easily (Wilkes, 1990), it may prove effective in bridging cultural differences in communication. Its ease of use and reliance on the phone system make it more accessible to a broad range of cultures. Thus, we ask:

Research Question 9: What functions does fax technology serve in the MNO?
Research Question 10: Does fax technology mediate the effects of power distance on communication?

The audioconference has been found useful for task-oriented meetings not mandating social presence (Christie, 1985). Audioconference users tend to find this medium more satisfactory for simple task accomplishment (Heimstra, 1982). When transported across cultures, however, this may not be an appropriate communication medium. Researchers speculate that in high-context cultures, ambiguity and misinterpretation may result from taking a message out of its nonverbal delivery context (Acker & McCain, 1990). Cultures may differ also in the way they signal turn taking. In a teleconferencing mode wherein visual cues are not present to coordinate patterns of speaking, familiarity with cultural differences in turn-taking styles may be crucial for those involved in both system design and use. Here, we ask:

> Research Question 11: How prevalent and effective is audioconferencing in controlling and coordinating MNO foreign subsidiary operations? What other functions does this form of teleconferencing serve in the MNO?
>
> Research Question 12: Is audioconferencing appropriate as a communication medium in high-context cultures?
>
> Research Question 13: Because cultures differ in their turn-taking styles, does audioconferencing hinder intercultural organizational communication between employees using different turn-taking styles?

Research indicates that the videoconference is particularly useful for complex information in which interaction is needed (Mathis, 1986). In other words, this medium may be most appropriate for situations in which transmitted messages gain impact via visual medium (e.g., in which maintaining friendly interpersonal relations is important). Unfortunately, designers of videoconference systems have omitted cultural variables in their design (e.g., Acker & Levitt, 1987). Also, in high-context cultures, human proximity may be irreplaceable, and any form of teleconferencing would be an inappropriate medium of communication.

Cross-cultural differences in the use of space might impinge on the design of culturally sensitive videoconference systems. Bretz and Schmidbauer (1983) accuse videoconference designers of ignoring the critical relationship between shot content, viewing distance, and virtual distance. What is now known about these relationships might be adjusted for the way cultures conceptualize space. On the basis of the limited knowledge we have regarding videoconferencing as a mode of communication, we ask:

> Research Question 14: How prevalent and effective is videoconferencing in controlling and coordinating MNO foreign subsidiary operations?
>
> Research Question 15: How do cultures differ in the way they conceptualize space, and can videoconference systems be designed to accommodate potential differences?

With the rapid dispersion of these new communication technologies, these research questions will demand answers. Given the unique international scope of MNOs, these issues may be even more salient for this type of organization.

CONCLUSION

The purpose of this chapter has been threefold. First, an attempt has been made to document the kind of environmental complexity that the MNO typically faces. It should be clear from this exposition that MNOs are very different from other organizations. Second, the literature on communication in MNOs has been reviewed. It should be evident that we presently know very little about communication in MNOs. Third, we have sought to provide a research agenda for future studies on intercultural organizational communication. The preponderance of the multinational corporation in today's global economy mandates that this research be pursued with vigor.

3

Minimizing Threats to the Validity of Cross-Cultural Organizational Research

JEFFREY C. ADY • University of Hawaii, Manoa

Organizations everywhere are experiencing a rapid transition due to increasing cultural diversity. Many organizational researchers have considered the cross-cultural nature of many organizations (e.g., Arensberg, 1978; Goodenough, 1978; Gregory, 1983; Likert, 1961; March & Simon, 1958; Strauss, 1978; Ting-Toomey, 1985; Van Maanen & Barley, 1982). The intersection of different cultures in an organization can present difficulties, particularly in the form of intercultural conflict, when culture-bound communicative behaviors and values clash (Ting-Toomey, 1985).

Researchers interested in the dynamics of cultures in organizations have directed their inquiries primarily to the comparative analysis of organizational practices (Adler, Doktor, & Redding, 1989; Wiio, 1989). Although these efforts have contributed to an understanding of some cultures' organizational norms, cross-cultural organizational research arguably has not established clear definitions of culture, as a grouping or an independent variable, in its inquiry. Such ambiguity also can characterize basic research design considerations such as variable selection and the control of threats to internal validity. Each point of ambiguity will be addressed in an agenda for cross-cultural research on organizational communication that seeks (a) a definition of culture that establishes meaningful boundaries for organizational research, (b) a clearer view of the organizational communication variables that are culture-variant or culture-invariant, and (c) a greater awareness of the threats to validity endemic to cross-cultural research on organizations.

ESTABLISHING BOUNDARIES: DEFINING CULTURE

The question of a researcher's definition of culture is vital, for when a researcher begins with culture as a grouping variable in cross-cultural research, the scope of the culture(s) involved affects the observations made. The same principle applies to boundary setting in any research activity (Dubin, 1978). As Shuter (1990a) noted, the vast majority of cross-cultural communication research has been directed toward theory validation, resulting in a focus on a handful of national or societal cultures. Shuter (1992) also observed that communication literature remains wanting of a good understanding of most national cultures and co-cultures—that is, discrete subsocieties definable by demographic characteristics such as ethnicity and regionality. But even the adequacy of the national and ethnic culture construct is challenged as some in society demand more attention to groups defined by gender, sexual orientation, and other co-cultures (Shuter, 1990a).

The organizational communication patterns of the groupings that follow from a researcher's particular definition of culture ought to be investigated vigorously. The need for activity of this nature should take on particular importance, given Triandis and Albert's (1987) view of culture vis-à-vis cross-cultural organizational communication as being defined by shared meanings, norms, values, linguistic and paralinguistic conventions, and frames of reference. A word of caution is appropriate, however; given the large number of definitions of culture that are offered in literature (see reviews by Atwood, 1984; Dodd, 1977), we may have to be satisfied that what is needed is a sensible and defensible definition of culture. A particular group might be judged to be a "culture," and therefore a group to be studied seriously in cross-cultural organizational research, to the extent that the attributes specified by a specific and clearly articulated definition of culture chosen can be observed. Culture as a grouping variable in cross-cultural organizational research must be defined sensibly and defensibly to identify clearly the characteristics of a particular group of people that mark it as a culture. An increasingly diverse—and divided—cultural landscape demands that we do no less.

CULTURAL VARIANCE/INVARIANCE: A GUIDELINE FOR VARIABLE SELECTION

Simon (1978) argued that variables appropriate for social science research are defined operationally to allow consistent measurement and to be valid indicators of—and have a reasonable and sensible relationship to—the hypothetical constructs they represent (p. 148). This argument suggests that in cross-cultural research in organizational communication, variables must, at minimum, be (a) operationalized carefully and (b) subjected to thoughtful consideration regarding the degree to which they may or may not be culture-variant. Operationalizations of variables therefore should have both theoretical and empirical bases.

The *theoretical base* is in the extant literature on cultural differences in organizational communication patterns and their implications for intercultural conflict in organizations. Womack's (1982) model described an interface between specific cultures, organizations, and the transnational organizational environment in which differences occur in the cultural elements of worldviews, thought patterns, beliefs, attitudes, values, rules, and value of conflict. Further theorizing regarding operationalization from the literature includes Porter's (1972) definition of culture, which includes meanings, beliefs, values, attitudes, concepts of self, the universe, status hierarchies, role expectations, spatial relations, and time concepts; and Pennington's (1985) typology of culture components, including worldview, language, schemata, beliefs, attitudes, values, temporality, proxemics, social relationships, and interpolation patterns (dealing with new information and change).

Such propositions regarding what is subject to cultural variation in organizational communication may imply that consensus exists regarding which variables actually do make a difference in cross-cultural organizational communication. But a thorough reading of research literature on cross-cultural comparisons of organizational behavior will reveal a historical division over the question of culture as a meaningful grouping variable in organizational behavior. Therefore, the empirical base for considerations regarding operationalization lies in the completion and syntheses of a large number of studies in comparative management. What is needed at this juncture is a notion of which variables in organizational communication have been found to be culturally variable and critical to effective cross-cultural organizational communication.

Considerable cross-cultural research on organizations has found communication patterns and styles that vary culturally. Lincoln, Olson, and Hanada (1978) found that Japanese workers favored superiors who made heavy demands on, and took personal interest in, subordinates; Japanese workers sought out relationships characterized by dependency with superiors and peers, whereas French workers avoided dependency (see also Lincoln & Kalleberg, 1990). Hou (1986) contrasted Western and Japanese management in terms of community emphasis, distinction between managers and workers, standardization of ranks and position, age and seniority as priorities in promotion, and attachment to the organization. Rosch and Segler (1987) discussed the importance to Western marketers of harmony and the primacy of internal group relations, high-context message information, introductory rituals, a long-term view, and personal trust in dealings with Japanese business counterparts (see also Ruffner & Ettkin, 1987).

Studies of Japanese subsidiaries around the globe (Dicle, Dicle, & Alie, 1988; Ishida, 1986) have identified several key characteristics of Japanese human resource management, including concern for the total person, class and ability egalitarianism, participation in workplace decisions, low formality in organization, flexible job descriptions, group-oriented behavior, and low turnover. Rehder (1988) concluded that for the Japanese, the key to constant innovation and improvement in Japan is people, and not technology. In comparing decision making in U.S., Japanese, and Chinese organizations, Weihrich (1990) found that in U.S. organizations, decisions are made at the top and by only a few. In Japanese organizations, they are made by all people at multiple levels of the hierarchy; in Chinese organizations, decisions are made at the top, but many other people are involved in operational decisions. Nonaka (1990) described the common practice in Japanese organizations of widespread sharing of knowledge and information among functions and specializations so that one worker can enter the specialty of the other, resulting in increased trust and loyalty among workers.

General calls for managers in multicultural organizations to be aware of culturally divergent subordinates' communication needs have been made by a number of authors (e.g., Stull, 1985). Darling (1986) noted that successful leadership in multinational organizations depends on managers having a flexible superior-subordinate communication style, and his opinion is confirmed by Abramms-Mezhoff and Johns (1989). Nystrom (1990) observed that different emphases are placed on the quality of vertical exchange between superiors and subordinates in the United States than in Japan and that care must be taken not to equate the two, particularly in research.

Researchers and practitioners have made similar observations regarding the review of culturally divergent employees' performance. Performance review itself is not questioned, but the way it is conducted has been identified as a culture-bound phenomenon. Perlmutter and Heenan (1983) observed that the multinational organizations they studied had used ethnocentric performance appraisal techniques, which were transferred overseas with little or no variation and with no foreign managers participating in their design. They concluded that this practice appeared to be the norm for most multinational and transnational organizations. Seddon (1987) noted that, although most performance appraisal systems being used have been developed in American and British organizations, they are incompatible with the cultural assumptions and work values in many non-Western and developing countries—

that is, ascription of outcomes to individual performance, frank and open discussions regarding employee performance, a contractual relationship between the organization and its employees, and the assumption that the employee has some degree of control over the outcome of the performance appraisal interview. This incompatibility raises the issue of the validity of these performance appraisal strategies—not for the cultures in which they developed, but for their cross-cultural validity. Seddon urged that appraisal tactics appropriate to specific, cultural assumptions and values be developed and implemented. Siegel (1984), in a study of Sudanese public service employees, found that workers favored a developmental performance appraisal system that included ratee participation in goal setting, use of multiple raters, the separation of development from other personnel decisions, specific performance goals, and day-to-day coaching instead of yearly appraisals. Siegel concluded by noting that these preferences were grounded in Sudanese cultural values.

The difficult part of operationalizing communication variables is finding a way to synthesize the many concerns and findings discussed above. The many efforts at examining cultural variation in organizational practices and preferences have generally not been synthesized into meaningful recommendations for approaching culture as a grouping variable in cross-cultural organizational communication research (an exception is Wiio, 1989). Researchers undeniably have identified loci of meaningful cultural differences in organizational patterns, but other variables investigated have demonstrated little cultural variation. Is there some principle that could generally answer the question, When does culture make a difference in organizational communication?

Frequently, it is assumed that management practices worldwide display more similarities than differences and that cultural influences on management practices are negligible. This is the thrust of the "culture-free" hypothesis (Joynt, 1985). Some writers have suggested that organizations around the globe have converged toward a Western-style pattern of organizing and communicating (e.g., Hickson et al., 1974). This position has been part of a larger debate in comparative management studies over the global divergence or convergence of management practices and organizational attributes (Joynt, 1985), and claims support from a large body of research. A crucial weakness of this position—and the research supporting it—is that it has focused on defining organizational universals (organizational variables that are more or less invariant across cultures) in searching for and finding similarities. Variables that are subject to change across cultures have been largely unnoticed by those arguing for a "convergence" solution to the controversy (Tayeb, 1987). Some management structures and principles may be universal, but the practices of management—the ways organizational structures and principles are made to work in specific populations in certain cultures—are undeniably different (Kleinberg, 1989; Lincoln, Hanada, & McBride, 1986; Lou & Borden, 1989; Tayeb, 1987). Adler et al. (1989) have described the debate in terms of two opposing viewpoints. The first perspective holds that organizational practices around the world have been converging and that ethnic and/or national culture is not an important factor in organizational life. The second perspective asserts that culture-variant organizational practices vastly outnumber culture-universal practices and that organizational practices are undergoing an increasing divergence. Adler et al. (1989) offer an exit to the dilemma by citing a large body of research whose findings on the formal level of organizations are inconclusive vis-à-vis the question of cultural variation. Findings on the informal organizational level, in contrast, strongly support cultural variation. Adler et al.'s (1989) review of the convergence-divergence debate suggests that, although formal and structural organizational variables may be etic (pancultural) variables, the a priori assumptions of cultures regarding communication patterns operate on the informal organizational level—much of the time out-of-awareness—and are emic (culture-specific) variables.

Adler et al.'s (1989) answer to the convergence-divergence debate supports observations by Lincoln et al. (1986), Tayeb (1987), Lou and Borden (1989), and Kleinberg (1989). According to Lincoln et al. (1978), most comparative organizational research focuses on formal structure, and the habits, customs, and values of their members and their cultural environment must be addressed. Maguire and Pascale (1978) and Pascale (1978) observed fewer differences between Japanese and American managers regarding the volume or direction of communication; however, the nature of that communication did vary significantly across cultures. Lincoln et al. (1986) found that operations technology and other structural variables made little difference between the Japanese and the Americans and that greater cultural philosophies guiding organizations were different. Tayeb (1987) found that structural variables such as organizational structure and functional specialization had little impact on differences observed between matched Indian and British organizations, and that other factors, such as communication patterns, were more meaningful. Furthermore, Kleinberg (1989) noted that a fairly uniform global business climate may exist but only at the level of necessary structural, organizational conventions; individuals from different cultures can have very different ways of cognition and valuation.

Wiio's (1989) comments regarding organizational communication research across cultures are particularly helpful in giving substance to the culture-variant and culture-invariant distinction. They also represent a unique approach in cross-cultural organizational communication research in that the nomothetic and theory-validation models driving most research across cultures in communication (Shuter, 1990a) are disavowed in favor of striving for an understanding of different cultures' organizational communication patterns, which is less constrained by the North American construct of what makes for effective organizational communication. Using the nomenclature of hardware and software variables, Wiio described the distinction in terms of the variables listed below:

Hardware Variables	*Software Variables*
Information sources	Social systems
Channels and their uses	Organizations
Number of messages	Trust
Code systems	Openness
Communication networks	Motivation
	Perceived need for information
	Topics of information
	Happiness
	Harmony
	Job satisfaction

Perhaps even more informative to the culture-variance distinction are several propositions offered by Wiio (1989) regarding the relationship between the two types of variables: (a) Hardware is a critical factor only in extreme conditions when there is too little or too much of it; otherwise software is the dominant factor, and (b) organizational communication hardware variables are more likely to be similar in different countries than are software variables.

Wiio thus offered an answer to the question of culture's influence on organizational communication, and his conclusions seem to be reflected in the findings of recent comparative management research (e.g., Adler et al., 1989). Such a corroboration between different disciplines strongly suggests a much-needed consensus in answering the questions posed by both sides of the convergence-divergence debate.

This consensus ought to be taken as a concrete guideline for which organizational communication variables would be likely to exhibit cultural variation and which variables would not. The basic logic of variable selection and hypothesis generation in cross-cultural organizational communication research would predict relative lack of variation for structural variables and relative variation for culture-specific variables. General expectations of observed differences between cultures vis-à-vis organizational communication variables should reflect that basic distinction between pancultural and culture-specific variables.

MINIMIZING THREATS TO VALIDITY

The assertions in this chapter echo Burgoon and Miller's (1990) desire for greater ecological validity. Indeed, the need for greater ecological validity in cross-cultural organizational communication research is the central thrust of this chapter. The validity threats of variable misselection, Types I and II error and nonequivalence, their implications, and ways to combat them therefore merit discussion in the next several paragraphs. A decision guide for minimizing validity threats is offered in Figure 3.1.

Cross-cultural research in general has been the concern of many methodologists and practitioners from a variety of disciplines. Concerns have included special threats to validity, methodological difficulties, and the motivations behind cross-cultural research. Notable among these works have been Berry (1980), Brown and Sechrest (1980), Hall (1986), Hui and Triandis (1984), Irvine and Carroll (1980), Kameoka (1984), Pareek and Rao (1980), Shuter (1990a, 1992), and Trimble (1988). For example, Berry (1980) noted that common criticisms of cross-cultural research are (a) it produces trivial, tautological, or highly abstract generalizations, (b) many generalizations are based on one-shot multiple comparisons between many cultures and thus do not provide an in-depth understanding of any one culture regarding the variable(s) in question, and (c) cross-cultural research sometimes compares "incomparables" from different societies, leading to distortions of reality for the cultures and variable(s) involved. Concerns of this nature have been shared with communication scholars such as Atwood (1984), S. Becker (1976), Casmir (1978), Hall (1986), and Shuter (1990a). Techniques to minimize these threats to the significance and validity of cross-cultural research generally take the form of calls for care in variable selection and close attention paid to equivalence.

Validity Threats Due to Variable Misselection

Cross-cultural research has been described as a methodological genre, rather than as a dedicated content field (Brown & Sechrest, 1980). The majority of communication research across cultures, to date, has been nomothetic and theory-extensive (Gudykunst, 1983, 1985;

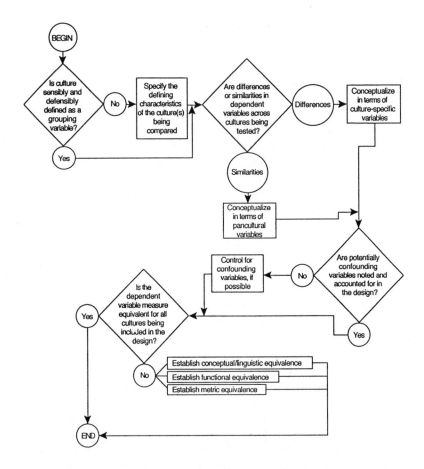

Figure 3.1. A Decision Guide for Minimizing Validity Threats in Cross-Cultural Organizational Research

Shuter, 1990a). As such, it must treat culture as an independent variable that is used to account for findings on a dependent variable(s) or an outcome measure(s), and culture therefore must be as free as possible from other, confounding, variables that may affect the dependent variable or measurable outcome (Brown & Sechrest, 1980). Confounding variables may inflate either Type I error (rejecting the null hypothesis because of erroneously inflated independent variable effects on the dependent variables) or Type II error (retaining the null hypothesis because of the failure to observe effects on the dependent variables that actually exist). Brown and Sechrest (1980) stated that Type II error is more likely to occur in cross-cultural research because of the ease with which culture is confounded by other variables. Variable misselection may lead to either type of error if a pancultural variable is mistakenly expected to exhibit cross-cultural variation or if a culture-specific variable is erroneously predicted to remain constant across cultures. Even if the researcher has avoided variable misselection, confounding variables may either deflate or inflate observed effects. Validity is threatened because the researcher is not truly measuring the desired variable.

Validity Threats Due to Nonequivalence

Equivalence occurs when a measurement yields comparable assessments for similar behaviors of respondents in different cultures. In Table 3.1, I summarize the following discussion of equivalence. Equivalence can be examined in three ways: Conceptual/linguistic, functional, and metric equivalences are all necessary conditions for construct validity in cross-cultural research (Brown & Sechrest, 1980). *Conceptual/ linguistic equivalence* exists if the measures used in differing cultures translate similarly (Berry, 1980; Hui & Triandis, 1984; Trimble, 1988) and can be established through back-translation and focus group validation of stimulus materials. *Functional equivalence* is established if the behaviors or events or objects described in the stimulus materials have similar experiential functions and properties in different cultures (Berry, 1980; Hui & Triandis, 1984; Trimble, 1988) and can be established through interview/focus group work with the stimulus materials in question in all cultures represented in the study. Work by Ticehurst (1992) assessing Australian employees' views of communication satisfaction and the Communication Satisfaction (COMSAT) Questionnaire is an example of a test of functional equivalence. Ticehurst found that the COMSAT questionnaire tapped different functions of communication satisfaction for Australians than it did for North Americans. *Metric equivalence* exists if the psychometric properties of tests used in cross-cultural research exhibit comparable interrelationships between independent and dependent variables and comparable correlation and/or factor structures (Berry, 1980; Hui & Triandis, 1984; Kameoka, 1984; Trimble, 1988). Similar factor solutions, strengths, and/or directions of effects, covariances, and interactions between independent variables should suggest metric equivalence; that is, respondents in one culture grouped items or stimuli in a measure similarly to that of respondents in another culture. A difficulty with metric equivalence, however, is

TABLE 3.1 Guide to Three Types of Equivalence

Equivalence Type	Requirements	Conditions for Equivalence
Conceptual/Linguistic	Similarity in translations of dependent measures	Relatively similar referents and descriptions
Functional	Similarity in functions and properties of behaviors described in stimulus materials	Behaviors described in stimulus materials have similar functions across the cultures being studied
Metric	Similarity in structure of psychometric properties of tests and data	Comparable factor structures, strengths, and directions of effects, covariances, and interactions

that such similarities are not guaranteed. True intercultural differences may mean that factor solutions, for example, are not similar. The researcher then must judge whether the desire for metric equivalence outweighs the practical necessities of the study in question (Berry, 1980).

There are many implications of the validity threats of variable misselection and nonequivalence for cross-cultural research in organizations. First, not all cultures will differ from each other in the same ways. Sudanese and North Americans may, for example, have quite different views of the meaning of evaluations for subordinates' performance, but North Americans and British may have similar ideas concerning that organizational function. This example implies that the effects of culture as an independent variable on an outcome or dependent measure or variable may vary along with the relative differences between cultures at the outset. The anticipation of effects for culture as an independent variable must be informed by the researcher's understanding of the degree of similarity between the cultures concerned, or else the researcher may be setting him- or herself up for inflated Type I or II error.

The answers offered to the convergence-divergence debate earlier may offer some guidance for variable selection. An implication of that discussion for variable selection is that what Wiio (1989) called "hardware variables" should be generally anticipated to exhibit less cultural variation than would "software variables"; although most cultures may employ some sort of performance appraisal function in organized activity, the interpersonal rules regarding that activity vary greatly among societies (Seddon, 1987). Whether one is looking for organizational variables that are more pancultural in nature or those that are more culture-specific, the distinctions and categories enumerated above should be kept in mind so that surprises due to research design and the interpretation of results may be minimized.

The possibility of confounding variables in cross-cultural research is increased by the presence of the same problem in organizational research. Inasmuch as organizational communication is affected by organizational culture (Barnett, 1988), cross-cultural research in organizations that defines culture as something other than organization-specific must account for the effects of organizational culture in the organization(s) studied in the research because organizational culture may well be contributing at least as much to dependent variable observations as does the culture otherwise defined by the researchers. Moreover, contingency theory warns against blanket generalizing across organizations (Lawrence & Lorsch, 1967) because the specific characteristics of individual organizations—including membership, organization type, and local environment, among others—potentially make every organization unique unto itself. Generalization, then, must be an activity informed by an understanding of the presence or absence of these and other potentially confounding variables. General research design in cross-cultural organizational research must control carefully for confounding variables that would inflate or deflate the effects of culture as an independent variable.

This same call for awareness holds true for equivalence. It is no longer sufficient simply to translate a measure into a target language in order to justify validity claims. Other kinds of equivalence must be established as well, and this means that the use of organizational assessment tools and other measures related to organizational communication study must undergo rigorous pretesting. In many cases, the decision to use a particular measure may involve a reasoned balance between the practical requirements for the study in question and the professional necessities for using truly equivalent instrumentation.

CONCLUSION

Research on intercultural relations in organizations has frequently been faulted for an overly glib and abstract discussion of "cultural differences" as the malady behind a host of organizational ills without offering meaningful explanations of the dynamics of the malady or offering suggestions as to the remedy. The abstractness and overgeneralized character of some of the historic literature generated by cross-cultural research identified by Berry (1980) has done some damage to the popular perception of the meaningfulness and significance of cross-cultural research, and this dissatisfaction also may taint perceptions of cross-cultural organizational research. What is needed is more work that identifies specific organizational variables that are experientially (not simply theoretically) troublesome for persons from different cultures who must work together in the world. This work must be thorough in minimizing the threats to validity that are special to cross-cultural research in designing research, measurement selection and employment, and interpreting findings. To further that end, here are four recommendations for cross-cultural research in organizational communication:

Recommendation 1: Culture, as a grouping variable in cross-cultural organizational research, must be defined sensibly and defensibly so as to identify clearly the characteristics of a particular group of people that mark it as a culture.

Recommendation 2: Pancultural variables generally should be anticipated to exhibit less cultural variation than would culture-specific variables.

Recommendation 3: General research design in cross-cultural organizational research must control carefully for confounding variables that would inflate or deflate the effects of culture as an independent variable.

Recommendation 4: The use of organizational assessment tools and other measures related to organizational communication study must be prefaced by rigorous pretesting in order to establish conceptual/linguistic, functional, and metric equivalence.

If cross-cultural research in organizational communication and inquiry into intercultural interaction in organizations are to address the exigencies of a culturally fractionated organizational milieu whose needs for understanding and accommodation are increasing, organizational communication theorists and researchers must formulate, agree to, and follow an agenda for action that provides a framework for sensitive and practical definitions of culture, a fuller understanding of when culture can be expected to make a difference in organizational behavior, and a greater awareness of requirements for research in organizational communication across cultures in order to enjoy an enhanced ability to claim internal and ecological validity.

II

CULTURAL BASES FOR COMMUNICATION IN MULTINATIONAL ORGANIZATIONS

4

Communication in Japanese Multinational Organizations

ALAN GOLDMAN • *Goldman and Associates, Scottsdale, AZ*

Pivotal to Western communication with Japanese multinational organizations (MNOs) is a cognizance of indigenous principles influencing intracultural and intercultural dimensions of interaction (e.g., Goldman, 1993a, 1993e; Starosta, 1993). Unless Western organizations integrate their business agendas with the influences of the host culture, they increasingly will face aborted expatriations, escalating Western-Japanese negotiating conflicts, ethnocentric MNO media coverage, and ill-fated attempts at transferring Japanese management practices.

In this chapter I examine a concept termed *ningensei* (human beingness) as central to Japanese multinational communication practices spanning strategic arenas of organizational, negotiating, proxemic, and performance protocols (see, BenDasan, 1970; Goldman, 1992b; Lebra, 1976, 1992; Yuasa, 1977). Embedded in Japanese culture, *ningensei* is traceable to fundamental Confucian presuppositions operationalized in contemporary organizations. It is argued that through investigations of relationships between indigenous cultural precepts and multinational practices, Western researchers and practitioners are better able to discern between *tatemae* (surface communication) and *honne* (communication of true intentions) and improve the interaction for expatriations and contact situations. I present this argument by (a) describing issues involved in MNO contexts, (b) analyzing the philosophical underpinnings of *ningensei,* (c) applying *ningensei* and related concepts to four communication patterns in MNOs, and (d) drawing conclusions and implications for researchers and practitioners.

BACKGROUND IN INTERCULTURAL ISSUES AND INEQUITIES

In the course of Western globalization, the specifics of culture often are overlooked or miscalculated, as witnessed in ethnocentric or Eurocentric approaches to international communication and management (Goldman, 1988, 1989a, 1990a, 1990c, 1993a; Hayashi, 1988; Hofstede, 1984). An insensitivity and a lack of preparedness on the part of North American and European management is particularly evident in joint ventures, mergers, relocations, and multinational negotiations, and within Western-based subsidiaries under Japanese majority ownership (e.g., Clark, 1979; Condon, 1984; Goldman, 1990a, 1990b, 1992d; March, 1990; Ouchi, 1981; Tung, 1984, 1988). This alleged lack of an intercultural orientation on the part of Western MNOs is reported repeatedly by scholarly and mass media sources on both sides of the Pacific and stands in stark contrast to the practice of leading Japanese multinationals (Goldenberg, 1988; Goldman, 1993a; Matsumoto, 1988; Neustupny, 1987).

Japanese MNOs have invested readily in culture-specific training and development in the post-World War II era, marked by widespread adoption of Western managerial and quality control innovations, in-house pedagogy addressing East-West cultural differences, and predeparture training (e.g., Condon, 1984; Luenemann & Knutson, 1993; Schonberger, 1982, 1986, 1987). It is commonplace within Japanese Fortune 500 MNOs, such as Nissan, Sumitomo, and Japan Victor, to provide ongoing Western culture training as a staple of multinational managerial, staff, and assembly-line human resource development (Goldman, 1992e). This training is provided during the course of the workweek, on company time and dollars. In most cases, cultural training is an extension of conversational English classes provided by companies with global agendas.

In contrast, Western MNOs and the corporate and academic communities have only recently collectively scrutinized Japanese managerial practices and interrelated cultural and communicative protocol (Hofstede, 1984; Luenemann & Knutson, 1993; Olaniran, 1993). Responding to trade frictions, reduced market share, Japanese competitiveness, and the opening of Japanese subsidiaries on this side of the Pacific, Western management of the late 1970s through the early 1990s attempted to transfer Japanese-styled group communication, superior-subordinate relations, decision making, quality circles, total quality management (TQM), and just-in-time (JIT) production methods to North American and Western European organizations (Berman & Hellweg, 1989; Condon, 1984; Hirokawa, 1981; Hirokawa & Miyahara, 1986; Okabe, 1983; Ouchi, 1981; Schonberger, 1982).

IN RESPONSE: INTRACULTURAL
AND INTERCULTURAL ANALYSIS

In response, I investigate in this chapter culturally based communicative behaviors within Japanese MNOs and extend the analysis into a cross-cultural perspective. From both intracultural and intercultural vantage points, the centrality of culture is depicted. Much as Japanese expatriate managers must wrestle with the cultural codes permeating behavior of Canadian, U.S., U.K., and Mexican "strangers" on assembly lines or at negotiating tables, so Western multinationals must invest in the "slower messages" of Japanese culture (Hall & Hall, 1987). As one of many indigenous principles operating in Japanese organizations, the centrality of *ningensei* provides researchers and practitioners with a "terministic screen" (Burke, 1968) for identifying patterns of Japanese intra- and intercultural communication.

An examination of *ningensei* and its relations to Japanese and Japanese-Western MNO communication calls attention to Giles and Pearson's (1990) position that "perceptions, ways of seeing the world, philosophical and linguistic traditions are amongst the important precursors to communication differences between cultures" (p. 3; also see Liu & Allinson, 1988). Being grounded in a fundamental understanding of Japanese philosophical tradition and intracultural codes, it becomes increasingly plausible not only to identify interpersonal and organizational differences and sources of intercultural frictions but also to work toward convergence and hybrid communication and values systems (Cousins, 1989; Giles & Pearson, 1990; King & Bond, 1985; Okabe, 1983; Ouchi, 1981). Because many Western MNOs are briefed insufficiently on Japanese and Eastern philosophical traditions (Liu & Allinson, 1988), communicators tend to be subsumed in what Japanese MNOs refer to as *tatemae* (the surface of communication) and bypass the deeper structure or *honne* (true intentions) of Japanese collectivism (Hall & Hall, 1987). According to Hayashi (1988), who employs a cultural anthropologist's approach to interaction in MNOs, it is vital to elaborate on the need to find culturally common ground via comparative analysis of oftentimes conflicting, indigenous, taken-for-granted cultural beliefs, attitudes, and values (for hybrid views of Western-Japanese communication and values, also see Giles & Pearson, 1990; Goldman, 1988, 1993c; King & Bond, 1985).

In this chapter I provide an intracultural and cross-cultural analysis of Western-Japanese multinational communication by situating the central role of culture (Japanese *ningensei*) within four areas of strategic interaction. Through a Western-Japanese comparison of four interaction categories central to multinational relations, the analysis and synthesis provide a framework for understanding differences. Protocols examined span national and MNO cultures, allowing for systematic identification of patterns of communicative behavior, differentiating interaction styles, points of conflict and tension, and developing common ground for adaptation and convergence. The four categories analyzed are (a) organizational behavior and protocols, (b) public table negotiations, (c) proxemic arrangements, and (d) speechmaking and oral presentations. Before examining each of these categories, it is necessary to examine first the Confucian bases for *ningensei* in Japanese culture and communication.

NINGENSEI IN JAPANESE COMMUNICATION PROTOCOLS

Much as Matsumoto (1988) situates Japanese national and corporate cultures within the emic framework of *haragei* (stomach or gut communication), I position Japanese multinational communication within the context of *ningensei*. Indigenous to national and organizational culture, *ningensei* (as a metaphor and working philosophy) permeates all facets of organizational and multinational communication. Consistent with *ningensei,* Japanese organizations place high priority on the nurturing, sustaining, and building of long-term interpersonal relationships and networks.

Ningensei can be understood in the light of Confucian philosophy and rule-governed behavior (note, however, that a Confucian interpretation of *ningensei* is but one of many possible vantage points). As a deeply rooted Japanese concept that influences social and business relationships, *ningensei* envelops and intersects with a variety of other indigenous Japanese practices and principles such as *honne* (true intentions or true communication), *tatemae* (surface communication), *haragei* (gut/stomach communication), *kokoro* (inner self), *wa* (group spirit), *amae* (interpersonal and organizational interdependencies), *giri* (obligations), *ie* (the Japanese family), *marugakae* (total involvement in family, group, or company), *kaisha* (group consciousness), *uchi* and *soto* (inside and outside—referring to social, family, or organizational boundaries), and *omote* and *ura* (front and rear). It can be argued that *ningensei* provides the Western outsider with a framework for better understanding strategic Japanese multinational protocols—ranging from organizational behavior and management theories, negotiating and conflict styles, and proxemic arrangements of offices and factory work areas, to delivering speeches before corporate audiences.

Ningensei literally translates into "humanity" or "human beingness" and orients Japanese to "invest so much sensitivity, compulsiveness, circumspection, and refinement to the creation or maintenance of smooth and pleasant social relationships" (Lebra, 1976, p. 6). *Ningensei* is an indigenous metaphor and symbol of a quality, style, and construct for interaction permeating Japanese social and corporate cultures (BenDasan, 1970; Goldman, 1992b, 1993a; Lebra, 1992; Yuasa, 1977).

In contrast to a more individualistic, adversarial, and direct Western style of management, *ningensei* breeds conciliatory, win-win game plans for negotiating, delivering persuasive oral reports, or managing conflict (e.g., see Goldman, 1992b). The *ningensei* influence underlies Japanese collectivist, indirect, and nonconfrontational behaviors within organizational families. Moreover, *ningensei* provides a source of illumination into the Japanese practice of seemingly uncharacteristic aggressive, adversarial policies outside of the *keiretsu* or corporate in-group (Doi, 1973, 1989; Lebra, 1992; March, 1990; Matsumoto, 1988; Nakane, 1970). *Ningensei* directs Japanese negotiators, managers, and expatriates toward the development and nurturing of relationships as the highest priority, in contrast to a more task and result oriented interpersonal communication of Western organizations.

Ningensei exemplifies four interrelated cardinal principles of Confucianism: *jen, shu, i,* and *li* (McNaughton, 1974). As purveyors and facilitators of warm feelings, Japanese *ningensei* requires *jen* (humanism). Shunning self-interest and individualism for the benefit of the in-group, the *jen* dimension of *ningensei* may be expressed in empathic interaction, caring for the feelings of negotiating, managerial, or worker associates, and seeking out others' views, sentiments, and true intentions. Mandating finely tuned skills of nonverbal observation and active listening, the *jen* dimension indicates a process, receiver-oriented approach to interpersonal and organizational communication (De Barry, 1959; Hall, 1959; Nivison & Wright, 1959; B. Schwartz, 1959; Shively, 1959; Yum, 1988).

A second Confucian principle intrinsic to *ningensei* is the practice of *shu,* or reciprocity. Closely related to *jen, shu* is explained by Confucius: "There has never been a case where a man who did not understand reciprocity was able to communicate to others whatever treasures he might have had stored in himself" (McNaughton, 1974, p. 28). Emphasizing the importance of reciprocity in establishing humanistic relationships, *shu* is the cultivation of "like-heartedness" (McNaughton, 1974) as a Japanese manager, public speaker, or negotiator attempts to feel as others feel and to step into their social reality.

Third, *ningensei* embodies the Confucian dimension of *i,* the concern with the welfare of the collectivity, group, or organization. Yum (1987a, 1987b, 1988) suggested that the principle of *i* directs human relationships toward "the betterment of the common good" (Yum, 1988, p. 377). The *i* component of *ningensei* surfaces in Japanese negotiators', workers', managers', and expatriates' commitment to the organization, group agendas, and to a reciprocity *(shu)* and humanism *(jen)* that is longterm, consistent, and looks beyond personal motivation. In the course of representing the greater interests of their organizations, Japanese negotiators specifically operationalize *i* in their forming of mutually dependent, long-term, obligatory interpersonal, organizational, and interorganizational (e.g., *keiretsus*) relationships. Reliant on human reciprocity (termed *amae*) (Doi, 1963, 1973, 1989), *ningensei* promotes organizational communication, negotiations, proxemic arrangements, and oral presentations closely linked to interdependent, ongoing relationships. Reciprocal networks of obligations keep individuals bound to each other and to the subsuming objectives of the company. The obligations incurred in the dance of *amae* may not be easily paid off or rectified, as it can involve expectations that debts be honored and met at much later dates, sometimes extending into the next generation (Doi, 1973, 1989; Lebra, 1976, 1992; Matsumoto, 1988). Moreover, reciprocity and mutual obligation to the common good of a corporation or group may require that individuals other than the original players make good on a debt, as indebtedness is ultimately the duty of the specific organizational network, family, or collectivity of which the individual is a part. According to the principles of *i,* debts, deeds, words, and relationships are not primarily located in the individual, but within collective group relationships.

Li, the fourth dimension of Confucianism vital to the operation of *ningensei,* refers to the outer manifestation and social expressions of *jen, shu,* and *i.* Japanese managers, workers, negotiators, and public speakers influenced by *ningensei* communicate according to the restricted codes of *li,* as their humanity, reciprocity, and commitment to the organization (and the organization's relationships) should be expressed in precise codes or predetermined manners. For example, the *meishi* ritual (the formal exchange of business cards) follows a standard, coded etiquette. The antithesis of an extemporaneous Western approach to greetings and business introductions, *meishi* is an operationalizing of *ningensei.* Japanese show their *jen* and *shu* via the exchange of business cards and pleasantries, their *i* through identification and allegiance to a company, and *li* in both verbal and nonverbal reverence acknowledging respect for individual rankings and organizational hierarchies.

Japanese *ningensei* is not communicable in a spontaneous and individualistic manner; rather, it necessitates a close adherence to culturally prescribed interaction codes within specified business and social venues and formats. *Li* is the intricate, composite interaction codes for expressing *ningensei* at negotiating tables, in printed and oral presentations, via proxemic arrangements in the workplace, and in all aspects of Japanese interpersonal and organizational relationships. Whether in Japanese verbal or nonverbal expressions, elaborate and extensive honorific systems guide the careful, stratified communication of *ningensei* (Brown & Levinson, 1978; Chao, 1956; Fukuzawa, 1969; S. Martin, 1964; McBrian, 1978; McIntire, 1972; Ogino, Misono, & Fukushima, 1985; Okabe, 1989; Slobin, Miller, & Porter, 1968). North American outsiders particularly are baffled by verbal and nonverbal expression of the *li* dimension of *ningensei* as the sheer complexity of a hierarchical, Confucian-influenced system of communication can present significant barriers to multinational interaction. Even in the case of Japanese who are fluent English speakers, U.S. negotiators report that the extensive honorific system is transferred noticeably to a "Japanized" communication through English as a second language (Goldman, 1989a; Neustupny, 1987).

Research by Brown and Ford (1964) distinguishing between first name address (FN) versus title plus last name address (TLN) is extended by Ogino, Misono, & Fukushima (1985) into a cross-cultural, North American-East Asian analysis having direct bearing on the *li* dimension of *ningensei.* Whereas North Americans need only a small increment of intimacy in order to shift from the honorific (TLN) to informal form of address (FN), Japanese and other East Asians require a long-term interpersonal relationship before informality is acceptable. However humanely Japanese negotiators, managers, workers, and public speakers may practice *ningensei,* the dimensions of *jen, shu,* and *i* are tempered by the linguistic constraints of *li,* codes of Confucian business and social etiquette that require adherence to rules of expression. This temperance is especially problematic to North American negotiators, expatriate Western managers, or U.S. assembly-line workers who may expect to move rapidly from TLN to FN address, only to be discouraged indirectly via the nonverbal behaviors of Japanese associates.

Organizational Behavior and Protocol

Building on an awareness of the centrality of *ningensei* to Japanese culture, we may now explore ramifications in the broad arena of organizational behavior. Clearly, the high-context nature of Japanese national and organizational culture allows for the fluid practice of the *jen, shu, i,* and *li* of *ningensei.* Close relationships are inseparable from the organizational structuring of alliances. Reciprocity between workers and management, commitment to the company, and fierce team players emerge from job security (Olaniran, 1993) and identification with the organization as a brethren "family" (*ie*) or "village" (Nakane, 1970). On the macro scale, the *li* of Japanese individualism is incorporated within gradations of collectivism: the department, company, *keiretsu,* or nation (Rauch, 1992). A *shu* dimension of like-heartedness is cultivated within and between Japanese organizations, and the *i* or collectivity receives priority over personal pursuits (e.g., careers).

As North Americans and Western European MNOs attempt to identify and adapt to *ningensei* during the early months of expatriations, it is common for them to experience the dissonance associated with being a stranger within a Japanese organization. Although the overall communicative demeanor of the hosting Japanese multinational is likely to be courteous, helpful, and polite, this behavior can be decoded easily as *tatemae* (surface communication). Having few in-depth ties or established relationships within a given Japanese organization, Western strangers feel the brunt of the *i* dimension of *ningensei.* True communication of intentions (*honne*) is not easy to access when you are outside the collectivity. Moreover, the *li* practice positions strangers within special *tatemae* forms of address and discourse (Nivison & Wright, 1959). With the exception of long-established Western-Japanese organizational alliances, the crucial force of *i* prevents *honne* or strategic adaptation to Japanese hosts.

Within the context of organizational communication, *ningensei* is difficult to penetrate. From the Japanese perspective, *ningensei* might be likened to *haragei* (stomach or gut communication; Matsumoto, 1988). It is difficult for Japanese to fathom that an outsider or *gaijin* (foreigner) could understand or participate in the decision making, human resource development, or management of a Japanese organization. In essence, *ningensei* has developed primarily within the intracultural organizational setting, as long-term allegiance to companies invites reciprocal, mutually dependent *amae* (relationships) with other Japanese. The high-context Japanese national and corporate cultures have perennially bred a concentration on cultivating restricted codes for in-group relationships (e.g., *keiretsus*), with attention paid only relatively recently (Meiji Period and Post World War II globalization periods) to the communicative and management styles of out-group organizations (Barnlund, 1989; Fukuzawa, 1969; Goldman, 1993a; Lebra, 1992; Reischauer, 1977). The slow, tedious, long-term nurturing of in-group, Japanese-to-Japanese *ningensei,* and closely affiliated decision-making rituals such as *matomari, nemawashi,* and *ringi* "requires that one be affiliated and identify with relatively small and tightly knit groups of people over long periods of time" (Yum, 1988, p. 379). Job or career mobility between organizations is highly restricted (a threat to *i*), and Japanese-to-Japanese *ningensei* is reciprocated between organizations that are compatible, reliable, in close proximity, and candidates for *jen* and *shu.*

The prospect of establishing a *ningensei* approach to communication with outside organizations presents difficulties for Japanese multinationals who may still proliferate a *nihonjinron* syndrome—that Japan and Japanese companies are for Japanese and cannot be understood by foreigners. Clearly distinguishing between in-groups and out-groups, Japanese organizations rooted in principles of *ningensei* may find it problematic to practice *jen, shu, i,* and *li* with Western multinationals.

Both at home and in Japan, Western multinationals must consider carefully the insider-outsider precepts of *ningensei,* as well as pay attention to many microanalytical factors precipitating *ningensei* in superior-subordinate relations, personnel and human resource policies, decision making and leadership, strategic communication for productivity, motivation and quality issues, and a myriad of managerial and workplace behaviors. Picture a typical *meishi* scenario unfolding between Japanese and Western MNO strangers: Western players have been briefed in the restricted Japanese code of business-card exchange but still may fall victim to starkly contrasting cultural protocols regarding formality and informality in address (the *li* dimension of *ningensei*). As outsiders to Japanese national and corporate culture, strangers likely will stumble on a Japanese reluctance to waive the formal for the informal mode of address (Ogino et al., 1985).

Within the Japanese organization, *keiretsu,* or political system is a strong presence of *jen, shu,* and *i,* but when Japanese interact with *Japanese* outsiders, a high level of competitiveness may prevail largely due to the lack of *i.* Whenever possible, the *li* of *ningensei* requires that the *tatemae* level of discourse remain civilized, polite, and as pleasant as humanly possible. But on the *honne* plane, the unstated true intentions may find expression in adversarial actions (e.g., Ishihara, 1990). The public rendering of hostile *honne* is a last resort as it challenges *kao* (face). Sometimes the abrupt appearance of confrontational communication catches both Japanese and *gaijin* by surprise, as witnessed in the days following the 1991 death of former Japanese Prime Minister Shintaro Abe. In the words of Barbara Wanner, writer for the *Japanese Economic Institute Report,* "despite outward shows of courtesy and politeness, Japanese politicians have proven to be as ruthlessly competitive as that Italian political mastermind Machiavelli could have wished" (1991, p. 1). Liberal Democratic Party officials publicly challenged the leadership of Abe's successor, Prime Minister Toshiki Kaifu, the compromise candidate. The rhetoric emerging from the Diet was harsh, not conciliatory; combative and demeaning, not an exercise in human beingness.

The *li* of *ningensei* does provide for a *tatemae* appropriate to both insider and outsider (e.g., *gaijin* or rival *keiretsu*) organizations, but the *honne* must be earned via a long-term agenda of *jen* and *shu* leading to *i* (alternatively termed *ie,* referring to family status). Accordingly, it is not surprising to find quick visits by U.S. automobile industry CEOs and former President Bush yielding much *tatemae* and little *honne* or *haragei.* A quick visit or two is hardly adequate to "melt the ice," and rather reflects the more jurisprudence, adversarial position of Western MNOs intent on "breaking the ice." Facing untutored, oblivious, or ethnocentric Western MNOs who do not grasp the strategic force of *i,* Japanese MNOs are prone to believe that the appropriate *ningensei* investment is lacking.

In Table 4.1, Japanese organizational protocol is juxtaposed with Western organizational protocol. *Ningensei* provides the cultural context or deeper structure for the Japanese side of the table. A composite of Western cultural forces contributes to the strong individualistic orientations of U.S., Canadian, U.K., and European multinationals. Careful study of the contrasting protocols gives credence to what Barnlund (1975) termed the nearly complete opposites of Western and Japanese social and organizational cultures. The potential for culturally based conflicts is formidable. Western MNOs and expatriate strangers typically are baffled by the subtleties of Japanese group orientation (*i*) and its myriad manifestations through language usage and interactions (*li*). Although aware of Japanese collectivism, Western MNOs find few parallels in North America and Europe for *amae* (Table 4.1, no. 11), *giri* (no. 12), *haragei* (no. 17), *tatemae* and *honne* (no. 8), *keiretsus* (no. 11), and *meishi* (no. 15), all of which identify and serve to further the insider- and outsider-oriented practices of *ningensei.*

TABLE 4.1 Japanese and Western Organizational Behavior and Protocol

Japanese Protocol	*Western Protocol*
1. Generalist workers	Specialist workers
2. Advancement by seniority	By accomplishment
3. Private, prescribed channels for grievances	Public arenas for grievances and disputes
4. Publicly conciliatory	Publicly more argumentative
5. Organizational relationships are highest priority	Tasks/goals are highest priority
6. Long-term organizational agendas	Shorter term organizational agendas
7. Primarily vertical upward and horizontal communication	More vertical downward communication
8. Clear distinction between *tatemae* and *honne*	Less distinction between surface communication and true intentions
9. Accessible informal channels for manager-employee communication	More formalized channels for manager-employee communication
10. Decision making via complete consensus	Decision making via majority vote or designated leaders
11. Amae (interdependencies) crucial in intra- and interorganizational communication (e.g., *keiretsus*)	*Amae* less pronounced and not publicly sanctioned (e.g., antitrust legislation)
12. Strong dependencies (*giri*) and commitments between organizations and employees	Less binding, more flux in commitments between organizations and employees
13. Organizational security via lifetime employment in large MNOs	More turnover, less security; layoffs, firings
14. Close workplace proxemics	More individualized work spaces
15. Ritualized, restricted formal codes for interaction	More informal; less restricted codes
16. Interactions more situationally bound	More ideologically bound
17. Valuing of intuitive, nonverbal communication (*haragei*)	Values analytical logic over intuitive communication
18. More reliance on face-to-face communication	Greater use of print communication

Western MNOs must work patiently toward inclusion or consideration for *i* status. It requires great insight into Japanese *ningensei* to perceive that the outward behavior of an individual corporate representative is bound by collective dictates of a system of debts (*giri*), the necessity of restraining from a communication of *honne* or *haragei* with corporate outsiders, and an allegiance to lifelong, multigenerational relationships to one's corporation and *keiretsu*.

It is in the light of *amae* and *giri* (manifestations of *jen, shu,* and *li*) that Western multinationals are further able to penetrate the veil and complexities of Japanese collectivism (*i*). Long-term, structured networks of intraorganizational relationships (Table 4.1, nos. 5, 6, 8, 10, 11, 12, & 13) operationalize *ningensei* via close worker and manager proxemics (no. 14), generalist work assignments and job rotation (no. 1), and high levels of worker feedback and participation (nos. 7, 9, 10, 13, & 17).

Growing Western and Japanese MNO interest in transferring Japanese-styled total quality management (TQM) to Western organizations has uncovered many problems, accentuating the differences cited in Table 4.1. Assuming that Western management is expected to implement TQM (perhaps by Japanese joint-venture partners) or has set its own TQM goals, the farther reaches of teamwork achieved via processes of Japanese *ningensei* are beyond reach on this side of the Pacific. Although Table 4.1 does not readily reflect Theory Y developments in Western organizations, and positions Western MNOs on the Theory X-individualism side of an individualism-collectivism continuum, few North American organizations ever escape a fundamental adversarial, antagonistic managerial-worker relationship. For example, assume that Western organizations readily learn from Japanese MNOs and see TQM as a means for simulating strategic aspects of Japanese national and organizational culture in the United States. Even a strong Theory Y, participatory management drift to the left will not significantly overturn long-standing pillars of staunch individualism. A close examination of Western MNO pilot TQM projects reveals that the pyramid is seldom sufficiently flattened. Extremely high and uneven CEO salaries prevail; workers are territorial, and proxemic arrangements are a major problem as managers resist attempts to convert individual offices to group space; and rapid turnover plagues the teamwork agenda of TQM. Even a cognitive appreciation for the *jen, shu, i,* and *li* of *ningensei* may not readily bridge the behavioral and affective gaps (especially regarding individualism-collectivism) between Japanese and Western organizations. What is more culturally responsive and realistic is experimentation with *ningensei*-Western managerial and communicative hybrids, as it is intercultural folly to attempt to closely mirror Japanese-styled TQM in the West. Short of creating a collectivist organizational island, Japanese and Western organizational protocols may be negotiated but not transferred, adapted but not adopted, shifted but not abandoned.

Public Table Negotiations

Japanese *ningensei* is strategized carefully within public table negotiations. As a primary channel of intraorganizational and multinational communication, negotiating provides a venue for examining, testing, and building relationships. As indicated in the broad investigation of organizational protocol, *ningensei* is a cultural context for dissecting and anticipating a plethora of negotiating behaviors: intrapersonal, interpersonal, group, organizational, intercultural, and multinational.

Western MNOs alongside politicians are constantly confused and even agitated by Japanese approaches to table negotiations. In the absence of extensive experience with Japanese negotiators, North American and European management frequently assume, erroneously, that Western approaches to public communication, bargaining, advocacy, decision making, and leadership are the international modus operandi (Condon, 1984; Goldman, 1990c, 1991, 1993a; Okabe, 1983).

This problem was evident in U.S. table negotiations with Japan during the early months of 1985, surrounding entrance of Western communication vendors into the then-projected April 1, 1985, deregulation date of the Japanese telecommunications industry. Japanese hesitation to reach rapid-fire decisions resulted in *The Japan Times* reporting that Japanese negotiators "refuse to get down to the nitty gritty" or reach "the bottom line" ("Japan refuses," 1985). Operating as ethnocentric and unofficial "partners" and "lobbyists" to the U.S. negotiating team, the Western-based international wire services set an agenda for public perception of the Japanese negotiators as evasive, slippery, stalling, ambiguous, misleading, tentative, and refusing to get to the point or make timely decisions (see Goldman, 1990b; March, 1990).

These largely inaccurate profiles can be interpreted, in part, as the response of Western MNOs and media personnel who fail to decode the *i* (collectivist) dimension of Japanese *ningensei*, and accordingly attribute U.S. and Western European motives to Japanese negotiating table behaviors. As high-context team players, Japanese negotiating teams communicate *jen, shu, i,* and *li* by valuing silences, engaging in less verbiage than Western counterparts, restricting nonverbal/physical messages, and frequently nodding their heads in seeming agreement. According to March (1990), these verbal and nonverbal behaviors may be decoded by North American and European negotiators as signifying that the minds of Japanese negotiators are being changed. From a Japanese perspective of *jen, shu,* and *li,* however, the negotiators must proceed slowly, as *gaijin* MNOs or competitive strangers only warrant the communication of *tatemae.* Moreover, *ningensei* requires the Japanese team to pay strict allegiance to the restricted codes of *nemawashi* and *ringi.* Unable to respond rapidly to Western MNOs' demands that individual Japanese players reach decisions at the table, the *i* of *ningensei* eluded the foreign negotiators and media and led to their assessment of Japanese "failure to get to the nitty gritty." Faced with a Western orientation of embodying aggressive, assertive statements and positions at public table negotiations, Japanese nevertheless will strive to keep up the appearance of *jen.* The continued onslaught of demands, arguments, and clever rhetorical arrangements of evidence may only further push Japanese negotiators into a defensive position, making them publicly agreeable (*tatemae*), but in truth (*honne*) less willing to yield or compromise.

In Table 4.2 the *ningensei*-influenced Japanese negotiating style is contrasted with a composite of Western negotiating protocol, philosophically rooted in Greco-Roman rhetorical tradition (e.g., see Goldman, 1992a, 1992b, 1993a; Okabe, 1983; Oliver, 1962). Prevalent throughout the Japanese side of Table 4.2 is the *ningensei*-styled preference for humanity, reciprocity, and a receiver orientation accompanied by a distrust for words and logic. BenDasan suggests that *ningensei* comprises the primary reality, whereas symbolic representations such as law, words, and reason remain only secondary; the Japanese thus are cognizant and respectful of "law behind law," "words behind words," and "reason behind reason" (BenDasan, 1970, p. 55, 85). Consistent with *jen* and *shu* dimensions of *ningensei,* Japanese negotiators see the human beingness of associates, but believe that true intentions (*honne*) are not revealed readily in words, contracts, and discursive reasoning (Lebra, 1976). Verbal agility, so central to low-context North Americans (Hall & Hall, 1987; Okabe, 1973), typically is viewed by Japanese negotiators as a "secondary reality," a surface, *tatemae* subterfuge masking *honne.*

The like-heartedness sought via the *shu* aspect of *ningensei* cannot be fulfilled through a publicly combative, individualistic verbal exchange of piercing, probing arguments—a jurisprudence-influenced communicative style closely aligned with Greco-Roman rhetoric (see Table 4.2, nos. 3, 4, 5, & 15). Rather, Japanese prefer a kind of nonverbal jousting and searching for elusive cues housing hidden motives, feelings, and unspoken agendas (see Table 4.2, nos. 15 & 16). In

TABLE 4.2 Japanese and Western Negotiation Protocols

Japanese Negotiating	*Western Negotiating*
1. Longer term	Shorter term
2. Strategic use of silences	Avoids silence
3. Indirect	More direct
4. Avoids public assertiveness	Values assertiveness
5. Publicly nonargumentative	More argumentative
6. Conciliatory	Values confrontational strategies
7. Formal business communication	More informal communication
8. Mostly group decisions (*wa*)	More individual power
9. Private decision making: *nemawashi* and *ringi*	Uses public tables for decision making
10. Priority given to forming lasting business relationships	Highest priority on tasks and pragmatic objectives
11. Avoids interruptions	Interruptions permissible
12. May use "go-betweens" for decision making	More direct face-to-face interaction for decisions
13. Understatement and hesitation in verbal and nonverbal	Prone to speaking in superlatives, exaggerations
14. Mixes business and social venues for decision making	More compartmentalized, separate approach
15. Uses *matomari* or "hints" for achieving group adjustment and saving face in negotiating	More directly verbalizes management's preference at negotiating table
16. Practices *haragei* (gut logic)	Practices more linear, discursive logic
17. Negotiating teams expected to publicly portray united front	Divisiveness is not uncommon

concert with the *i* of *ningensei*, Japanese negotiating behaviors attempt to defend, save, and give face for all involved persons, avoid public disagreements at all costs, and cultivate a long-term campaign approach to negotiating (see Table 4.2, nos. 1, 3, 6, 10, & 13). Any public divisiveness is antagonistic to the principle of *shu*, as Japanese negotiators must build reciprocity with associates. It is thought that public decision making, ultimatums, overstatements, exaggerations, impatience, overly direct language, and verbosity are philosophically and interpersonally incompatible with the common good (*i*) and the development of obligatory, long-term, interdependent relationships (see Table 4.2, nos. 1, 3, 6, 8, 11, & 15). Moreover, the Confucian concept of *i* leads to a patient approach to negotiating and breeds distaste for a strict task-orientation demanding immediate results (March, 1990).

Ningensei cannot result from the segregation of business and social communication (see Table 4.2, no. 14), as the prospects for *jen, shu, i,* and a growing understanding of *li* suffer. Goldman (1993a) reported that Japanese negotiators conduct *tatemae* business in an "appropriate," formal venue during prescribed meeting hours. In addition, Japanese negotiators tend to blur the line between personal and public relationships by encouraging an informal continuation of *ningensei* outside the negotiating table and within social arenas of cabarets, restaurants, bars, golf courses, hot springs, and country club settings. By developing a more holistic, all-encompassing, personalized relationship through extended social contact, Japanese anticipate that *shu* will be served and that *i* becomes increasingly possible. Reciprocity, warm feelings, humanity, and mutual obligations grow out of personal relations and into public negotiating venues.

Of the opinion that many Western MNOs put primary emphasis on discursive, analytical argument, placing ultimate faith in logical discourse and argumentation, Japanese recognize that the *li* of *haragei* is where the East-West line usually is drawn (Goldman, 1992b; Matsumoto, 1988). Epitomizing the cultural and language barriers that hinder Western-Japanese MNO negotiating, *haragei* is a challenge for Japanese to explain to North American and European business associates. Matsumoto stated, "It's tough even for Japanese to explain it in words. It takes a Japanese to understand *haragei*. If you can't feel it, it proves you're a *gaijin*" (Matsumoto, 1988, p. 8).

For many Japanese, the subtleties of *li* and *i,* expressed through the *haragei* of *ningensei*, are inseparable from *kimochi* (emotions) or *ormoiyari* (caring) as "being warm . . . [is] . . . likely to be used to avoid situations of conflict" (Matsumoto, 1988, p. 8). Located somewhere between the heart and the head (affective and cognitive), *haragei* leads to an acute receiver-oriented approach to cultivating relationships. It requires a shift from the more Western MNO notion of "table" negotiations to a more all-inclusive negotiating process or campaign. *Haragei* is characterized by indirectness, an adversity to public questioning at negotiating tables, an avoidance of saying no in public, pregnant pauses and silence (for time to consider situations and people and to interpret nonverbal behaviors), an unstated acceptance of differences in views, and little need to publicly reduce uncertainty when dealing with anticipated paradox, contradictions, and ambiguities (Hall, 1973). Through the use of predominantly nonverbal *haragei,* Japanese are schooled in resolving potentially embarrassing negotiating table situations, as opinions and differences should not be expressed publicly. By the use of facial and paralinguistic nuances, Japanese negotiators may subtly and indirectly acknowledge conflict within a public venue, but the preferred channel for negotiating conflict is private, personal interaction.

In Japanese-Western interaction, the *haragei* of *ningensei* prepares Japanese, ironically, to "stomach" the meeting of East-West negotiating and interpersonal styles, resulting in a variety of *(tatemae)* concessions, while the *honne* remains more concealed. As decision makers, Japanese reserve the most genuine and fluid *haragei* and *honne* for proven intraorganizational and family interactions among familiars. Even the readily briefed and culturally sensitized North American or European expatriate usually will be excluded from the in-group rituals of *nemawashi* and *ringi* (see Okabe, 1983), as Japanese engage in their gut-level decision-making rituals largely behind closed MNO doors. Disputes are reserved for private rooms and corridors, as the table negotiation is equated with *tatemae.* Only after reaching complete private consensus *(ringi)* will Japanese negotiators be able to reveal their positions at the table (under unusual circumstances, a high-ranking negotiator may be extended decision-making powers at the table).

Proxemic Arrangements

Hall (1973, 1976, 1983), and Hall and Hall (1987) reported distinct proxemic orientations of Western and Japanese organizations. Although there are some significant variations between U.S., U.K., German, and other Western MNOs' approaches to corporate spatial arrangements (Gudykunst & Kim, 1984; Prosser, 1989), the gap is far greater between Western and Japanese proxemics. In contrast to the group-space orientation of *ningensei,* the more individualist and lower context Western MNOs generally share a primarily fixed approach to office space, as widespread use of walls and doors conclusively communicate territoriality. There is a starkly contrasting absence of a fixed proxemic, individualist spatial arrangement within both the Japanese corporation and home. Sliding paper and wood doors (*shoji,* screened doors) tentatively separate rooms, and it is commonplace for Japanese organizations to position many desks and "offices" in a large, undivided room (although used in the West, it is far less common).

Expatriate North American and Japanese representing their MNOs may not be prepared for the showdown between proxemic protocols. The European transplant, for instance, often is thrust into the *jen, shu,* and *i* of *ningensei* as he or she has to adjust abruptly to an almost complete lack of physical privacy and to a cognitive, affective, and behavioral "sharing." Even those fortunate enough to be issued an office with a door may soon find that a door, a receptionist, and a telephone do not act as hindrances to the group-space orientation of Japanese associates. Much as the *shoji* screen offers minimal separation between rooms and individuals, Japanese corporates are accustomed to communal space in the home, office, and village (Nakane, 1970). It is difficult for Japanese to respect privacy when it is not something they are particularly cognizant of (e.g., *shu* and *i*) until in close quarters with Westerners (Goldman, 1993e).

Assuming that the *i* or collectivism is "obviously" operationalized through group space, a brief knock on the door and a sudden entrance by a Japanese manager may violate the proxemic code of a startled German or U.K. expatriate. The incidence of Western-Japanese proxemic violations and conflicts are numerous and particularly difficult to avoid, due to their unexamined and unconsciously learned origins (Goldman, 1993b; Hall & Hall, 1987). Cases illustrating Western-Japanese proxemic conflicts are viewed on the production lines in Japanese MNO acquisitions, subsidiaries, joint ventures, and manufacturing plants based in the West. Populated by Western and Japanese line workers, many Westerners have difficulty adjusting to the U-shaped Japanese production line and the closer proxemics and nonverbal reciprocity structured between workers. Western workers are far more familiar with I- and L-shaped lines, wherein they are positioned to view the side or back of fellow workers, allowing for more privacy, anonymity, and distance (Goldman, 1989b; Schonberger, 1982). The U-shaped line employed by many Japanese just-in-time (JIT) and total quality management (TQM) plants positions workers in arrangements that make them visible and physically, nonverbally, and verbally accessible to one another. Western line workers complain that they have no privacy, and they initially prefer the relative insulation of their own space (Goldman, 1993d, 1993e). Moreover, Japanese proxemics serve as a springboard for job rotation on production lines (highly uncommon in Western factories until recent implementations of TQM), as workers are strongly urged to develop competencies at a variety of workstations, positions, and jobs.

The closer Japanese proxemic relationships can be better understood within the context of Japanese *ningensei.* Thrust into what may be

TABLE 4.3 Japanese and Western Proxemic Protocols

Japanese Proxemics	*Western Proxemics*
1. Primary use of semifixed space	Focus on fixed space
2. Less personal space	More personal space
3. More group work spaces	More private offices
4. More accessible vertical communi- cation	Fixed and intentional barriers constricting vertical interaction
5. U-shaped factory lines	L-shaped factory lines
6. Maximum visibility among workers	Physical arrangements may hinder visibility among workers
7. Less hierarchical, more participatory proxemics	More hierarchical approach to spatial arrangements
8. Spatial arrangements to promote generalist workers	Spatial arrangements to promote specialist workers
9. Physical arrangements to promote rapid information flow	Physical arrangements to promote downward information flow
10. Proxemics establishes inter- dependencies (*amae*)	Proxemics establishes autonomy of individual workers and departments

viewed as an unstated method of operationalizing the *i, amae,* and *giri* of Japanese collectivism, the Western line worker or expatriate manager may experience a fundamental collision of proxemic protocols. Proxemic arrangements enforce the *li* of *ningensei,* as team work is structured into Japanese work space. Whereas many management theories, both East and West, talk about individualism and collectivism, the clash of individual versus group space tends to cut into the affective and behavioral nerves of a joint venture.

Table 4.3 presents broad differences in Western and Japanese corporate and manufacturing plant spatial arrangements. All Japanese proxemic characteristics cited in Table 4.3 contribute to the structuring of a highly participatory approach to superior-subordinate and lateral communication. By minimizing distances and barriers, both vertically and horizontally, Japanese spatial arrangements enforce the collectivism of *jen, shu, i,* and *li* dimensions of *ningensei.* The close, face-to-face situating of Japanese workers facilitates more frequent and active communication (sociopetal orientation; see Sommer, 1969). In comparison,

Western organizational proxemics typically separates individuals of similar or different expertise and rank from one another (sociofugal orientation; see Sommer, 1969), structuring more individualism, a growing desire for personal space, less upward communication, more downward communication, bottlenecking, information gatekeeping, and a slower information flow (Goldman, 1989b, 1993a, 1993d; Sommer, 1969).

One of the most serious sources of culture shock is the onslaught of an unknown proxemic; what follows are attempts at negotiating Western and Japanese proxemic protocols in multinational joint ventures. As indicated in a case study, *Nippon Inc. v. Raleigh Ltd.* (Goldman, 1993d), U.S. line workers and management may agree in principle to Japanese-styled TQM and JIT as part of a joint venture arrangement with Japanese majority owners, only later to discover that personnel are not willing to give up their hard-earned offices and private territories in the name of any management theory. Frequently, Western managers and workers experience the participatory and group proxemics of Japanese companies as a spatial invasion and lack adequate preparation or impetus for appreciating or interculturally adapting to an alien proxemic protocol. Although Japanese *ningensei* philosophy may prompt that the *i, amae,* and *giri* be put into practice through a restructuring of a Western subsidiary's work space arrangements, there is little precedent in Western corporate culture for this radical change (Goldman, 1993e).

It is recommended in Western-Japanese joint ventures that special and separate attention be given to proxemic protocols, as they are highly problematic. A database is readily available through a variety of MNO "laboratories" on both sides of the Pacific. It is also quite likely that a myriad of proxemic hybrids are emerging as in *Nippon Inc. vs. Raleigh Ltd.,* in which the U.S.-based partner eventually adapted a Theory Z amalgam (Goldman, 1993d). Aspects of individualism and private space were maintained in league with a 5-year plan toward partial structuring of group space. Quite simply, a Japanese group proxemic provides a physical context for the development and practice of *ningensei,* as Western separateness and privacy is the antithesis of *i.*

Speechmaking and Oral Presentations

Another arena in need of closer national and corporate culture scrutiny is speechmaking and oral performance protocols. Despite the internationalizing of corporations and communication systems, little culture-specific assistance in speechmaking is available to Western corporates facing Japanese audiences (Dei, 1989; Goldman, 1988,

1989a, 1992c). This lack of preparedness is reflected further in the sparse Western research conducted on speechmaking and international rhetoric (Okabe, 1973, 1983, 1989).

Western MNOs increasingly face Japanese audiences and now must expand their heterogeneous concept of "audiences" to include cultural strangers. Japanese who speak English alternately assume the roles of audience and speaker before Western MNOs, as epitomized in such highly mobile, international speakers as Sony Chairman Morita and former Japanese Prime Minister Nakasone. According to Dei (1989), Nakasone is the Japanese exception; he is a world statesman whose code switches when writing and delivering speeches to Western or Japanese audiences. Evidence from Western and Eastern sources, however, suggests that both sides appear to maintain their indigenous cultural expectations regarding speaking styles and do not easily code-switch as speakers or listeners (Barnlund, 1989; Goldman, 1992a; Okabe, 1973). An assertive, projecting, forceful, argumentative U.S., U.K., or German corporate speaker may be unprepared for a Japanese public-speaking code characterized by modesty, reserve, humility, and conciliatory rhetoric (see Dei, 1989). Whether presenting a position paper at a professional convention or board meeting, engaging in an extended monologue at multinational negotiations, speaking at a press conference, or being interviewed in a roundtable format, the confrontation (silent or vocal) of Western-Japanese protocols is inevitable.

Only the most thoroughly Westernized Japanese MNO speaker is remotely comfortable with the Greco-Roman-influenced adversarial formats (Goldman, 1993a, 1993b; Okabe, 1989). Moreover, to view that special medium of communication termed "speech" as an *individualized* art and skill contradicts the need to establish and sustain *i* (the collectivity). Although the great Western orator can mobilize the collectivity, it is contrary to Japanese human beingness; rather, it is through nonverbal, intuitive, less direct channels of *haragei* that interrelationships tend to be established.

Table 4.4 lists key characteristics of Japanese and Western presentational protocol, emphasizing deeply rooted national and corporate culture differences. Underlying the direct, confrontational, challenging, analytic, verbose, dramatic speaking style of Western communicators is a 2,000-year-old Greco-Roman rhetorical tradition (Oliver, 1962). Contemporary MNO management subscribe to and perpetuate this assertive style of rhetorical advocacy in their speechmaking and approach to presentations. Although presentational protocols derived from Aristotle, the Sophists, Demosthenes, Cicero, Quintillian, and the latter-day elocutionists still survive in Western national and organizational cultures

TABLE 4.4 Japanese and Western Presentational Protocols

Japanese Presentational Style	*Western Presentational Style*
1. Indirect	Direct
2. Nonargumentative	Argumentative
3. Face saving	Challenges face
4. Synthetic, configural logic	Analytical logic
5. Favors nonverbal communication	Favors verbal communication
6. Favors *haragei* (gut communication)	Favors verbal eloquence
7. Slower, more patient speakers	Fast speakers
8. Indirect eye contact	Direct eye contact
9. Reserved style	Projecting style
10. Smaller gestures	Larger gestures
11. More formal	More informal
12. Avoids public expression of emotions	May express emotions
13. Presentations speak to the motives of *kaisha* or group consciousness	Presentations may be motivated individually or collectively
14. Presentations reflect *ie* (household) or *uchi-no* (one's workplace)	Presentations may reflect individual communicative style
15. Total involvement (*marugakae*) in company provides the framework for speech	Individual expertise/specialty may take priority over affiliation
16. Speaking agility is linked with *haragei,* like-heartedness with audience, and relation to an organizational family	Speaking agility is more a function of individual capacity, training, and eloquence
17. Success in public speaking depends on speaker's relations with audience, or audience-centered skills	Success in public speaking is more commonly speaker- and message-centered

(though partially transformed by the demands of the electronic media; see Jamieson, 1988), this approach is at odds with Japanese perceptions of speechmaking (Goldman, 1992c; Okabe, 1973; Yum, 1988).

In the *li* of *ningensei,* a Confucian view of presentational speaking casts the eloquent speaker as a master of a kind of *gaijin tatemae.* Assuming that words are a secondary reality (BenDasan, 1970), the master of words (the Western wordsmith) is a peripheral, secondary communicator. The *li* of Confucian *ningensei* situates the "great orator" as a Sophist in the most pejorative sense of the term. Although a knowledge of Western Greco-Roman rhetorical traditions may allow a Japanese MNO to appreciate a non-Japanese based performance protocol, it is no simple matter to switch, negotiate, or achieve a bi- or multicultural approach to something as fundamental as speech.

Ningensei, as a central metaphor of a Confucian philosophy that frames Japanese communication, positions *honne* and *haragei* as largely unattainable through verbal eloquence. The speechmaker, orator, and jurisprudence-modeled debater (e.g., at multinational meetings) addresses audiences more through the discursive, analytical logic of the West, not via the listening, intuitive, finely tuned interpersonal skills central to *jen, shu, i,* and *li.*

Fundamental to the contrasting presentational protocols is the individual communicator's relationship to his or her organization. As part of a collectivity or *i,* the Japanese corporate speaker is first and foremost a representative or mouthpiece of the *kaisha* (Table 4.4, no. 13). He or she brings expression to the group consciousness and verbalizes and nonverbally encodes according to the mind and will of the corporate *ie* (household) or *uchino* (one's workplace). Individual communicative style or personal rhetorical imprint is not a strategic component of this *ningensei* process (and probably would be discouraged) and is more relevant to the Western leader (Table 4.4, no. 14). Similarly, in presentations of importance to Western-Japanese MNOs, many Western speakers use the words of both their specialization and corporate culture, whereas Japanese usually express the language of Nissan, Sumitomo, or Japan Victor Corporation (see Table 4.4, nos. 13-16). Furthermore, the *shu* (like-heartedness and reciprocity) and *i* (collectivity) orient Japanese speakers to frame their presentations less from the vantage point of the specialist and more from the perspective of the Nissan generalist (Table 4.4, nos. 15 & 16). What is permissible via the *ningensei* context is the *li* or language of company, affiliation, rank, and corporate culture—not the exulted Western-styled expression of personal opinions or individual egos (Table 4.4, nos. 13-16). Hence, the notion of the charismatic speaker, for instance, is more applicable in the West.

Of considerable importance for Japanese oral presenters is the secondary reality of words, juxtaposed with the primary importance of the relationships between speaker and audience, and the *ethos* of the orator (Table 4.4, no. 5). According to Lebra (1976, p. 5), "In dealing with symbols . . . the Japanese seem socially oriented. The truthfulness or value of a given symbolic system is likely to be judged by the personality of its producer or sender, or by the kind of relationship obtaining between its sender and receiver."

Relationships are more the precursors of MNO presentations than the result of individual or collective orations (Table 4.4, nos. 14-17). If engaged totally in the organizational collectivity (*i* and *uchino*), this *marugakae* allows the Japanese insider to address an already established interpersonal and group network. Especially during the early going of an MNO joint venture with Westerners, the Japanese speaker maintains more of an outsider status, and the relational solidarity is lacking for public address. Accordingly, from a Japanese perspective, a presentational situation constitutes one of the least desirable formats for early MNO communication with Western partners. But in character with Western national and corporate culture and presentational protocol, the speaking venue frequently is "forced" on Japanese negotiators, guests, and expatriates.

Also of significance is the *ethos* of the communicator who produces speeches. In multinational communication between Western and Japanese partners, presentational protocol reveals differing perceptions regarding what constitutes credibility. Japanese *ningensei* positions *ethos* as closely correlated to the *i* and *li,* linking speaker and organization. In other words, a speaker who lacks allegiance to the organization or who may not embody appropriate rank and status (achieved through seniority and allegiance more than accomplishment) is not worthy of substantive, moral, or ethical stature. High Japanese *ethos* ratings correlate most favorably with those speakers who are top-ranking corporate team players. Whereas Western protocol views *ethos* as more derivative of achievement and expertise, Japanese cannot separate these variables from *marugakae* or *uchino* (Table 4.4, nos. 14 & 15).

As a secondary reality of *ningensei,* spoken and written words do not carry the weight or *ethos* attributed these channels by Western national and corporate cultures. The longer term establishment of *honne* and the communication of *haragei* orient Japanese multinationals more toward the encoding and decoding of nonverbal behaviors, feelings, intuitions, and overall relationships. For Western MNOs, the business presentation is conceived of as a high priority verbal format; Japanese *ningensei* points toward the suspect status of oratory and the propensity of the eloquent speaker toward deception (Table 4.4, nos. 16 & 17). The U.S., U.K., or German corporate representative pays careful attention to the sculpting of the phrase, the powers of analytical logic, and the importance of beginnings, endings, transitions, tropes, and figures (Table 4.4, nos. 4-6). Such elements are cornerstones of Western rhetoric. But the

Japanese speaker or listener is prone to gloss over the importance of analysis and arrangement of arguments, as the *haragei* and *honne* predispose business communicators to look for the "words behind words . . . the reasons behind reasons" (BenDasan, 1970, p. 177). It should be expected that the oral presentation occupies a *tatemae* position in the Japanese business agenda and, moreover, that the celebrated position of speaker and speechmaking is held to be a *gaijin* innovation, channel, and venue. Japanese give strict attention to the nonverbal encodings of this foreign medium, as Japanese communicative code is more restricted and precise in the expression of body language, facial expression, paralanguage, breathing, eye contact, and silences (the *li* of *ningensei*).

The secondary status attributed to speechmaking and orators is also applicable to Japanese perceptions of the written word. Although written documentation, data, statistics, and precise evidence generally is expected of Western corporate speakers (as hard copy backup), the status of the printed word or the written typed contractual agreement are merely verbalizations subject to the individuals and groups involved and pending uncertainties. As situations change, people have priority over words, laws, and contracts. The indirect, ambiguous communicative style deeply exudes the spirit of *ningensei,* a concept that encourages mutual, collective responsibility and a sharing of good and bad results. To "embalm" or "freeze" a detailed MNO agreement into printed form is indicative of a Western response to uncertainty reduction. A flexible, oral agreement and a growing interpersonal reciprocity (*jen* and *shu*) are Japanese alternatives for uncertainties. The win-lose, adversarial nature of the oral or written word that usually sets the agenda for MNOs' future is contrary to the like-heartedness of *shu*.

A SUMMARY NOTE TO RESEARCHERS AND PRACTITIONERS

Lurking between the words of Japanese-Western contracts, behind the arguments of speakers, silently implicit in proxemic arrangements, and thinly veiled at MNO negotiating tables is the imprinting of culture. *Ningensei* requires a probing curiosity and a time-consuming anthropology that understandably eludes the fast messages of Western MNO communicators. Vague *gaijin* or outsider notions of Japanese collectivism or group consciousness only hint at the complexities of interpersonal and corporate relationships, leaving Western theorists and practitioners unprepared for its myriad manifestations in proxemics, speechmaking, table negotiations, and overall organizational protocol. Divorced from the slower messages of culture, Western researchers or MNO negotiators and managers are doomed to "tourist status." The message of *ningensei* is of the overwhelming influence of national (and corporate) culture, a force that drives Japanese individuals and MNOs to adapt, yield, or be unyielding to Western (and other Asian or Japanese) cultural or corporate strangers. From the perspective of Japanese *ningensei,* there is reason to believe in a profoundly conservative, ritualistic bent to culturally learned behaviors—even in the advent of this global information era and the internationalizing of business. It is difficult to imagine a sudden Japanese appreciation or acceptance of adversarial table negotiations, argumentative speakers, the pursuit of individual careers over loyalty to one's organization, or a conversion to individualized offices and work spaces. On the other side of the Pacific, Western MNOs should exercise extreme caution before retaining a TQM consultant (or other "international" management consultant) who advocates the unimportance of culture in the course of transferring collectivist Japanese organizational practices across national borders. To the contrary, management theories and organizational protocol are inseparable from national, ethnic, and racial cultures.

A significant line of research might entail the reframing of ongoing intercultural and international communication research questions and theory building within non-Western cultural contexts (e.g., Shuter, 1990a; Starosta, 1993; Yum, 1988). Quite simply, current Western-born hegemonies, paradigms, and/or terministic screens of intercultural competency, uncertainty reduction, compliance gaining, intercultural adaptation, intercultural communication apprehension, power-distance, masculinity-femininity, and individualism-collectivism require "reframing" of Japanese intracultural and intercultural presuppositions (Fishman, 1982; Giles & Pearson, 1990; Goldman, 1992b, 1993e; Hayashi, 1988; Hildebrandt & Giles, 1983; Jahoda, 1988; Lagmay, 1984; Shuter, 1990a; Starosta, 1993; Wetzel, 1988). For example, the established international "robustness" of Hofstede's dimensions does not survive the "Confucian work dynamism" (CWD) cultural dimension when applied to Japan and other Asian countries. Closely paralleling some of the pillars of *ningensei* examined in this chapter, Giles and Pearson make a case for incorporating an indigenous perspective and examining the applicability of Western theories in Eastern cultures:

> Questioning the Western bias inherent within Hofstede's dimensions, the Chinese Culture Connection (1987) used *Chinese*-generated values and identified four Chinese cultural dimensions: "integration," "Confucian Work Dynamism" (CWD), "human heartedness," and "moral discipline." These

with the exception of CWD, were significantly correlated with three of Hofstede's dimensions. Particularly notable is that the CWD was found to be unique to Eastern contexts—especially the "Five Economic Dragons" (viz., Hong Kong, Taiwan, Japan, South Korea and Singapore) and found to be significantly correlated with Gross National Growth. (1990, p. 4)

Apparent in the research of Giles and Pearson (1990), Bond (1988), and Goldman (1992b, 1993a) is a cultural mandate necessitating that Western researchers anticipate the equivalent of a "CWD factor" whenever crossing national, cultural, racial, and ethnic boundaries. Within the framework of *ningensei,* the brainstorming reader will conjure up any number of Western correlations to the *jen, shu, i,* and *li* dimensions. But unlike the Chinese Culture Connections' depiction of CWD, *ningensei*'s incompatibility with Western MNO communication protocol may be largely a function of the interplay of all four dimensions. Without a scrutinizing of the *li* dimension, for example, it is probable that a "fast reading" Western critic would liken *jen* and *shu* to a Theory Y MNO organization; but this is hardly the case. The interplay of dimensions shows both vertical and horizontal features, a composite of Theory X and Y orientations, and a multifaceted nurturing of teamwork (*i*) that makes use of close, shared proxemic space but maintains elements and reinventions of an ancient Confucian hierarchical approach to address, honorifics, and verbal interaction (the *li* dimension).

EPILOGUE

Western MNOs of the late 20th century must realize increasingly that the success of international agendas is contingent, in part, on cultural preparedness. By recourse to Japanese *ningensei* in an analysis of four dimensions of multinational communicative protocol, this study stresses the importance of identifying cultural differences, sources of ethnocentrism, and the prospects for intercultural adaptation. The high premature return rate of Western managers and families from Japan and additional cited evidence of corporate and cultural insensitivities can be cognitively, affectively, and behaviorally reduced by an examination of the centrality of culture. Far too often, U.S. presidents, North American and European CEOs, and heads of state underestimate the powerful grip that respective national and corporate cultures have in joint ventures, trade, and diplomacy. As indicated throughout this study, the clash of cultural protocols is particularly evident in the light of Western social scientists' and practitioners' confusion of Japanese *tatemae* with *honne, soto* with *uchi,* and *omote* with *ura.*

The intercultural shortcomings of Western MNOs in the midst of global agendas is witnessed in the failure to recognize the Japanese predisposition toward carefully orchestrated, rule-governed, collectivist communication. The building of relationships and human beingness (*ningensei*) takes priority over the success, failure, or compliance-gaining prospects of individual speeches, negotiations, contracts, or performances. Giles and Pearson (1990), Barnlund (1975, 1989), and Nakanishi (1986) called attention to the "length and type of relationship" as an "important mediator" in willingness to self-disclose. It should be evident that "members of some cultures may be more willing to self-disclose to outgroup members than others" (Giles & Pearson, 1990, p. 16) and that "self-disclosure itself may be perceived differently by various cultures; while it may indicate friendliness and openness to Westerners, Japanese may use other criteria to assess such attributes" (Giles & Pearson, 1990, p. 16; also see Nakanishi, 1986). From the *ningensei* framework, the prioritizing of long-term relationships is pivotal for *jen, shu, i,* and *li,* and close correlations are to be drawn between self-disclosure (a rough translation is *kokoro,* or "inner self") and *honne* (see Matsumoto, 1988). Under the influence of *ningensei,* communication campaigns take priority over shorter term strategies as self-disclosure and *honne* require human beingness. Future research into Japanese-Western MNO communication can take notice of the differences between the shared social realities of interactants and can strive to define the philosophical, symbolic, and interactional codes of specific cultures (Berger & Luckman, 1967; Giles & Pearson, 1990).

By increased investment in understanding Japanese philosophical, psychocultural, sociocultural, and organizational codes, Western management accelerates the cultural adaptation process and alleviates some of the conflicts that abound in trial-and-error interaction, ethnocentric table negotiations, and xenophobic corporate diplomacy. A growing sensitivity to Japanese expectations may lead Western management down a path of cultural convergence whereby North American and European MNOs knowingly adapt to more "Japanized" communicative behaviors and managerial policies (or Japanese to more Westernized protocols). For example, in the case of the return of total quality management (TQM) from Japan to the United States and Western Europe (via joint ventures, mergers, acquisitions, and subsidiaries), some organizations have undertaken radical restructurings based on Japanese models of closer proxemics, just-in-time production, quality circles and teamwork, decentralized communication systems for interpersonal and group interaction, and increasingly participatory management styles (see Cusumano, 1988; Feigenbaum, 1961; Hayashi, 1988; Schonberger, 1982, 1986, 1987).

Additionally, a growing knowledge of *ningensei* and other indigenous Japanese concepts may allow Western MNOs to better assess the prospects for "family status" with Japanese partners (e.g., there has been much concern among U.S. representatives in the Structural Impediments Initiative between the United States and Japan that the Japanese *keiretsus* are a major stumbling block in breaking through Japanese "family lines" and into Japanese consumer markets; see Ostrom, 1991, pp. 5-7). Research must produce a better understanding of both the Japanese nuclear and work families (Hambata, 1990; Kawashima, 1949; Murakami, Kumon, & Sato, 1979; Nakane, 1967) as a precursor to strategizing longer term Western-Japanese MNO alliances. It is possible that evidence will point toward the folly of implementing Japanese-styled collectivism in some Western MNOs, while others may discover blueprints for successful transitions, hybrids, or coexistence with Japanese MNO partners. Especially in Western MNOs eager to adapt to Japanese protocol, a *marugakae* (total involvement) may be expedited by such cultural analysis and preparation. It is vital at this point that Western and Japanese researchers document these MNO contact situations, managerial transfers, and hybrids and report them in the form of case studies.

Evidence of cultural convergence in Western-Japanese speechmaking and oral performance protocols was cited in the *Asahi Shimbun* daily newspaper of Japan, noting that some Japanese professionals were becoming increasingly argumentative and confrontational after frequent attendance at conventions with North Americans ("Marked change in communication," 1981, p. 3). Goldman (1988, 1989b) and Okabe (1983) reported that this convergence of Japanese and Western approaches to communication and organizational protocols, termed "Z-Communication" (also see Ouchi, 1981), offers a means for reducing ethnocentrism, managing conflicts and misunderstandings, and reducing flight and frustration in MNO business.

By creating in-house corporate laboratories for simulating Western-Japanese communication and providing cross-cultural briefings, Western management may increase both the culture-specific knowledge base and repertoires of MNO players. The degree of convergence or adaptation to Japanese norms may be guided by power, pragmatics, and expediency; surely even greater adaptation is called for in situations of Japanese acquisitions and takeovers of struggling Western plants. In contrast, mergers and joint ventures may be viewed in a more egalitarian fashion, as more parity in corporate financial investments requires a highly sensitive juggling of cultural and communicative protocols.

Much as Western global marketing campaigners painstakingly discovered the specifics of Japanese culture and readjusted after internationally heralded advertising blunders, so too can MNOs view their premature return rate of expatriates, negotiating standoffs, superior-subordinate conflicts, and the superiority of some of Japan's consumer industries as signals indicating a need for closer examination of Japanese culture. Soon to be expatriates, U.S. and U.K. management and staff working under Japanese majority ownership, and personnel and human relations specialists are in dire need of intercultural tools for interacting more effectively with Japanese. In this chapter I have provided both insider and outsider facets of Japanese MNO communicative behavior and illustrated that thicker descriptions of Japanese collectivity are in order. *Ningensei* provides this central, Confucian-based metaphor as a pivotal framework for appreciating the intricacies of Japanese MNO communicators. Finally, in the process of scratching the surface of an intracultural and intercultural analysis and juxtaposing Western and Japanese MNO protocols, other researchers are invited to unravel the *tatemae* and seek the *honne* of *ningensei*.

5

Communication in Latin American Multinational Organizations

LECIA ARCHER • *University of Colorado, Boulder*
KRISTINE L. FITCH • *University of Colorado, Boulder*

One of the biggest challenges to multinational enterprise is adjusting to cultural differences between the international organization and the host culture. Not only must organizations adapt to the marketing environment, but transplanted individuals also must learn to adapt their behavior and policies to fit the cultural beliefs and values of the host country. A major barrier to effective organizational communication in any multinational organization is the culture-specific nature of the training, theories, and experiences that guide the practices of workers—usually managers—from the parent company. Few of those workers believe they can carry on business in Latin America in exactly the same way as in the United States. The understanding is that cultural differences will influence communication and other practices in the workplace and that there is the need to deal with those differences in some way. Pinning down what the cultural differences are, however, and their impact on organizational life is complicated. Usually, that learning is done in the context of experienced managers passing on their views, in prescriptive form, to less experienced people. Cultural specifics are discussed only as they inform particular scenarios faced by managers; connection into a broader system of cultural meaning is elusive at best. Often, traits are discussed as "cultural" that seem very likely to be a more complex mix of individual disposition, environmental constraints, and situational variables. An example from Kras (1989) is illustrative:

> [Mexicans] have an extremely well developed ability to conceptualize and perceive problems in global terms, identifying all the influences and visualizing the ramifications . . . But the practicalities of implementation and problem solving in everyday business situations are generally not addressed. . . . Programs and projects, conceived, planned and produced on paper, are often not put into practice or are left uncompleted because of unforeseen difficulties. Problems are left unsolved, resulting in lower productivity and a negative effect on personal motivation. (p. 49)

We get no sense from this description which governmental, business, or environmental factors account for "unforeseen difficulties." A pattern of behavior is described as typical, highly problematic, and rooted in "culture"—presumably a historically transmitted, shared system of beliefs and premises. It is difficult to imagine what belief system would incorporate acceptance of "leaving problems unsolved" that have negative impact on productivity and personal motivation.

In this chapter, we offer a view of a less fragmented approach to culture, in the interest of both refining organizational communication theory and paving the way for prescriptive research that can be grounded in a deeper understanding of culture and its manifestations. We begin by reviewing previous research on Latin American organizations. Next, we examine Latin American societies in general and the implications of societal beliefs for organizational communication practices. Then, we describe *padrinazgo* and *palanca,* two aspects of interpersonal beliefs in Latin American societies that have a pervasive impact on organizational life. We discuss the implications of these two practices for organizational communication research and practice in terms of power, motivation, and formal and informal communication.

PREVIOUS RESEARCH
IN LATIN AMERICAN ORGANIZATIONS

There is far less empirical research into Latin American organizations than exists for some other regions of the world. Thus, the literature review below, though not based on as extensive a fund of preexisting work as would be desirable, gives a reasonable sense of what does exist. Some researchers have tied organizational practice to economic development, often advocating broad systemic change with the implication that conformity in cultural practices would help nations develop economically. Others have applied U.S. management theories to Latin American work environments in the interest of improving some aspect of the organization. Finally, prescriptive treatments such as those alluded to earlier have offered descriptions of work practices generally, without giving a broader sense of the culture.

Extant research can be summarized across those broad areas in a roughly chronological progression. Early organizational scholars who provided prescriptions to managers implied that organizations would be the same everywhere if the societies in which they operate could discourage or do away with unproductive cultural values (e.g., Estafen, no date; Lauterbach, 1966; Rehder, 1968; Saeed, 1986). For example,

Riquelme Perez (1968), in an analysis of managerial development in Chile, suggested that *connectionalism,* the tendency to staff according to extended familial and friendship relations, "is retarding Chilean aspirations for achievement and must be considered as a major constraint to social and economic development" (p. 134). He recommended staffing based on a rational system and depending on technical skills much like the bureaucratic systems operating in the United States. This viewpoint implied that the ways of the developed world were better and that if organizations in "underdeveloped" societies were to contribute to development, they had to function in ways more similar to U.S. organizations. Lauterbach (1966), in his book on Latin American enterprise, suggested that changing organizational practice is not always wise, nor necessarily possible. Although this caveat suggests some measure of openness to cultural difference, he went on to say that "gradual change in [casual work habits] is not impossible" (p. 184). By describing the work habits of Latin Americans as "casual," Lauterbach offered a U.S. American viewpoint with no sense of the cultural context in which work habits are formed. Given the relative instability of Latin American governments, for example, what looks to U.S. Americans like a casual attitude may be the most rational strategy for dealing with economic and political instability and for maintaining the extremely important personal network of connections in an organization.

More recent research, though somewhat more sensitive to the integrity of other cultural systems, still proposes changes in practice that are heavily tied to the researchers' own culture or the culture in which particular theories of management originated (e.g., Hostalcio Costa, Diegues Fonseca, & Dourado, 1989, cited in Amado & Vinagre Brasil, 1991). The basis for such work is quite often a particular theory of organizational practice slightly adapted to fit another cultural context. For example, in researching international alliances, particularly U.S. and Japanese companies with Mexican *maquiladoras,* Teagarden and von Glinow (1990) pointed to differences between cultures to determine which contextual factors must be modified to make human resource management more effective. These authors showed their awareness of a fundamental difference between cultures when they quoted a *maquiladora* manager saying,

> Mexico isn't just another state. You have to understand the culture—when to kiss and hug, and when to keep your distance. Until we really got a handle on the Mexican culture [through employment of a Mexican human resources manager] we were pouring training dollars down the drain. (p. 33)

Although the authors emphasized the importance of understanding Mexican culture, their suggestions for dealing with Mexican workers are still fairly superficial, using U.S.-based strategies for dealing with cultural differences rather than operating within cultural norms. For example, they gave anecdotal evidence that job-related and personal-needs training is important for workers who move to job sites far from their families, but did not explain how training can replace a supportive family system. The authors also recommended that supervisors use performance appraisals to make more personal contact with employees, to show that the employees are viewed as people, not simply as workers (p. 45). However, how far periodic work-related contact—which is, additionally, evaluative—would go to constitute personal contact with supervisors is questionable. A more systemic approach to this kind of prescription would involve learning a rhythm of work life that revolves around personal relationships and, as will be discussed later, learning how to fit into it to some extent.

Finally, some recent work on cross-cultural management training techniques emphasizes learning about other cultures and their languages to enhance success in cross-cultural management (e.g., Brislin, Cushner, Cherrie, & Yong, 1986; Harris & Moran, 1987; Kras, 1989). Often, the resources suggested for doing so are limited to traditional literature on the history, political system, and economic structure of the country. These then are supplemented with lists of prescriptive statements. The connection between historical and/or political descriptions of culture and the lived experience of organizational life is extremely loose, such that the do's and don'ts of cross-cultural management trainers present a simplistic and/or fragmented view. For example, Harris and Moran (1987) gave this advice for doing business in Latin America:

> Deals are never concluded over the telephone, usually not even by letter, but in person. Don't call anyone by his or her first name unless the person has made it clear they are ready for it. When in doubt, be formal. Dress conservatively and use calling cards of good quality and in the local language. (p. 376)

This may be sound advice for the U.S. manager conducting business in Latin America. However, the prescriptions themselves do not provide an understanding of the premises and values governing interaction in the cultural context, an understanding that is essential for making decisions in specific situations. In the next section we outline some cultural features of Latin American societies and their implications for communication in Latin American multinational enterprises.

LATIN AMERICAN SOCIETAL TRAITS

In 1991, Latin America comprised 20 countries with an estimated population of more than 447 million people (Hoffman, 1993). A variety of indigenous, African, and European cultures exert strong influence on Latin America, with the strongest influence being Spanish and Portuguese. With the Spanish and Portuguese colonists came a Napoleonic code of laws, the influence of feudalism, and family-oriented, patriarchal societies. Although plainly there are important distinctions between Latin American countries, these nations are culturally similar in a number of ways. Davis (1971a) pointed out that despite local and national differences, there are probably more meaningful similarities among the nations within the Latin American region than among the countries of Africa, Asia, or Europe.

Latin American countries were traditionally agrarian. Although considerable urbanization has occurred during the past generation, the legacy of that very recent past is seen in strong needs among the middle and upper classes for a social hierarchy that clearly distinguishes them from lower status persons. This pervasive orientation to class differences carries over into organizational life in numerous ways, including an expectation of formality (from styles of dress to use of titles in speaking and referring to people of high rank) and a sharp distinction between mental and manual labor (e.g., suggestions that professionals should make their own coffee or photocopies can be highly offensive).

Generally speaking, Latin Americans are taught from an early age to accept authority from their parents and elders. In an extensive literature review, Rehder (1968) found that empirical research supports the claim that Latin Americans are more apt to rely on authority structures to deal with uncertainty than to attempt to find other types of solutions. Historically, this likelihood may derive from the *patrón* relationships common on Latin American plantations and ranches. This was an unequal but reciprocal arrangement between the owner and his workers or tenants, which tied members of different social classes together in enduring relationships. Tenants and workers owed the *patrón* a certain amount of labor in return for housing, tools, a place for their own gardens, and protection in legal disputes and other difficulties. *Patrones* were expected to take a personal interest in the welfare of workers and their families, addressing them by first names, caring for them when they were ill, participating or contributing to their celebrations, and so on. Often the *patrón* served as godfather for the children of loyal workers, which created the *compadrazgo*[1] or godfather system in which a *patrón* was expected to sponsor or provide protection for a godchild. Thus businesses became familial, although unlike U.S. families, social class differences existed between different members of the arrangement. This cultural practice carried over into handicraft shops, mines, and small factories (Gillin, 1971). Ties to kin and *patrón* are still pervasive and profoundly powerful in Latin American societies.

In Latin America, as anywhere, the attitudes and beliefs of organizational members are instilled in them by parents, church, and schools for many years before they become members of a business organization. One dimension of organizational life in which this influence is particularly noticeable is the importance of personal relationships for doing business. Although many Latin Americans now are employed by large organizations, personal relationships remain far more central to organizational life than they are in the United States and other industrialized countries. A legalistic undercurrent permeates most of organizational life in the United States, a legalism that is paired intimately with the written word. Wrongs are documented in paper trails and addressable in courts of law, for example; written statements of company policy count as directives that are, at least sometimes, taken seriously. A parallel in Latin America is the pervasive existence of networks of personal relationships against the background of a lifetime of experience that suggests they are the best, most reliable resource for getting things done.

This parallel holds true for relationships across hierarchical levels as well as within them. The legacy of the *patrón* system from colonial days is a view of authority as more absolute and potentially whimsical, creating a greater dependence of subordinates on the goodwill of superiors. Highly centralized decision making and authoritarian delegation—of tasks, but not authority, for example—are widespread expectations, although certainly not invariably the case. At the same time, compliant subordinates often expect protection and favors from their superiors: leeway in completion of work-related tasks, exceptions to company policies, soft-pedaled criticism, even promotions. Having good relationships with the boss and with co-workers, who also may be in a position to protect or grant favors, is thus a demonstration of merit at least as crucial as other aspects of job performance.

A MULTINATIONAL PROFILE
OF WORK-RELATED VALUES

Hofstede's (1984) multinational study of four cultural traits provides some insight into Latin American society, with implications for how meaning is negotiated and how work gets done. Further, Hofstede's survey data illustrate why certain U.S. organizational practices may be difficult to implement into Latin American multinationals. Although quantitative data may be of limited usefulness in knowing precisely what the values and beliefs of a culture are, the data for Latin American countries show similarities and provide a meaningful starting place for analyzing organizational communication. In this section we overview three of the four traits: power distance, uncertainty avoidance, and individualism. The fourth trait, masculinity/femininity, is not addressed because of wide variation in the ratings among Latin American countries.

Power Distance

Power distance (PDI), according to Hofstede (1984), is "the degree of inequality in power between a less powerful individual (I) and a more powerful other (O), in which I and O belong to the same social system" (p. 71). The index is based on survey data from subjects who were asked their perceptions of their superiors in terms of whether they felt afraid to disagree; whether their boss was autocratic versus persuasive or used a paternalistic decision-making style; and whether the subjects preferred a consultative or nonconsultative decision-making style in their superior. Less educated persons, who constitute a higher percentage of the population of workers in Latin American countries, tend to have higher PDI or tolerance for inequality. Hofstede's (1984) data included seven Latin American countries: Mexico, 81; Venezuela, 81; Brazil, 69; Colombia, 67; Peru, 64; Chile, 63; Argentina, 49. A high number shows a greater tolerance for unequal status among members of a social system.

All of the Latin American countries surveyed had higher power index ratings than the United States (40). The implications for the impact of high PDI as a societal phenomenon on organizations in Latin American societies are a greater centralization of decision making, steeper hierarchical structures, a large proportion of supervisory personnel, and low qualifications of lower strata workers (Hofstede, 1984). Latin Americans, for the most part, are more likely to accept differences in status and authority and prefer to be directed by those with legitimate authority over them rather than make their own decisions. These interpretations fit with Kras's (1989) claim that in Mexico, because of their respect for authority, "young executives never question or even comment on a decision of their superiors, even if they totally disagree with it" (p. 47). Authority rarely is delegated to subordinates because that would decrease the authority and status of the manager. The owner of a business usually is seen as the ultimate authority in a firm (Davis, 1971a), delegating authority only to a few trusted employees. Nevertheless, "even when these individuals are given responsibility, . . . they have no decision-making powers" (p. 176).

Uncertainty Avoidance

Uncertainty avoidance (UAI) is the degree to which one can tolerate ambiguity. The questions for deriving this figure asked about whether rules should/should not be broken, how long employees would work in the present company, and the frequency of tension (stress) at work. The premise for this last question as an indicator of uncertainty avoidance is that when people feel more stress, they have a stronger need for security or certainty. The uncertainty avoidance ratings for seven Latin American countries were as follows: Peru, 87; Chile, 86; Argentina, 86; Mexico, 82; Colombia, 80; Venezuela, 76; Brazil, 76.

The UAI ratings for Latin American workers are significantly higher than that of U.S. workers (46). According to Hofstede (1984), the implications for organizations in a high UAI society are more approval for loyalty to organizations, preference for group decision making over individual decision making, overall satisfaction with the organization, clear hierarchical structures, and a preference for clear requirements and instructions. Because of the sense of fatalism or personal lack of control perceived by Latin Americans (Gillin, 1971; Harris & Moran, 1987; Kras, 1989), the more uncertain one's view of the future, the more one will rely on what one can be certain about: family ties and established extended kinship ties ensuring loyalty.

Individualism

Individualism (IDV) is the relationship between the individual and the collectivity, the emotional dependence of a person on his or her social group. The IDV is based on questions about the need or desire for personal recognition and the freedom to adapt one's own approach to a job. The IDV scores for seven Latin American countries were as follows: Argentina, 46; Brazil, 38; Mexico, 30; Chile, 23; Peru, 16; Colombia, 13; Venezuela, 12.

Workers from all Latin American countries that Hofstede surveyed scored lower on individualism than U.S. workers (91). Hofstede (1984) suggested that workers in more collectivistic societies have greater emotional dependence on organizations and that organizations need to take more personal responsibility for their members than U.S. organizations. Latin American workers tend to conform more than those in individualistic societies and be more particularistic. That is, people are thought of in terms of in-groups and out-groups to a great extent, beyond their individual achievements. Social relationships are more predetermined by in-group membership than by personal affinity. Latin American societies are low IDV and very particularistic. Technical skills are not sufficient; to be successful requires being connected, even in large organizations. Being plugged into the group can lead to more successful organizational life. Unlike in the United States, work and personal life are not separated; getting jobs more consistently relies on whom you know than what you know. In many U.S. organizations, the norm is to talk very little about one's family, because such disclosure implies blurring of an important line between public and private life or even privileging of the family over work. In Latin American organizations, it is inappropriate *not* to ask about someone's family (Kras, 1989). This behavior may be related to the traditional relationship between the *patrón* and the tenant in which the *patrón* (boss, manager) knew the tenant's (employee's) family as well as the worker. For multinational firms, managers imported from individualistic cultures may have much more difficulty being accepted by their subordinates than will employees who are members of that culture because of the lack of in-group status and tendency toward individualism. Further, Latin American employees will be less likely to accept relocation to other areas far from their families and other in-groups. The need for connections, authority, and a class-based system builds a rationale for something other than legal-rational structure as the defining principle for Latin American organizational life. We offer an explanation of the something else in the form of a case study.

PALANCA AS ORGANIZATIONAL CONTROL

We turn now to a case study based on ethnographic investigation in Colombia to describe a pervasive principle of interpersonal relationships with particular relevance to organizational life. This analysis of *palanca* (literally, a lever; interpersonally, a connection) is drawn from data collected as part of a larger study. Although *palanca* is described here as a Colombian phenomenon, we proceed with the assumption that there is both commonality and difference in other Latin American countries.

Data were collected in three time periods: 10 months in 1987, 6 weeks in 1989, and 3 months in 1992. Sources of data were interviews, participant and nonparticipant observation, and document analysis. Approximately 600 hours of observation were conducted in diverse settings: schools, manufacturing organizations, government offices, banks, and other corporate settings. In-depth interviews, ranging from 2 to 10 hours in length, were conducted with approximately 18 informants. Those interviewed ranged in age from 18 to 65 and represented diverse occupations: doormen, maids, teachers, lawyers, economists, psychologists, priests, and an academic department head. Documents consisted of newspaper and magazine articles, classroom materials and school bulletins, advertisements, letters of recommendation, professional newsletters, and several books written about Colombia. Analysis followed the steps of Spradley's (1979, 1980) Developmental Research Sequence, incorporating as well several descriptive categories from Hymes's (1972) model of the interaction of culture and spoken life.

The data of primary interest for examining the concept of *palanca* were observations of and narratives about organizational life. A cultural perspective on organizational processes requires exploration, not just of what happens, but also of what the people involved believe about what happens, how, and why. Thus, *palanca* is described here as more than an objective interpersonal process. It is certainly that: Colombians do observably pursue varied goals by way of relational connections. Beyond its observable status as an interpersonal process, the concept of *palanca* connects with other values and beliefs to form the basis for a powerful cultural myth.

Palanca, as described by Colombians, is the most purely instrumental form or aspect of an interpersonal relationship. "To move a *palanca*" or "to shake out a *palanca*" is to use a relationship like a tool to obtain some objective. Objectives that may be sought by way of *palanca* include services, jobs, or authorizations that are restricted or inaccessible because of either institutional rules and procedures or status as scarce resources. Acting as a *palanca* to transcend scarcity and/or rules is viewed as a favor, and sometimes as an obligation, of interpersonal relationships. The favor may be extended directly or accomplished by way of intermediaries between the person seeking the favor and the person able to grant it. Loosely speaking, the favor of serving as a *palanca* implies an obligation to reciprocate, if possible.

Because *palanca* involves transcending rules or scarcity, it is inherently hierarchical action. Serving as a *palanca* often requires a position within an organization controlled by or responsible for enforcing such rules. Generally, the greater the magnitude of the favor, the higher must be the status of a potential *palanca* in order to secure the desired objective. Thus, *palancas* tend to be of the same or higher status than intermediaries and beneficiaries. People's most frequent contacts are usually with others whose positions are within a limited range of their own, such that the status of the *palancas* one has access to (and the magnitude of favors one may expect to obtain from them) is related to one's own status.

Beyond hierarchical position, *palanca* rests fundamentally on interpersonal connection between the provider and the beneficiary. When the service required is provided easily, the position sought unimportant, or the scarce goods not terribly risky or difficult to secure, the relationship may be minimally close. When stakes are higher—when the service desired is difficult even for the *palanca* to obtain, the position is one that will affect directly the future and/or reputation of the provider, or the goods are very carefully controlled—a significantly higher degree of trust and friendly feeling must exist.

As mentioned above, *palanca* may be viewed as a cultural myth, as well as an interpersonal process. Philipsen (1987) described cultural myths as contributions to the cultural conversation in that they provide a model to which members of the culture can orient themselves in seeking to give purpose and dignity to their lives. *Palanca* provides such a model among Colombians, wherein the oppositions of capricious organizational life are overcome by way of establishing interpersonal bonds, with certain responsibilities and expectations incumbent on them. *Palanca* functions as a symbolic narrative that provides bases of harmonious thought and action: By establishing contact with adequately powerful others, individuals transcend institutional rules, procedures, and scarcity. The *palanca* provides the favor because of the interpersonal bond with the beneficiary. This myth, in its most idealistic form, claims that no earthly end is unachievable, given enough interpersonal bonds with others. There is a limit to what any individual may do; there is virtually no limit on what may be accomplished by *palancas*. Certainly, individual merit is recognized, discursively real, and at times a necessary precondition to secure a *palanca*. Providers are not foolish enough to promote someone who will make them lose credibility. Still, the worth of a person rests just as crucially (and often more so) on his or her connections to other persons of influence as on his or her individual capabilities.

Moral judgments of using *palanca* to get a job, admission to an educational institution, and so forth are, for the most part, positive, resting on the assumption that an interpersonal bond is the basis for extending the favor. Certain related practices that rely on money or trickery, rather than kinship, friendship, or other personal association, are viewed much more negatively. Bribery, falsification of documents, and use of *tramitadores*—people who make their living by performing bureaucratic duties for a fee, often shared with a contact inside the organization—are evaluated harshly. Yet lines between *palanca* and other, more unsavory forms of influence are, not surprisingly, sometimes blurred. A public instance of such ambiguity occurred when a former president of Colombia was granted an annulment of his Catholic marriage after 35 years and several children. There were jokes and some outrage among Colombians, and the often stated assumption was that he "must have bought someone off." The someone, of course, would have to have been a very high ranking Vatican official. Exactly how the annulment was obtained is immaterial. There probably was some basis in ecclesiastical law for the action, yet the wealth and political power of the petitioners clearly influenced the outcome as well. There was no political or social price to pay, whatever public opinion might have been. Within a few years, the former president was appointed Colombian ambassador to, of all places, the Vatican.

Palanca, as both a cultural myth and an interpersonal process, embodies basic belief premises about persons and relationships that are pervasive in the Colombian interpersonal ideology (cf. Fitch, in press, for further discussion of interpersonal ideology). The most basic of these premises is that human beings as individuals are necessarily incomplete entities. Although every individual has unique characteristics and experiences, a person's identity is largely constituted by relationships to other individuals. The events and emotions of life are relatively meaningless to the extent that they are experienced individually, rather than in the context of an interpersonal bond. By the same token, the institutions in which a person may aspire to be educated or employed, the speed and convenience with which he or she may expect to accomplish goals within an organization, the certainty with which he or she may hope to secure quality medical, legal, and other services—key aspects of who that person is—are dependent on the interpersonal bonds that exist with other persons.

The quality of interpersonal bonds is evaluated according to, among other aspects, the degree of *confianza* that exists between human elements. *Confianza* is a feeling of trust, interpersonal closeness, and commitment to shared effects in the future, based on similarity of worldview and derived from common experience (which is derived, in turn, from the contact that facilitates *palanca*: kinship, being class-mates, teammates, co-workers, etc.). Some degree of *confianza* must be created in order to seek the benefits of a *palanca:* The bigger the favor being asked, the more *confianza* is required. Although seeking *palanca* is an instrumental process, there must be some semblance of interpersonal connectedness that implies willingness to take on the possible responsibility of reciprocating.

Finally, among the circumstances that define a person's life experiences, outlook, and range of interpersonal bonds is the positioning of all persons in several parallel status hierarchies. Some of these hierarchies are the family, the Church, the State, and a social system characterized by widely disparate levels of economic and educational status. Human elements necessarily occupy positions of unequal status relative to one another in those hierarchies, and those of higher status naturally exercise authority over those of lower status. The hierarchy must exist for order to be maintained; the opposite of hierarchy is not equality, but anarchy. Still, the rules and procedures that are the most visible symbols of that order may be disregarded or transcended when an interpersonal relationship of *confianza* obtains.

A closely related form of interpersonal connection through which organizational life is structured is also derived from the assumption of hierarchy as a logically pervasive aspect of human existence. This form is *padrinazgo*, godparenting someone, in which a person of lower status who shows exceptional promise is helped by someone of higher status to advance. The help offered might involve moral support and financial backing, in addition to specific access to jobs or institutions, and thus goes beyond the usual purview of *palancas* as relatively transitory interactions. Godparenting someone over an extended period of time involves providing access and/or scarce resources and comes about as a result of an interpersonal relationship. Because it is predicated on an assumption that the beneficiary is particularly deserving, it is viewed as a more noble instantiation of the *palanca* myth.

Although the notion of *palanca* as we have discussed it here is based completely on Colombian data, evidence from other research in Latin America suggests it is a pervasive structure of belief and organizational practice (see discussion of Venezuela by Perez Perdomo, 1990; of Chile by Davis, 1971b; of Brazil by Amado & Vinagre Brasil, 1991; and of Mexico by Kras, 1989).

At this point, it is possible to summarize the thrust of the literature reviewed and the case study in several characteristics of the climate of Latin American organizations that could have significant implications for organizational communication in multinationals in that region: (a) a strong belief in hierarchy that includes separation of social classes; (b) a pervasive emphasis on interpersonal connections as the basis for interaction, within and outside of organizations; (c) a view of the future as tenuous and uncontrollable, especially with regard to government and the business environment; (d) a workforce that is in some ways more stable, due to less geographical mobility and greater loyalty to the organization; and (e) a view of laws and rules as more often symbolic than real in their consequences.

We move now to describe an ethnographic approach to organizational communication research and practice in Latin American multinationals that can produce both theory and prescriptions more truly saturated in Latin American culture. By *ethnographic* we mean to suggest both a research methodology (explored in depth elsewhere; see Carbaugh, 1988; Saville-Troike, 1982; Schwartzman, 1993, for description and exemplars) and an approach to prescription based on the following premises about culture, language, and organizations.

First is a fundamental assumption that cultures are coherent systems of premises and beliefs that are basic and profound. Notions of what kind of entity the self is (e.g., primarily an individual vs. primarily a set of bonds to other people), what kinds of relationships are most desirable among people (e.g., egalitarian and compartmentalized vs. hierarchical and, to some extent, personable), and what kinds of communication practices best accomplish what is most important in life, including organizational life (e.g., open and honest vs. deferential and highly constrained by formality) are all culturally saturated ideas. As such, they are basic principles that vary enormously in different cultures. Predictably, they underlie many of the problematic situations encountered during intercultural contact. Too often, the immediate situation is all that is analyzed; the cultural foundations for observed behavior are given less attention. From this approach, a thorough understanding of the cultural systems is the starting point for extrapolation to concrete situations.

Second is the assumption that culture extends beyond the walls of organizations and that cultural beliefs are pervasively, often invisibly, influential in people's perceptions and actions. A commitment by a multinational organization to doing ethnographically grounded research and training thus would involve in-depth examination of important cultural institutions such as schools, family, voluntary organizations, and, where possible, successful native businesses. It also would involve a commitment to taking seriously the idea that business practices in the host country have an integrity and logical force to them that can be discovered and, in turn, be implemented in the training of managers from the parent organization.

Third is an assumption that language and culture are inextricably interwoven, such that to learn one effectively is to learn the other. Learning to speak Spanish, from this view, is only part of the communicative preparation necessary. Learning how to use language is equally important to do business in Latin America: when to be direct or indirect, how to perform and interpret speech action, public versus private contexts for particular kinds of talk, and so forth. This assumption may sound merely like a push for managers who are more fluent in the language of the host country. Although the desirability of linguistic fluency cannot be overstated, far more critical is attention to the norms and beliefs of the host culture about the *uses of language.* Even when the language of most frequent use is that of the manager, there are significant cultural differences in understandings of how and when to criticize, inform, ask questions, give orders, make suggestions, give compliments, and so forth. The cultural beliefs that constitute those shared understandings are a major focus for investigation, from this approach, and prescriptions focus on being able to recognize and respond to those kinds of expectations when they differ from one's own.

Fourth, as may be apparent from the assumptions listed above, an ethnographic approach centers on questions about the systemic connections between cultural beliefs and the varied behaviors they generate. For that reason, it is not an approach that lends itself to simple answers, lists of cultural traits, or formulaic responses to clearly defined types of problems. It does offer more comprehensive insight into a culture and cultural differences that may be at the heart of many related situational difficulties, though not in any immediately obvious way. This approach is not antithetical to prescriptive research; there is no reason why ethnographically grounded findings cannot be put into practice in the form of guidelines and strategies. The possible difference is the serious commitment to illuminating the logic behind native practices in detail, with the assumption that members of any culture do things the way they do for historically valid reasons. From this view, any move to change practices or policy is grounded in, it is hoped, a respectful understanding of the integrity of the system.

Based on these assumptions, the central question for an ethnographic approach to multinational organizations in Latin America is this: How does a system that revolves around hierarchically organized interpersonal connections work? That broad question can be broken down into more specific ones related to some traditional areas of organizational communication research.

IMPLICATIONS OF *PALANCA* FOR LATIN AMERICAN MULTINATIONALS: POWER, MOTIVATION, AND FORMAL COMMUNICATION

Power

Power is the ability to influence outcomes even in the face of resistance. *Control* is an exercise of power. Most studies of organizations are concerned with control, whether the focus is on controlling individual employee behavior (e.g., human resources theories), material resources (e.g., scientific management), or interaction at the organizational level (e.g., culture management, critical theory). In other words, most theories of organizations are concerned at some level with the power of superiors to control subordinates. In U.S. organizations, legitimate power, or the power afforded by an organizational position, is seen as very important because those with legitimate power also have reward and coercive power over their subordinates.

With the assumption that power and control will emerge, not through legal-rational policies, but through interpersonal interactions and social class-based status, several questions arise. How are bases of power defined and obtained? How is the emphasis on connections with others balanced with the need for technical skills? What are the advantages and drawbacks of strongly hierarchical organizations as compared to egalitarian ones? How is personal power enhanced by connections, and in what ways (and under what circumstances) is that power mitigated by other needs and functions of the organization? What force do rules and policies have in societies wherein courts of law are not such ready enforcers? What other ways do organizations have to enforce regulations when they know that rules often may be subverted by informal networks?

Motivation

Training seminars for managers often are based on some version of human resource theories, which usually stress the development of the individual through empowerment. Further, nearly all undergraduate and graduate textbooks on organizational communication, management, and organizational behavior recommend human resource theories of motivation, which generally are based on the work of Abraham Maslow (1970). Managers are encouraged to include their subordinates in the decision-making process, provide a climate of trust in which employees can say what they think without fear of reprisal, and foster the individual growth of employees through meeting organizational goals. Human resource theories of motivation suggest that an individual can work toward self-actualization by achieving organizational goals once the lesser needs (e.g., hunger, security) are met. Presuming that self-actualization may be defined differently in collectivistic cultures than in individualistic ones raises several questions. How do tenuous views of the future affect the goals that workers strive for? How, if at all, is that changeable by job security and a merit-based system of rewards and punishments? What kinds of communication intended to motivate are most effective in public as opposed to private? What accounts for the impression among non-Latin Americans that Latin Americans are characterized by a casual approach to work (e.g., what specific relationships and tasks are considered to take precedence over work responsibilities)? Under what conditions do Latin Americans prefer or expect to be told what to do, and under what conditions would it be potentially insulting to be told what to do? Are decision-making structures such as participative management, self-directed work teams, and high-involvement organizations (Likert, 1961) workable alternatives in Latin American multinational organizations? What kinds of retraining or reprogramming, if any, could make them effective? What kinds of relationships between superiors and subordinates are most effective for organizational goals? What kinds of communication patterns, for example, strike a useful balance between the need to take a personal interest in employees while maintaining the hierarchical distance expected of a leader? What signs of personal status are particularly valued, and how can managers be sensitive to the motivational impact of their distribution to workers?

Formal and Informal Communication

Formal communication is based on implicit or explicit rules that govern who must report to whom and what the communication should contain. *Formal communication* flows upward, downward, and horizontally. *Informal communication* occurs outside the lines of formal communication and also can flow upward, downward, and horizontally. U.S. organizations privilege formal communication and formal authority over informal communication for getting work done, at least in a public and symbolic sense. That is, although the importance and pervasiveness of informal communication is recognized increasingly in organizational communication literature, there remains a shared understanding of accountability on some level to the formal procedures of the organization. What happens informally is generally regarded as less factual than what happens formally; it is less real in its believability and thus in its consequences. In the Weberian sense, U.S. organizations are very techno-rational. The association of formal communication with real, and of informal communication with unreal, reinforces the separation between work and personal life expected of workers in that culture.

The greater emphasis on interpersonal connections and the lower degree of reliance on formal rules and laws in Latin American organizations lead to a general expectation that informal communication has a different structure, meaning, and importance. A number of questions about the nature of informal communication and its relationship to formal communication thus arise: What relationship, if any, exists between job descriptions (written or unwritten), negotiated understandings of workers' responsibilities, and work-related sanctions? In what circumstances is written communication more effective than oral communication (for clarity, emphasis, to get attention; to remind, reward, punish, thank, commemorate, etc.)? Under what circumstances, if any, are formal chains of authority observed, and when are they bypassed? Where no formal lines of communication exist, how does it occur? Where and why do informal networks break down? How can multinational managers (who are generally, after all, foreigners) discover the important contacts outside the organization with whom personal contacts are necessary for efficient business operation? That is, what sorts of questions can obtain that kind of information, and to whom may they be addressed? How can they make those contacts once they are identified? How can they find out what sort of reciprocation (thanks, favors, cash) is expected?

Finally, the importance of interpersonal connections that we have emphasized here suggests that ethnographic research in Latin American multinations can refine what currently is known about interpersonal networks as a feature of organizational life. Questions that might be pursued in this vein include: To what extent is network analysis, as practiced in U.S. organizational communication research, revealing of the extent and influence of interpersonal connections in Latin American organizations? What supplementary measures, if any, are needed to complete the picture? What can Latin American connectedness suggest in the way of improving the efficiency of informal communication in U.S. organizations?

CONCLUSION

In this chapter we have proposed a cultural approach to the study of organizational communication in Latin American multinational organizations. Based on research on organizational practices, societal traits, and work-related values, a profile of several dimensions of organizational environments in Latin America was constructed. That profile, along with a case study of *palanca* in Columbia, in turn, formed the background for a description of an ethnographic approach to organizational communication research that focuses on interpersonal processes and the values attached to them that have implications for the workplace.

We argued throughout that a primary limitation of much current work on Latin American organizations centers around descriptions of problematic situations and immediate solutions to them with limited grounding in culture as a system of premises and values that extend across both difficult and pleasurable encounters. This approach, we would add, does not prepare multinational managers to function effectively in the wide variety of situations inevitably encountered in complex intercultural interactions. Nor does it lead to refinement of existing theory by way of substantive documentation of differences. An ethnographic approach that investigates the host culture on its own terms as a crucially important context for organizational life progresses toward both of those objectives.

Like much research, we closed by raising perhaps more questions than we have, in any real sense, answered. Proposing a cultural approach to the study of multinational organizations is intended to be only a first step toward understanding organizational communication in Latin America.

NOTE

1. Two closely related terms are used to describe this relationship, depending on the dialect: *Compadrazgo* is the relationship between parents and godparents of a child; it also refers to a clique, ring, group, or cabal. *Padrinazgo* is sponsorship, patronage, favor, or protection.

6

Communication in Multinational Organizations in the United States and Western Europe

DONALD P. CUSHMAN • *State University of New York, Albany*

SARAH SANDERSON KING • *Central Connecticut State University, New Britain*

> The global corporation is the most powerful human organization yet devised for colonizing the future. By scanning the entire planet for opportunities, by shifting its resources from industry to industry and country to country, and by keeping its overriding goal simple—worldwide profit maximization—it has become an institution of unique power. The world managers are the first to have developed a plausible model of the future that is global. They exploit the advantages of mobility while workers and governments are still tied to particular territories. For this reason, the corporate visionaries are far ahead of the rest of the world in making claims on the future. (Barnett & Muller, 1974, p. 363)

Central to these various visions that multinationals have for colonizing the future are alternative conceptions of the role that organizational communication can most appropriately play in colonizing the future. In this chapter we explore in detail the role that communication must play in operationalizing two successful multinational organizational operations that find their roots in the United States and the Western European core markets. In so doing, we (a) explore the link between multinational corporations and rapid increases in economic development, (b) explicate the alternative conceptions of the appropriate role that communication plays in successful American and Western European multinational corporations, and (c) draw some conclusions regarding the role of organizational communication in the emerging global economy. Each of these issues is examined in turn.

THE LINK BETWEEN MULTINATIONAL
CORPORATIONS AND RAPID ECONOMIC DEVELOPMENT

It is old news that nearly one-fifth of the world's population lives on less than $1 per day and that in parts of Africa the average is going down (World Bank, 1993). The new news is that another one-fifth of the world's population whose annual income had been between $2,000 and $5,000 have watched, during the past 20 years, their annual income double, triple, and quadruple (World Bank, 1993). What exactly is the difference between these two groups?

The difference hinges on taking advantage of three facts. First, during the past 20 years, world trade has increased three times as fast as the world's gross domestic product ("Remembering," 1992). This datum means that all of those nations and corporations involved in international trade had the potential to grow three times faster than those not involved. That is exactly what happened to such nations as Singapore, Taiwan, Hong Kong, Spain, Portugal, Mexico, and Argentina and to such corporations as General Electric (GE) and Asea Brown Boveri (ABB) ("Explaining," 1992).

Second, to effectively participate in world trade, corporations had to locate within nations where governments would modify their economic policies to allow for effective competition. "Over the past forty years a single model of governmental economic policy has emerged for all nations who wish to participate in this increase in world trade" ("Explaining," 1992, p. 15). The generalization of such a model does not imply that all governments or all economies are alike; it merely suggests broad central tendencies in the economic policies of most nations as they begin to participate in the world economy.

Third, a new model for economic development has emerged that creates a unique role for multinational corporations to play in the diffusion of practical knowledge to less developed nations. This theory was outlined in a dissertation by Paul Romer, now at the University of California at Berkeley, titled "Dynamic Competitive Equilibria With Externalities, Increasing Returns, and Unbounded Growth" ("Explaining," 1992).

This theory modified classical economic theory, which argued that economic growth was based on the appropriate use of land or natural resources, labor, and capital. The new theory put forward four major factors of economic growth: capital, labor, practical knowledge (or how to make things), and new ideas as measured by patents on technical and practical knowledge with important market applications. Romer thought this theory could explain rapid economic development as it exists today where such small island nations as Japan, Hong Kong, Singapore, and Taiwan have experienced rapid growth yet have little land or natural resources. This theory has several unique features that warrant further discussion.

First, the new theory recognizes that knowledge of how to make things, or practical knowledge, is central to economic development and can raise dramatically the return on investment. In addition, it acknowledges that education and/or new ideas that cannot be translated into practical knowledge have only a limited or delayed effect on economic growth and will retard the payback on investment.

Second, practical knowledge is a factor of production that must be paid for by foregoing consumption and investing in practical knowledge training, generation, and diffusion. Education as such must be broadened from a liberal arts base to a practical and technological knowledge base. More significantly, it elevates practical knowledge of production processes to an equal status with professional and scientific knowledge. The discovery and diffusion of such knowledge, as well as training in the use of practical knowledge, is as likely to take place at work as in a formal educational system. Thus, multinational corporations are becoming the primary investors in, and the laboratory for discovery and teaching and diffusion of, such knowledge to workers at all levels of formal education and to some who have little or no formal education.

Third, investment in the use of such knowledge over extended periods of time will spur rapid national growth. However, investment at the same time will spur the further accumulation of practical knowledge. Multinational corporations are the chief source of such investment. They are also the chief laboratory for developing and diffusing such knowledge. However, they will only establish and maintain a significant presence in countries where the government establishes the appropriate economic conditions for the competitive participation in world trade.

Finally, a sustained investment in practical knowledge can raise permanently a country's growth rate while at the same time driving down the price of such products to one's citizens, thus immediately raising their overall quality of life.

In short, to pursue rapid economic development, a nation, or more specifically a nation's government, must do three things: (a) make the necessary economic reforms to create a favorable climate for corporations to gain access to world trade and the global marketplace, (b) gain access to practical knowledge by attracting multinational corporations to the country, and (c) gain access to significant investment capital for necessary infrastructure development by attracting multinational corporations to the country. Such access has led Mexico, Argentina, Spain, Portugal, Indonesia, Malaysia, Thailand, Hong Kong, Singapore, Taiwan, China, and South Korea to experience rapid growth, along with an appreciable increase in the quality of life for their citizens.

Throughout this discussion, we have talked about attracting multinational corporations to one's country, however, we must acknowledge the differences in the cultural roots of various multinationals and their implications for communication and host country development. Let us address this issue in some detail.

COMMUNICATION IN SUCCESSFUL WESTERN EUROPEAN AND UNITED STATES MULTINATIONAL ORGANIZATIONS

We begin this inquiry by noting three realities. First, in all nations there are more small and medium-sized companies that do not participate in world trade directly than those that do. The vast majority of these firms, however, are suppliers for multinational firms involved in the global economy (Ellis & DelValle, 1993). Second, not all multinational firms are successfully participating in world trade. However, we selected two successful firms in which to examine effective organizational communication. Third, not all successful multinational firms reflect the roots of the cultures from which they grew. However, we selected firms that do reflect those roots in order to gain an insight into the regional differences in multinational organizations whose roots are in the United States and in Western Europe. These multinational corporations are the General Electric Corporation, with roots in the U.S. core market, and Asea Brown Boveri Corporation, with roots in the Western European core market.

Our analysis of each of these firms proceeds in three stages. First, we explore the cultural and economic roots of the firm. Second, we explore the nature, function, and scope of the firm. Third, we explore the communication patterns employed by each in generating, disseminating, and employing practical knowledge and investments.

The General Electric Corporation

Corporations, like individuals, are a product of their economic and cultural roots, their present circumstances, and their future visions.

GE's roots in the American core market. The U.S. core market is unique in the world. It consists of 250 million relatively homogenous, high-consumption customers. It is the least constrained and most internationally competitive market in the world. U.S. corporations are among the most productive in the world, have the lowest wage rates of the big three economies, have the lowest average increase in manufacturing costs, and lead the world in exports ("America the Super-Fit," 1993; Malabre, 1992; O'Reilly, 1992), In short, the United States is one of the largest, most competitive markets in the world. Its consumers have access to a broad range of products at very low prices. Its corporations are faced with low margins and what Fraker (1984, p. 34) identified as "rapidly changing technology, quick market saturation and unexpected competition which creates a volatile business climate."

GE's nature, function, and scope. The General Electric Corporation is the fifth largest industrial organization in America, with sales of $62.2 billion, third in profits with $4.7 billion, and second in stockholder equity with $73.9 billion (Faltermayer, 1993). GE has 13 businesses, operates 200 manufacturing facilities in the United States and 130 abroad in 24 countries, has 284,000 employees, and exports $7.1 billion in goods each year. Let us briefly explore GE's (a) leadership style and (b) corporate goals and values.

In 1981, Jack Welch became CEO of the General Electric Corporation. He viewed the CEO of a multinational corporation as a global warrior. Welch (1988) recalls his early vision:

> At the beginning of the decade, we saw two challenges ahead of us, one external and one internal. Externally, we faced a world economy that would be characterized by slower growth with stronger global competitors going after a smaller pie. In the context of that environment we had one clear-cut major competitor: Japan, Inc. . . . powerful . . . innovative . . . and moving aggressively into many of our markets. Internally, our challenge was even bigger. We had to find a way to combine the power, resources and reach of a big company with the hunger, the agility, the spirit and the fire of a small one. . . . The product businesses had to achieve global leadership positions in cost, quality and technology. (pp. 1-2)

In an attempt to operationalize this vision, Welch led GE through a radical transformation. Welch began this transformation by cutting GE's 150 independent business units down to 13, each positioned in a high growth industry in which GE ranked number 1 or 2 in market shares. Welch shed more than 150,000 workers, 1 out of every 4 employees. He cut management by 50%, decentralized, built a new executive team, revamped the corporate culture, restructured the operating division, and replaced 12 of 13 independent business leaders, primarily with American managers. Being a global manager, according to Welch, is a frame of mind and not primarily a matter of ethnic background.

By 1988, Welch had, for the most part, implemented his initial vision and could begin to see a new vision for GE in the 1990s:

> The world is even tougher and more crowded. Korea and Taiwan have become world-class competitors, as hungry and aggressive as Japan was in 1981. Europe is on fire with new entrepreneurial spirit and leadership that is among the world's best. Many of its most aggressive companies, like Electrolux and ASEA of Sweden, Philips of Holland, and Siemens and Bayer of Germany, are after our markets through acquisitions and joint ventures—just as we are going after theirs. At the same time, the Japanese are more sophisticated and aggressive than ever—building servicing plants outside Japan, including dozens just over the Mexican border. (Welch, 1988, p. 3; reprinted by permission.)

The 1990s, according to Welch (1988, p. 4), will be a "white-knuckle decade for global business . . . fast . . . exhilarating" with many winners and losers. But GE, according to Welch, is ready. His transformational vision, mobilization, and institutionalization in the 1980s put GE in position to meet these new threats head-on with minimal stress and with the communication, speed, flexibility, and efficiency of a creative firm. Welch (1988) illustrated:

> We approach the '90's with a business system, a method of operating, that allows us to routinely position each business for the short- and long-term so that while one or more are weathering difficult markets, the totality is always growing faster than the world economy. . . . To go with our business strategy, we've got a management system now in place and functioning that supports that strategy—one that is lean, liberating, fast-moving—an organization that facilitates and frees and, above all, understands that the fountainhead of success is the individual, not the system. (p. 40; reprinted by permission)

Jack Welch's leadership has won him the acclaim of business communities in the U.S., Europe, and Asia. He has won Foreign World's Outstanding Leader in the World award and numerous other top management awards. More than 20 of his former top managers now head successful multinational corporations, and when IBM and GM sought to hire a new CEO, he was at the top of their list, along with several of his former assistants.

In addition to leadership style, goals and values are also significant. GE's corporate goals and values are clear and simple: (a) become the most competitive corporation in the world, (b) become the nation's most valuable corporation, (c) develop a skilled, self-actualizing, productive, and aggressive workforce capable of generating and employing practical and technical knowledge, and (d) develop open communication based on candor and trust (Cushman & King, 1994, Chap. 4). We have examined briefly the volatile business climate in the U.S. that gave rise to General Electric Corporation's prominence as a multinational firm and have explored the nature, function, and scope of GE's operations by investigating its radical transformation in leadership style and goals and values since 1981. We are now in a position to examine its unique patterns of communication aimed at generating, disseminating, and using practical and technical knowledge to fuel corporate growth.

The communication patterns employed in generating, disseminating, and employing practical and technical knowledge at GE. At the heart of GE's attempts to fulfill its goals within its corporate values while generating, disseminating, and using practical knowledge is a unique continuous improvement program called Work Out, developed by Jack Welch. Five dynamic communication processes, each with its own theoretic rationale, currently form the basis for such a continuous improvement of organizational co-alignment processes based on world-class benchmarking. These are (a) negotiated linking, (b) a New England town meeting, (c) a cross-functional teamwork, (d) a best practiced case study program, and (e) a responsive R&D program.

In a Negotiated Linking Program, a unit or function is created within an organization whose purpose is to scan continuously the globe in order to locate resources in the form of customers, partners, technologies, and/or consultants that are capable of enhancing an organization's competitiveness. Such resources may include land, labor, capital, market entry, distribution channels, technology, and training. This unit then (a) interacts with the unit holding the potential resource in order to locate its interests, concerns, and contributions to co-alignment; (b) develops the form of co-alignment preferred by both units, such as acquisition, joint venture, alliance, partnership coalition, collaboration, licensing technology leasing, transfer, and/or training; and (c) determines the world-class benchmarking targets in market shares, productivity, quality, flexibility, and/or rapid response time to be met before co-alignment can take place. The organizational negotiated-linking program then formulates the negotiated co-alignment agreement aimed at mobilizing external practical knowledge for organizational usage.

In a New England town meeting, a unit or function is created within the organization to implement a worker continuous improvement program within a New England town meeting format. Its goal is to improve an organization's productivity, quality, flexibility, adaptability, and/or response time. It is an attempt to eliminate nonessential, nonproductive, or "bad" work and to replace it with "good" work. These New England style town meetings last from 1 to 3 days. They begin with the division head calling together 20 to 100 workers, suppliers, and/or customers. Subsequently, the division head opens the meeting with a presentation of key market issues, the organization's vision in responding to these issues, how the organization and its competitors are responding to this vision, and specific organizational needs for increased productivity, quality, flexibility, adaptability, and rapid response time. The division head leaves at this point in the meeting. Thereafter, teamwork facilitators take over and generate a list of bad work to be eliminated and good work to be undertaken in responding to the various areas of concern. The group then is divided into teams of 5 to 10 members to analyze, discuss, and debate potential areas for improvement. Each team then provides a cost-benefit analysis and action plan for the solutions recommended. The division head then returns and listens to a cost-benefit analysis and action plan from each group. The division head acts on all high yield ideas by selecting a team champion, training the team champion in project management, empowering a team to implement the change, and setting performance targets, measurement criteria, time frame, and feedback procedures. The worker improvement team then implements the action plan. New England town meetings create practical knowledge within a unit.

To establish a Cross-Functional Teamwork Program, a unit or function is created to set up cross-functional teams that are assigned the task of mapping the decision, implementation, and review levels of important organizational processes. The cross-functional team then is asked to evaluate and make improvements in the process mappings. This procedure is accomplished in four steps: (a) developing a clear understanding of the process goal, (b) identifying the necessary and sufficient critical success factors for achieving that goal, (c) mapping and improving the essential subprocesses to meet these critical success factors, and (d) rank ordering each subprocess and evaluating its productivity, quality, flexibility, adaptability, and how to make improvements. The unit and/or function then implements the change process and fine tunes its subprocesses. Cross-functional teams create across unit or process practical knowledge.

With the Best Practice Case Study Program, a unit or function is created to scan one's own organization and the globe for world-class competitors and to study how various parts of these organizations succeeded in setting world-class benchmarking standards in productivity, quality, flexibility, adaptability, and response time. This unit usually locates such organizations and makes a site visit, develops a case study of the processes involved, and trains personnel at its own organization in ways to adapt these innovations to its organization. This unit then sets up monitoring and feedback procedures for and implements the change. A Best Practices Program serves to disseminate practical knowledge.

Finally, for an R&D Program, a unit is formed of scientists and engineers to develop new products and processes. At GE, 20% of the budget comes from corporate headquarters, 80% from each product division. Each business unit includes a member of the R&D staff so that this person can be made aware of the unit's practical needs. Then, where feasible, the R&D center attempts to meet those needs. The R&D unit's funding depends on creating usable practical knowledge for each product division (Cushman & King, 1993).

By the end of 1993, more than 70,000 GE employees participated in 3-day workout town meetings with remarkable results. In GE's plastics division alone, more than 30 workout teams were empowered to make changes. One team saved GE plastics $2 million by modifying one production process, another enhanced productivity fourfold, while a third reduced product delivery time 400% ("Workout," 1991). Another business, NBC, used workout to halt the use of report forms that totaled more than 2 million pieces of paper a year (Stewart, 1991). GE Credit Services used workout to tie its cash registers directly to the mainframe, cutting the time for opening a new account from 30 minutes to 90 seconds. Similar results have been reported from workout projects in GE's other businesses, demonstrating a remarkable companywide reorientation of co-alignment processes between worker capabilities and organizational needs.

While this internal transformation of GE's value chain was taking place, Jack Welch also realized that other global organizations were achieving greater productivity, quality control, flexibility, adaptability, and rapid response time than GE, even with the workout program in place. In the summer of 1988, GE began its Best Practices Program. GE scanned the globe and located 24 corporations that had outperformed GE in some area. They then screened out direct competitors and companies that would not be credible to GE employees. Welch invited each corporation to come to GE to learn about its best practices and, in return, to allow GE people to come to the other companies to study their best practices. About half of the companies agreed. They included AMP, Chaparral Steel, Ford, Hewlett Packard, Xerox, and three Japanese companies. GE sent out observers to develop case studies and to ask questions. These best practices case studies were turned into a course at Crotonville, GE's leadership training center, that is offered to a new class of managers from each of GE's 13 businesses each month (Stewart, 1991).

Finally, as GE's top management team reviewed the projects that had been successful from both their workout and best practices programs, they noticed a difference in the types of product that saved up to 1 million dollars and those that saved 100 million dollars. The latter always involved changes in organizational processes that spanned the entire value chain. They cut across departments and involved linking with suppliers and customers. All emphasized managing processes, not functions. This finding led GE to establish its cross-functional team-work program aimed at mapping and then improving key organizational processes. Such process maps frequently allowed employees for the first time to see and understand organizational processes from beginning to end. They also demonstrated the need for a new type of manager, a process manager who could co-align an organization's total assets. It allowed employees to spot bottlenecks, time binds and inventory shortages, and overflows.

Since implementing such a cross-functional teamwork program, GE Appliances has cut its 10-week manufacturing cycle in half, while increasing product availability 6% and decreasing inventory costs 20%. The program has cost less than $3 million to implement and already has returned profits 100 times that (Stewart, 1991). Product mapping programs also have provided an empirical basis for changing how GE measures its management and workers' performance. GE now employs world-class cross-functional process benchmarking standards to evaluate its various business performances and to award its bonuses and merit awards for process improvement practical knowledge (Cushman & King, 1993).

These, then, are the five dynamic communication processes developed by GE for generating, disseminating, and using practical knowledge in order to meet GE's goals. GE's results have been dramatic. During those 13 years, sales rose from $27.9 billion to $62.2 billion; profits rose from $2.9 billion to $4.7 billion; stock appreciation went from $31 per share to more than $93 per share. More significantly, GE is one of only eight multinational corporations to make a profit in each of those 13 years. Each of GE's 13 businesses ranks number one or two in market shares, its productivity increased over 110%, and it became the third largest U.S. exporter (Cushman & King, 1994).

The Asea Brown Boveri Corporation

In 1987, the Swedish electrical engineering firm, Asea, with a strong presence in the Scandinavian market, merged with its Swiss counterpart, Brown and Boveri, an electrical engineering firm with a strong presence in the Swiss and German market, to create ABB. ABB's intent was to become a major player in Europe and the European Economic Community (EEC), where its chief competitors would be Germany's industrial giant Siemens, Britain's GEC and Northern Engineering, and more than 40 smaller national firms. National preference for products in Europe was such an ingrained habit that local producers normally had a definite and decisive advantage. However, the large R&D costs of developing state-of-the-art nuclear and steam electric generators was such that an American firm, General Electric, and a Japanese firm, Hitachi, were beginning to make inroads into European markets.

ABB's roots in the European core market. The European core market is unique in the world. It consists of 460 million relatively diverse consumers distributed across 25 countries. Within Europe is the 13-nation EEC, which was to form a common market by 1992 in order to accelerate the economic growth of its members. Problems with the European Exchange Rate Mechanism, however, have halted a monetary union; problems with the ratification of the Maastricht treaties have halted a political and economic union; plans to remove frontier passport checks for citizens of member countries have been postponed due to opposition from Britain and Denmark; problems with French farmers threaten to torpedo a world trade agreement; and Europe is sliding into a major recession (Moseley, 1992).

Equally ominous is public opinion throughout Europe, where voters are bringing down government after government that had been involved in the EEC negotiations (Whitney, 1993). Economic union has been plagued by government subsidies to major local industries and the letting of large government contracts to those same corporations. In addition, unemployment is mounting (11%); government deficits are soaring due to liberal social programs; interest rates are too high (7%); and market growth is nonexistent (0.01%), with imports from both the U.S. and Japan rising (Javetski, Toy, Templeton, Melcher, & Rossant, 1993).

European consumers are facing high prices, restricted access to world products, high taxes, and declining wages. Europe's corporations are confronting flat market growth, high interest rates, high labor costs, and tough outside competition. Many of Europe's largest corporations are dependent on government subsidies for survival at a time when the EEC wants such support cut to zero. Thus, most European corporations are moving production facilities offshore in an effort to cope with these problems.

ABB's nature, function, and scope. ABB is the 14th largest industrial corporation in Europe, with annual sales of $28.3 billion; 27th in profits, with $587 million; and 66th in stockholder equity (Woods, 1992). ABB has eight business segments and employs 240,000 workers in Europe, North America, South America, and India. Let us briefly explore ABB's leadership style, as well as its corporate goals and values.

In 1987, Percy Barnevick, the former CEO of Asea and the chief architect of the merger with Brown and Boveri, became the president and CEO of ABB. In attempting to build a new vision for his firm, he was confronted by three contradictions. The European and global markets for electrical systems and equipment were regulated, controlled, and financed by national and state governments with a preference for local sourcing to meet local regulations, suggesting the need for a large number of small local firms. However, the large costs for R&D in developing and maintaining state-of-the-art equipment, the need for economies of scale in manufacturing and marketing, and the price competition that would come from such large firms as Siemans, General Electric, and Hitachi suggested the need for a large multinational firm. These opposing economic and political forces created three internal contradictions: The new firm needed to be global and local, big and small, centralized and decentralized all at the same time (Taylor, 1991).

Barnevick came up with a unique strategy to resolve the contradictions, a vision that all European corporations and business schools are watching with excitement as ABB attempts to create a clean, lean, and mean pan-European firm that is competitive internationally, yet with a uniquely European structure ("Asea-Brown-Boveri," 1988; Cohen, 1992). Barnevick's vision was to create a loose confederation of nationally recognized local firms that could be chained together through a global coordination center. Such a firm could plan and resource globally, while responding and adapting locally (Taylor, 1991).

In an attempt to operationalize this vision, Barnevick undertook three moves. First, he sought to acquire or form joint ventures with nationally recognized local firms with a reputation for quality and service in each of the major markets in Europe and the United States. ABB has acquired or taken minority positions in 60 companies, investing $3.6 billion over 4 years (Taylor, 1991).

Second, Barnevick downsized all of his units to make the organization lean, mean, rapid in response, and agile. For example, when Asea Brown Boveri was merged, he reduced the corporate headquarters' staff of 2,000 at Asea and 4,000 at Brown and Boveri to 100. Barnevick has cut more than 50,000 employees in a wrenching process of consolidation and rationalization—layoffs, plant closings, and exchanges between countries—during the past 4 years.

Third, Barnevick restructured ABB in order to cut duplication, ensure high quality and productivity, and develop a globally responsive R&D program. For example, when one internal unit is more productive than another, he has the latter study the former and then moves both facilities to a common location. He hired a former GE executive to restructure ABB's global R&D operation. He concentrated ABB's 11,000 R&D employees in three main centers in Vasteras, Heidelburg, and Baden and in six smaller product centers. This move was essential for creating an R&D team that could generate technical and practical knowledge for the more than 50 business centers while becoming a high quality, low price producer ("Asea-Brown-Boveri," 1988).

Asea Brown Boveri's corporate goals and values are also clear and simple: (a) to become the most competitive corporation in the world through global planning, coordination, and sourcing with deep roots in local markets, (b) to be a low cost, world-class technology and quality provider of products and services, and (c) to employ communication effectively in thinking globally and acting locally. Clearly, these objectives are reflected in Barnevick's leadership.

We have explored briefly the contravailing economic and political forces operating in Europe that gave rise to Asea Brown Boveri's prominence as a multinational corporation. We explored the nature, function, and scope of the firm, its leadership style, and corporate goals and values. We are now in a position to examine its unique patterns of communication aimed at generating, disseminating, and using practical and technical knowledge to fuel corporate growth.

The communication patterns employed in generating, disseminating, and using practical and technical knowledge at ABB. At the heart of ABB's attempts to fulfill its corporate goals within its value system while generating, disseminating, and using practical and technical knowledge are a unique (a) R&D system, (b) matrix management system, and (c) internal benchmarking system. Let us explore each in turn.

In 1988, ABB consolidated and focused its R&D program, clustering its 11,000 R&D personnel into three main and six small research centers. Craig Tedmon, a former R&D manager at General Electric, was brought in to head the R&D effort. He immediately shifted most of the funding for R&D to the various business areas to be spent by them pursuing their various technical and practical needs. Each R&D center immediately dispatched staff members to each business area to try to obtain business to support its R&D unit.

By 1991, ABB business units and central headquarters were spending $2.3 billion a year, or 8% of sales, on R&D. That was a sum greater than that of any of ABB's major competitors. One important result of this R&D effort was ABB's development of the X2000 high-speed train. While the French, German, and Japanese engineers developed similar trains, they each required new track beds that are flat with gentle curves. ABB's engineers developed a special suspension system for their train that allowed the train to run on existing conventional tracks, seriously reducing the cost of installing a high-speed system. The train and several like it won the Amtrac contract for high-speed trains to be employed in the U.S. between Boston and New York and will reduce the 230-mile run from 4 hours plus to 2 hours plus (Rapoport, 1992).

Beyond R&D, at the heart of every firm's organizational communication system, are the communication processes involved in organizational integration, coordination, and control. At ABB, this communication system must also resolve ABB's internal contradictions—namely, to be global and local, big and small, centralized and decentralized in reporting. For ABB, this is accomplished through a unique matrix management communication system (see Figure 6.1).

At the top of the communication system is CEO Percy Barnevick. Immediately below him is a 13-member executive committee consisting of Swedes, Swiss, Germans, and Americans. They meet every 3 weeks at a different ABB facility around the world. They are responsible for establishing and coordinating the global strategy and performances of the various product divisions or business areas and the various geographic areas of country managers.

Directly below the executive committee are business sector managers (BAs) and country or regional managers (CAs). Rapoport (1992, p. 78) explained:

Two bosses for everyone. Barnevick's master matrix gives all employees a country manager and a business sector manager. The country managers run traditional, national companies with local boards of directors, including eminent outsiders. ABB has about 100 such managers, most of them citizens

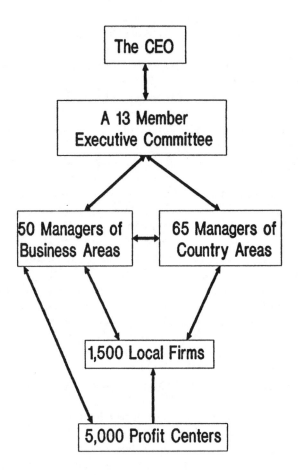

Figure 6.1. ABB's Communication System

of the country in which they work. Of more exalted rank are 65 global managers who are organized into eight segments: transportation, process automation and engineering, environmental devices, financial services, electrical equipment (mainly motors and robots), and three electric power businesses: generation, transmission, and distribution.

Located worldwide, business area managers (or BAs) are responsible for optimizing business on a global basis. These managers set the strategies, hold worldwide factories to cost and quality control standards, allocate export markets to each factory, share expertise by rotating people across borders to create mixed national teams to solve problems and scout talent, and are responsible for building a culture of trust and open communication.

Country managers (or CAs) in the developed world are organized as national enterprises and in the underdeveloped world as regional enterprises with presidents, balance sheets, income statements, and career ladders just like any other firm. These managers report to the BA managers and the executive committee.

Just below the BAs and the CAs are the local business managers and the profit center managers. The business managers are 1,500 local businesses with strong local reputations. Within each business are various profit centers or self-sustaining product units. ABB has more than 5,000 such profit centers. ABB's 1,500 local businesses have an average size of 200 employees. The 5,000 profit centers have an average size of 50 employees.

Communication within this matrix system is the glue holding the firm together. Barnevick (cited in Taylor, 1991, p. 104) illustrated:

> **Communications.** I have no illusions about how hard it is to communicate clearly and quickly to tens of thousands of people around the world. ABB has about 15,000 middle managers prowling around markets all over the world. If we in the executive committee could connect with all of them or even half of them and get them moving in roughly the same direction, we would be unstoppable. But it's enormously difficult.

To solve this problem, Barnevick argued that employers must overinform their employees by sending the same messages through the duplicate channels of the matrix and by having the CEO and executive committee hold meetings frequently with all levels of the matrix in order to communicate a common, repetitive message.

The third key communication system is internal benchmarking. Whereas technical knowledge is developed between business centers and the three main and six regional R&D centers, practical knowledge is developed by employing internal benchmarking teams between various local firms and profit centers. In both cases, the matrix management system must initiate the interchange. Sune Karlsson, vice president of the power transformer business in Mannheim, Germany, initiated a benchmarking change in his Muncie, Indiana, plant. Taylor (1991, p. 96) detailed the main features of Karlsson's model for change.

> Karlsson's approach to change is in keeping with the ABB philosophy: show local managers what's been achieved elsewhere, let them drive the change process, make available ABB expertise from around the world, and demand

quick results. A turnaround for power transformers takes about 18 months. In Germany, for example, one of the company's transformer plants had generated red ink for years. It is now a growing, profitable operation, albeit smaller and more focused than before.

Creating pressure for various local firms to improve requires internal competition, coordination, and open communication. Taylor (1991, p. 97) reported:

Every month, the Mannheim headquarters distributes detailed information on how each of the 25 factories is performing on critical parameters, such as failure rates, throughput times, inventories as a percentage of revenues, and receivables as a percentage of revenues. These reports generate competition for outstanding performance within the ABB network—more intense pressure, Karlsson believes, than external competition in the marketplace.

The key to turning such internal competition into constructive (not destructive) change is to build a culture of trust and open communication and then to create the opportunities to initiate benchmarking studies and to facilitate the training of teams to initiate change. ABB has three such forums for initiating change and focusing training teams. They are (a) the BAs' management board meetings, (b) Karlsson's staff visits to sites, and (c) the regular meetings of functional coordination teams within Karlsson's staff.

ABB's R&D centers, matrix management systems, and internal benchmarking systems are the three dynamic communication processes developed for generating, disseminating, and using technical and practical knowledge in order to meet ABB's goals. ABB's results have been dramatic. During the 6 years of ABB's existence, sales went from $18 billion in 1988 to $28.3 billion in 1991; profits went from $550 million in 1989 to $1.1 billion in 1991 and $587 million in 1991; while stockholder value tripled (Woods, 1992). ABB is considered to be one of the top technology competitors in electrical systems, robotics, high-speed trains, and environmental control (Cohen, 1992, p. 91; Rapoport, 1992, p. 76).

CONCLUSIONS REGARDING COMMUNICATION IN MULTINATIONAL ORGANIZATIONS

The present inquiry appears to have taught some valuable lessons. First, multinational corporations are the primary laboratory for discovering, disseminating, and using technical and practical knowledge.

Second, the effective use of technical and practical knowledge is a catalyst for rapid national and organizational development through the participation in world trade. Third, successful U.S. and European multinational organizations have a unique nature, function, and scope because they arose from different roots.

More specifically, GE, a successful U.S. corporation with roots in the U.S. core market, is characterized by technological breakthroughs, quick market saturation, and unexpected competition, which has made the business environment volatile. ABB, a successful European corporation with roots in the Western European core market, is characterized by multigovernment preferential contracts and subsidies to local firms, creating a noncompetitive multidomestic market in Europe.

On the one hand, GE stabilized its presence in the volatile U.S. core market by focusing on businesses that had the core capabilities to be first or second in market shares in a high growth area. On the other hand, ABB stabilized its presence in the multigovernment preference and subsidization of local industry multidomestic European market by acquiring and linking together well-known local firms to create economies of sourcing and scale in the global market.

GE accomplished its corporate strategy and goals in developing, disseminating, and using technical and practical knowledge to achieve rapid economic growth through the communication processes involved in a well-integrated, coordinated, and controlled continuous improvement process involving self-managed teams, cross-functional teams, benchmarking, linking, and R&D programs. ABB accomplished its corporate strategy and goals in developing, disseminating, and using technical and practical knowledge through the communication processes involved in an R&D, matrix management, and internal benchmarking program.

We are now in a position to explore the major lessons for organizational communication theory from the communication similarities and differences found in these two successful multinational organizations.

Similarities

The most obvious similarity between these two firms is that each has a strong, articulate leader who can communicate a clear vision and form a management team capable of ruthlessly pursuing that vision in a systematic and credible manner. This characteristic clearly and directly supports the communication theory involved in *transformational leadership.*

In addition, both firms have developed a method for achieving high productivity, high quality, and low product costs and for rapidly getting those products to market by employing teamwork, benchmarking, and clearly articulated performance targets. This characteristic directly supports the communication theory involved in *high-speed management* (Cushman & King, 1993).

Finally, both firms have focused on the communication relationship found between a firm's goals, structure, and culture in an attempt to develop trust in an open communication system. This characteristic clearly and directly supports the communication theory involved in *continuous improvement programs.*

Differences

Market differences in the roots of these two firms have led to major differences in their operational communication systems, with significant implications for the development of organizational communication theory.

The goals, strategies, structures, and processes to be communicated by GE are succinct, open, and flexible, while at ABB they are open, complicated, and rapid. GE's goal is to become the most competitive corporation in the world by being number one or two in market shares in a high growth area through developing low cost, high quality, high customer satisfaction products, while employing such continuous improvement processes as self-managed and cross-functional teamwork, internal and external benchmarking, acquisitions and joint ventures, and a world-class R&D system. Note that GE has given a succinct and open statement of goals to be number one or two in market shares in a high growth business by developing low cost, high quality, high-customer-satisfaction products. GE has left open and flexible which business to enter and leave and what strategies, structures, and continuous improvement processes its 13 businesses are to rely on, based on shifting customer needs and competitors' means for attempting to meet those needs.

ABB, on the other hand, also wants to be the most competitive firm in the world by leaving open its specific goal but specifying the strategy and structure for achieving the goal. This strategy involves global planning, coordination, and sourcing with deep roots in the local markets, acquiring or joint venturing with firms that have quality products and high national recognition, employing matrix management to overcome the firm's three contradictions, while employing the processes of internal benchmarking, acquisitions and joint ventures, and world-class R&D to develop products. This strategy is difficult to put in place and is complicated to maintain. It is difficult in Europe, the U.S., and Asia to acquire and/or joint venture with competing firms unless they are in trouble. It is complicated to matrix manage these firms once acquired. Finally, to employ global economies of scale as one's primary strategy is limiting, and matrix management as one's only structure is a rigid approach to competition in a rapidly changing global economy.

GE's method of communication with its stakeholders is comprehensive and optimally effective, while for ABB it is limited and suboptimally effective. GE seeks to communicate to its customers that it is a low cost, high quality, and high-customer-satisfaction product provider; to its employees and management that it is a "win-aholic" organization that allows for control over one's career; and to stockholders it is the nation's most valuable corporation in terms of assets and return on investments (Welch, 1993). GE believes that the optimally effective method for communicating these messages is in an interpersonal context where one has an open and trusting interaction among stakeholders of equal status. Thus, all stakeholders are included in New England town meetings, where they can make suggestions for improving GE as an organization and where management must respond instantly that they will or will not implement the change suggested and why. These suggestions and responses are taped and reviewed by top management to make sure management treated the suggestions in an open, trustworthy, and action-oriented manner ("Workout," 1991).

ABB, on the other hand, addresses only a portion of its stakeholders (customers and workers) in a direct manner and relies primarily on the repetition of messages from management to influence each of them. Such a solution is, according to most recent research, limited and suboptimal in orientation (Larkin & Larkin, 1993).

The communication at GE within its corporate culture and work teams attempts to be self-motivating, creative, and process oriented with a strong sense of individual and team responsibility, while ABB attempts to be supervisory motivating, focused, and with a strong sense of unit responsibility (Barnevick, as cited in Taylor, 1991; Welch, 1988).

Finally, the communication leadership training for ABB attempts to develop a multicultural, articulate, and globally experienced management team, while GE attempts to develop a culturally articulate and globally focused management team (Barnevick, as cited in Taylor, 1991; Welch, 1988). The main difference here is that ABB selects managers from different countries, employs English as a common corporate language, and rotates these managers through different cultures to give them experience. GE selects primarily American managers, teaches them to think globally, and places a limited number abroad.

In conclusion, what lessons can we learn from our inquiry? First, it is clear that both rapid national and corporate growth depends on (a) access to world trade, (b) a stable economy with a convertible currency, (c) the generation, dissemination, and use of technical and practical knowledge, and (d) the major catalyst in this process being the multinational firm.

Second, while both GE and ABB are attempting to become the most competitive firm in the world, GE has become the most competitive firm in the U.S., while ABB has yet to become the most competitive firm in Europe. According to *Forbes* in 1991 and 1992, based on an index of corporate competitiveness that includes sales, profits, assets, and market value, GE is number one in the U.S. According to *Fortune*'s rating of the Global 500 employing these same measures, ABB is only the 33rd most competitive firm in Europe ("The Forbes 500s," 1993, p. 198).

Third, it is clear that transformational leadership, high-speed management, and continuous improvement programs taken together provide the broad outline of an important general theory of organizational communication in the 1990s. Equally important but perhaps less obvious are the discoveries that an organization's (a) goals, strategies, structures, and processes to be communicated effectively must be succinct, open and flexible; (b) stakeholders must all be addressed as equals through interpersonal communication; (c) communication within a corporation's culture and work teams must be self-motivating, creative, and process oriented, with a strong sense of individual and team responsibility; and (d) communication leadership training must attempt to develop a multicultural, articulate, and globally experienced management team.

In short, as Jack Welch (1993, p. 88), stated:

> To create change, direct personal two-way communication is what seems to make a difference: exposing people—without the protection of title or position—to ideas from everywhere, judging ideas on their merits. . . . Another thing I've learned is the value of stretching an organization by setting the bar higher than people think they can go. The standard of performance we use is: Be as good as the best in the world. Invariably, people find ways to get there, or most of the way. (reprinted by permission of Doubleday)

III

DIVERSITY AND ADJUSTMENT
IN MULTINATIONAL ORGANIZATIONS

7

Intercultural Challenges and Personal Adjustments

A Qualitative Analysis of the Experiences of American and Japanese Co-Workers

YOUNG YUN KIM • *University of Oklahoma, Norman*
SHERYL PAULK • *University of Oklahoma, Norman*

Nearly five decades after Northrop (in his book *The Meeting of the East and the West* [1946/1966]) offered a vision of intercultural interface, approximately 600,000 Americans work for Japanese-owned and operated companies in the United States today (Morrow, 1992, p. 19). For these Americans and their Japanese counterparts who work daily side-by-side, Northrop's vision *is* their reality. To them, the notion of effective intercultural communication takes on a special urgency in the intense daily grind of the multinational organization. Its imminent significance comes to the forefront as they attempt to bridge their differences and communicate effectively.

The academic search for helpful insights into the increased Japanese-American interface has been essentially a series of systematic attempts to delineate the cultural differences between these two groups. The prevailing aim of the researchers has been to improve the mutual understanding of the group-level cultural differences. Studies such as Condon's (1984) work have identified differences in various cultural dimensions, including the respective values underlying organizational protocol, providing a comparative insight into the behavioral practices that affect the communication of these two cultural groups (see Benedict, 1946; Haglund, 1988; Nakane, 1970).

AUTHORS' NOTE: This chapter is based on a study directed by the senior author and funded by the Office of Research Administration, University of Oklahoma. We gratefully acknowledge the collaboration of Jiro Sakai and Ezhar Tamam during the data collection and analysis phases of this study, and of Richiko Ikeda during the data collection phase. All three are graduate students in the Department of Communication, University of Oklahoma.

The value orientation of individualism/collectivism (Triandis, 1988), along with the perceptual orientation of high-context and low-context communication (Hall, 1976), often have been employed to explain cultural differences in communication and interpersonal relationships (Barnlund, 1974, 1989; Barnlund & Yoshioka, 1990; Hsu, 1985; Nomura & Barnlund, 1983; Stewart, 1972; Triandis, Brislin, & Hui, 1988). Cultural differences in specific verbal and nonverbal behavior have been an issue in several studies (Becker, 1988; Hall, 1976; Ishii & Bruneau, 1988), while others have emphasized the inherent difficulties and implications presented by the language differences of the two groups (Condon, 1984; Okabe, 1987; Rowland, 1985). Also examined are Japanese/American cultural differences in time orientations (Hall & Hall, 1987), rhetorical styles and strategies (Okabe, 1987), conflict orientations (Cushman & King, 1985), facework (Cupach & Imahori, 1991), face negotiation in conflict (Ting-Toomey, 1988), attitudes toward decision making (Stewart, 1985), and uncertainty reduction and attribution patterns (Gudykunst, Yang, & Nishida, 1985).

In other studies, the impact of Japanese and American cultural differences in work orientation has been examined (Cathcart & Cathcart, 1988; Haglund, 1988; Hall & Hall, 1987; Kumara, Hara, & Yano, 1991). Differences in the respective managerial philosophies and styles have been identified as well in other studies (Ouchi, 1981; Pascale & Athos, 1981; Pegels, 1984). Particularly notable is the work by Hofstede (1984) in which the four work-related cultural value dimensions of individualism-collectivism, masculinity-femininity, power distance, and uncertainty avoidance were identified as universal dimensions on which organizational practices in more than 50 cultures were compared, including Japan and the United States. Further differences related to the management styles of the two cultures have been explored, including managerial attitudes toward decision making (Kume, 1985), the Japanese consensus-building system (Stewart, 1988), criteria for promotions (Beatty, McCune, & Beatty, 1988), structural factors in multinational organizations (Triandis & Albert, 1987), and organizational cultures in Japan and the United States (Chikudate, Barnett, & McFarland, 1990).

Indeed, these and related studies have provided many useful insights into the cultural differences in Japanese and American organizational and communicative patterns. Moving beyond and building on the existing insights, the present study attempts to develop a detailed understanding of the way cultural differences actually are played out in the daily interactions of American and Japanese co-workers. Based on the premise that not all cultural differences would be equally pertinent and consequential to their performances as co-workers, the present study explores those cultural differences that truly make a difference from the experiences and views of the workers themselves. In addition, this study explores the various ways that Japanese and American co-workers have tried to cope with the problematic cultural differences in their own actual dealings with each other. Rather than imposing existing concepts and theories related to managing cultural differences and intercultural communication, this study is devoted to ascertaining the reality of the workers themselves as reported by them and to exploring the rich, experiential insights into the respective organizational and communication prototypes operating in the two cultural groups that are articulated in the existing literature.

Answers to these and related issues have been sought in the present study from a series of one-on-one interviews with Japanese and American employees at a subsidiary of a large Japanese multinational corporation during May-August 1991. In this chapter, we focus on those aspects of our study that deal with (a) the cultural differences that Japanese and American co-workers experience as sources of communication difficulties between them and (b) the strategies these co-workers employ to cope with such difficulties.

THE STUDY: METHODS AND PROCEDURES

The company that was investigated in the present study is located in the central-southern region of the United States. It manufactures computer peripheral devices and is a wholly owned subsidiary with a president who oversees the three primary areas of manufacturing, engineering, and administration. A total of 306 American employees and 13 Japanese employees work at this facility, with 50 of the American staff and 10 of the Japanese staff holding management positions. Because all but three of the Japanese staff are managers, interaction between American and Japanese employees is concerned primarily with operational decision-making objectives. Of the 306 American employees, only about 30 of the American staff members have direct daily contact with the 10 Japanese on the staff. Approximately 75 other American workers deal with the Japanese staff only occasionally, and the remainder have minimal contact with the Japanese staff.

Interviewees

Of the 30 American employees who interact with Japanese employees daily, 12 were selected by the company administration to participate in this study, along with 6 of the 10 Japanese employees. The selection of interviewees was determined on the basis of their regular daily engagement in communication with their Japanese and American counterparts. An analysis of the interviewees' profiles shows that, despite the limited number of participants and their nonrandom selection, they were representative of the overall profile of all those employees who were involved thoroughly in intercultural activity.

All of the interviewees had been employed by the company for a period ranging from 18 to 60 months, with the average term of employment being 42 months. The 18 interviewees consisted of 12 males, most of whom were in their 30s and held positions in middle and higher levels within the company and had a college degree. Most of the six females involved in the interviews were in their 30s, held positions in middle or low levels within the company, and had an educational background consisting of a 2-year college or vocational degree. Table 7.1 presents a summary of the interviewees' profiles.

Interview Procedures

The research team consisted of the principal author and four graduate students specializing in intercultural communication. Two were Japanese nationals who worked as an interviewer-recorder team for all of the Japanese employees. The 12 American employees were interviewed by another interviewer-recorder team that consisted of an American interviewer and a recorder from Malaysia. The American interviewer worked for the company being researched and was a fluent English-Japanese bilingual. Each interview, which lasted 30 to 45 minutes, took place in a small private conference room at the interviewee's convenience and was tape-recorded and transcribed in its entirety. All but one interview with an American was conducted during work hours, while the Japanese interviewees preferred the interviews to take place after office hours.

The definite advantages of having an insider on the research team included the fact that interview scheduling was handled with efficiency and sensitivity and that the interviewees felt more comfortable to speak freely, take their time, and draw explicit examples because of their familiarity with the American interviewer. Biases that could incur by the inclusion of someone directly involved with the company were minimized by having the two-person interview team verify each other's observations and by excluding this company employee from the coding process.

TABLE 7.1 Interviewee Profiles

Identification Number	Job Category	Gender	Age	Education	# Months at Company
Americans					
A01	Manager	M	40s	4+	24
A02	Manager	M	30s	4+	54
A03	Manager	M	20s	2	54
A04	Supervisor	M	20s	4+	30
A05	Supervisor	M	30s	4+	36
A06	Engineer	M	30s	4+	54
A07	Engineer	M	30s	4	54
A08	Manager	F	30s	4	51
A09	Supervisor	F	40s	2	56
A10	Secretary	F	30s	2	37
A11	Secretary	F	30s	2	32
A12	Secretary	F	40s	2	18
Japanese					
J01	Manager	M	50s	4	60
J02	Manager	M	40s	4	55
J03	Manager	M	40s	4	30
J04	Manager	M	20s	4	47
J05	Manager	M	30s	4	45
J06	Coordinator	F	30s	4+	30

NOTE: 4+ = More than 4 years college education
4 = 4 years college education
2 = 2 years college or vocational education

The Interview Schedule

This study incorporated both qualitative and quantitative methods of data collection. The interview schedule consisted of both structured questions and open-ended questions dealing with five topic areas: (a) *background characteristics* including age, gender, educational background, length of employment, and current job description, (b) *communication interaction patterns* dealing with the extent of intercultural interaction both at work and outside the workplace, (c) *psychological profiles* based on 24 statements to which the interviewees assessed themselves on 5-point Likert-type scales covering a range of specific communicator characteristics that were considered to be potentially facilitative (or hindering) to intercultural communication effectiveness,

(d) *intercultural communication experiences* using open-ended questions concerning free impressions of interviewees regarding their comparative experiences of working with in-group co-workers and out-group co-workers, the general difficulties they perceived in working with out-group co-workers, and a specific incident that was particularly problematic in terms of communicating with out-group co-workers as well as the methods they used to cope with these difficulties, and (e) *perceived characteristics of the competent intercultural communicator* asking for interviewees' own characterizations of those American and Japanese co-workers who are notably capable and effective in dealing with out-group co-workers. At the conclusion of each interview, debriefing questions were asked to allow the interviewee to make any additional comments about his or her experience at the company and to express his or her opinions and feelings about the interview itself.

The interview questions originally were composed in English. Interview questions for the Japanese were translated and then pretested among the three Japanese-speaking members of the research team by using appropriate back-translation methods. In terms of the interviewing procedures, the Japanese employees were interviewed (in Japanese) by the two Japanese team researchers, while the American employees were interviewed (in English) by the non-Japanese researchers. A comparison method of translation was used for the Japanese interview responses with some back-translation involved. These translations then were verified by a professional translator.

Data Analysis

Of the quantitative and qualitative data obtained from the interviews, the present analysis is based on a portion of the qualitative verbal responses that are relevant to the interviewees' personal experiences of intercultural interaction at the company. Specifically, the interviewees' comments, observations, and testimonials in response to the following interview questions serve as the bases for addressing the two research issues posed at the beginning of this chapter—that is, (a) to investigate the cultural differences that truly make a difference from the experiences and views of the American and Japanese workers themselves and (b) to identify the ways these two groups of workers have tried to cope with their own problematic intercultural communication situations.

Throughout the process of qualitative coding and data analysis, every effort was made to avoid preconceptions and expectations so as to allow the results to naturally emerge from the data. The open-ended verbal data were analyzed in several stages. First, all distinct elements in the raw data in response to the questions of cultural differences and coping strategies were identified. These elements were cross-checked for reliability by three of the research team members to verify that all relevant points made by the interviewees were coded and to ensure that the coders agreed on specific assignments to the coding categories. The elements then were grouped into common categories based on emerging themes of problematic differences and coping strategies. This procedure was followed by another cross-checking of the research team members. Interpretation of the results was conducted by each member of the research team, who verified and confirmed each other's results with the other members. In this manner, the data were reduced to form a composite picture of the interview data. Categories were integrated gradually into the three final categories: (a) language and communication, (b) work style/orientation, and (c) management style/orientation. The findings of these categories are presented below, followed by a section on the strategies that the interviewees reported to have employed in their dealings with out-group members.

SOURCES OF COMMUNICATION DIFFICULTIES

All of the interviewees involved in this study were keenly aware that differences between the Japanese and American co-workers do indeed exist, and all participants readily voiced their views on these differences. Table 7.2 provides a summary of the key sources of communication difficulties; each is described in detail below.

Language and Communication Behavior

Various challenges in communication are attributed by both American and Japanese interviewees directly to differences in language and verbal and nonverbal communication behavior. This category of differences emerges clearly as one of the most salient issues in the minds of most interviewees.

Language. Differences in language distinctly emerge as the most serious source of the difficulties in their everyday interaction. Indeed, all of the Americans and half of the Japanese emphatically stressed this point. According to the majority of the American respondents, the *misunderstanding of terminology, poor pronunciation,* and *inadequate English grammar* make communication with the Japanese co-workers not only difficult and time-consuming but also frustrating. Many of the misunderstandings, according to the interviewees, are specifically due to the language barrier. Two American interviewees complained that

TABLE 7.2 Sources of Communication Difficulties

Category	Reported by Americans	Reported by Japanese
I. Language/Communication Behavior		
Language	J inadequate use of terminology	The necessity of using English
	J inadequate pronunciation	A speaking rapidly
	J inadequate grammar	
Verbal/Nonverbal Behavior	J lack of verbal clarity	A lack of intuitive understanding
	J lack of verbal specificity	A focus on speaking
	J verbal indirection	A poor listening
		A emotional communication
		A need for detailed instruction
Communication Channel	J reliance on written communication	
II. Work Style/Orientation		
Work Performance	J redundant and detailed work format/procedure	A need for specific job assignment
		A unwillingness to devote necessary time to learn
Information Transmission	J unclear job definitions	A job overspecialization
		A need for detailed and clear-cut job explanation
		A tendency for rushing to conclusions
Company Knowledge and Loyalty	J absolute adherence to "the company way"	A lack of understanding and support for company philosophy
		A unwillingness to compromise personal interests
III. Management Style/Orientation		
Hierarchy	J strict status concerns	A emphasis on individual career
	J superior attitude toward subordinates	A casual and informal relational orientation
	J expectation for all employees to think like managers	A lack of a sense of responsibility toward superiors
	J managers' lack of concern for subordinates' needs	A lack of broad, long-term company perspective
	J managers' lack of specific feedback/praise for subordinates	
	J frequent job transfers	

TABLE 7.2 Continued

Category	Reported by Americans	Reported by Japanese
	J lack of respect for female workers	
	J lack of respect for outside vendors	
Decision Making	J lengthy decision making	A tendency to make hasty decision
	J time-consuming *nemawashi*	
	J manager's involvement in every decision	
	J exclusion of A in decision making	

NOTE: A = American, J = Japanese

the constant *need to speak in simple English* to accommodate the Japanese slows communication and makes it difficult to express fully one's own opinion. One American interviewee described: "I speak in almost broken English to make sure that I get the meaning across. . . . It slows important communication. It gets so slow, so frustrating . . . oftentimes I don't understand what they are saying because of poor pronunciation." Two more Americans explain that as a consequence of this difficulty, some Americans tend to avoid initiating conversations, and add that this language barrier impedes socializing outside the company with Japanese co-workers.

From the viewpoint of a number of Japanese interviewees, the language difficulties stem from the perceived *rapidity* of American speech. One Japanese interviewee stressed that the Japanese are handicapped because they are *forced to use English* and that communication would be much faster and efficient if conducted in Japanese. As one Japanese interviewee explained: "The most difficult thing is English. . . . I try to understand by using my imagination and guessing what they are saying. I get my job done using 80% imagination and 20% English, or maybe it's the other way around."

Verbal/nonverbal behavior. Nine of the 12 American interviewees pointed out the Japanese tendency toward *ambiguity and indirection,* as opposed to the American tendency toward *explicit and straightforward* verbal and nonverbal behavior. Both groups agreed that this communication style difference does indeed result in unclear communication and piecemeal information. The prevalent feeling between both groups was that the Japanese tend to be less explicit than necessary, while the Americans require more complete information than what the Japanese deem necessary or are capable of providing. Such verbal and nonverbal characteristics have some American interviewees at a loss as to how to go about a job and makes them feel unsure about how the Japanese feel toward the Americans. One American interviewee expressed frustration in having to "constantly read the Japanese mind because they often do not say what they mean." Another American reported: "What they say is not always what they mean. I had one Japanese boss who told me that it was my responsibility to be able to read his mind." On this matter, at least three Japanese interviewees expressed their own frustration at constantly having to provide full and precise explanations to the Americans. From the perspective of these interviewees, the Americans lack intuitive understanding and demand to be told everything in detail, including specific outcomes before taking action.

This communication-style difference appears to be particularly problematic in situations of disagreements and confrontation. American interviewees point out that whereas the Americans tend to be more assertive, ask more questions, and involve themselves in more heated debates, the Japanese tend to *avoid confrontations.* This perceived tendency led the Americans to view the Japanese as being reluctant to disagree or to say no, which often results in misinterpretations and an inability to discuss opposing viewpoints freely. One Japanese interviewee illustrated this problem succinctly: "One thing Americans hate the most is when something is 'under consideration,' or when you say 'I'll think about it later,' or 'I'll do as much as I can' or 'I'll do my best.' They don't like this at all. To Americans, these sayings mean 'I'm not doing anything.' But, for the Japanese, these are the best ways to respond." Another Japanese noted that the American predisposition to debate each issue makes the Japanese question whether the American employees actually oppose an idea or are arguing for arguments' sake because they have been schooled in debate.

Further insights are provided by Japanese interviewees, who pointed out that Americans tend to have more of a *speaking focus,* contrasted with the Japanese *listening focus.* As one Japanese interviewee put it: "The most important thing in communication is to listen to the other person. Americans think talking is communication. I think the Japanese feel communication begins with listening to other people."

Communication channels. Additional comments made by the Americans concern differences in communication channels. The majority of the American interviewees contrasted the Japanese reliance on written communication to the American use of oral or verbal communication. Four American interviewees found the differing use of communication channels to be problematic in that it substantially slows down the communication process. One of them commented: "Just give up [talking] and go write. Writing English seems to be a better [channel of] communication [for the Japanese] . . . because they can read it; they can look up the words if they don't understand and take their time." It should be noted, however, that this problem of relying on written versus face-to-face communication channels was unrecognized by any of the Japanese interviewees: No Japanese interviewee linked any of his or her difficulties with differences in the use of communication channel.

Work Style/Orientation

Along with the above language and communication differences, both Japanese and American groups identified troubling differences in the way they view their work and the way the two groups relate to one another as they carry out their daily responsibilities. As one Japanese interviewee noted: "Problems often occur when our Japanese company has a certain way of getting the job done and encourages the employees to do it that way. Then, some of the Americans say that they have been doing it a different way in American companies. When this happens, both sides get emotional."

Work performance. A strong sense of frustration emerges from the American interviewees' comments that the Japanese work style is *inefficient.* Half of the American interviewees pointed out that the Japanese strict emphasis on seemingly insignificant details in work formats and procedures are time consuming and often redundant. Some Americans also found it difficult to work because they thought the Japanese bosses are reluctant to delegate work and often do not complete one job before starting another. These factors contributed to the American workers' feeling that they can never get caught up in their work and that they are "working in a pressure-cooker atmosphere."

However, the Japanese saw the American counterparts as requiring excessively detailed and clear-cut explanations and conclusions even when they cannot be given easily. According to one Japanese interviewee: "The Americans don't have any background [knowledge about] what it takes to do the work here at this company. . . . There are a lot of things they don't know about the business practices of this Japanese company." Some Japanese interviewees also noted that Americans tend to focus on *overspecialization* and prefer *clear-cut work roles* that limit their general knowledge of the way the company operates, unlike the

Japanese employees, who "know a little bit about everything." One Japanese interviewee suggested that the American workers' lack of general knowledge may be attributable to their *unwillingness to devote the necessary time* to learn, particularly after quitting time, when necessary. On this point, an American interviewee observed: "The Japanese will work until 10 o'clock every night and be back to work at 8 o'clock the next morning."

Information transmission. A related set of problematic work style/orientation differences stems from divergent cultural expectations about how work-related information should be presented in making job assignments and reporting through the chain of command. Three American interviewees, for example, pointed out the difficulty they have with the *lack of clarity in the way Japanese managers define and prioritize tasks.* One of them made this point by stating: "It has been frustrating at times when I'm the only American in a meeting and I have no idea what's being done, what is said, and I feel like I'm wasting my time sitting there. . . . It is frustrating because I know I'm not getting all of the details. Maybe later on they're going to wonder why something wasn't done." Another American interviewee observed: "The Japanese don't share information with anyone. They keep the information to themselves."

The Japanese interviewees, however, indicated that they are frustrated because the Americans do not understand the Japanese tendency to focus on company philosophies or concepts rather than on specific and clear-cut tasks and job instructions. They thought the Americans' need for detailed instructions and explanations is very time-consuming. They added that the American tendency to *jump to conclusions* is ineffective and creates problems. This difficulty is explained partly by one Japanese interviewee as stemming from the vast difference between the Japanese *nemawashi*-style (meaning, negotiating under the table) and the American style of open, explicit information dissemination. Another Japanese interviewee commented that the Japanese have a greater understanding of what is going on throughout the company than the Americans do and that, because of this, the Japanese do not feel the need for as much instruction as the Americans.

Company knowledge and commitment. The Americans' lack of understanding concerning the company's philosophies and basic principles was pointed out by both American and Japanese interviewees. A number of American interviewees observed that due to the Japanese custom of lifetime employment, most of the Japanese employees are trained in one company and have the attitude that their "company way" is the only right way. They noted that this unquestioning loyalty of the Japanese employees to the company results in tunnel vision, preconceived ideas, and narrow perspectives. As a consequence, they thought that many of the Japanese are *not willing to listen or adjust* their views precisely because of their company loyalty. Most of the American interviewees found the Japanese dedication to their company to be excessive. One American interviewee described: "Americans have perhaps a bit more balance in their priorities. Although work is important, family and recreation and quality of life outside of work are equally important to their career." On this point, one Japanese interviewee agreed when he points out that by spending too much time at work, the Japanese, unfortunately, tend to ignore other important aspects of their life, such as their families.

In contrast, the Americans' *lack of loyalty* was seen as a source of difficulty to a number of the Japanese interviewees. Two Japanese interviewees, for instance, commented that American staff members have difficulty understanding and actively supporting company philosophies. Other Japanese interviewees expressed the belief that Americans tend to be primarily *interested in their individual future goals,* rather than collective company goals, as opposed to the Japanese tendency to see work as a responsibility to be fulfilled. In the words of one Japanese interviewee: "If American employees think that what they are doing at this company is useful for their future careers, they usually do their job well. They will accept some severe criticism just because they think this criticism is beneficial for themselves." To some of the Japanese interviewees, this American focus on self-interest is associated with a work orientation that lacks responsibility. One Japanese interviewee commented: "Whenever a problem arises, Americans will always have an excuse. . . . If you permit too much of this, Americans will take advantage of it and use it all of the time. On the other hand, when the Japanese make a mistake . . . they don't try to explain themselves because they know they are partially at fault."

An additional insight was offered by two American interviewees who noted that it takes time to build a relationship with the Japanese, whereas Americans tend to form relationships much more quickly. This dichotomy presents a problem because the Japanese employees are transferred back to Japan just when good relationships are about to be formed. One American interviewee pointed out that this *continual transfer* of Japanese staff members makes the American employees hesitant to get close to new Japanese employees.

Management Style/Orientation

In the previous section we identified the discrepancies between the Japanese and the Americans in their work style and orientation, but several sources of difficulties also emerged in the way the company is managed. Here, we focus on the way the company management is structured hierarchically and the way the company makes decisions on management issues within that structure.

Hierarchy. Differences in other aspects of work orientation regarded as sources of communication difficulties by the individual American interviewees include the *strict hierarchical system* in which the *status-conscious* Japanese are placed in an overriding position, allowing them to make most of the evaluations and judgments. One American interviewee described: "The differences I've found have been in the positions, how you treat positions. There are expectations of 'I'm this level' or 'I have a certain position that must be met.' That seems to be more pronounced with some Japanese." This hierarchical management system was seen by many of the American interviewees as problematic in that it allows the Japanese bosses to treat subordinates as "students to be taught in the appropriate ways." As one American interviewee described: "Part of the Japanese way is that, in their hierarchy system, [they] give you a basic idea and let you work on it and suffer a little bit . . . and you come back with your first rough draft and then you get corrected . . . and you work on it again and then eventually they'll show mercy and you'll be done." Similar observations were made on this issue by other American interviewees, who pointed out the authoritarianism of Japanese bosses reflected in their public reprimands of American workers.

Relatedly, the issue of gender, raised only by the American female interviewees, is a bone of contention for the interviewees who felt as though the Japanese bosses do *not treat female employees with respect* and do not like to delegate responsibility to females or allow females to take the initiative. As a result, the female interviewees thought their jobs are frustrating and lack any challenge. One interviewee added that the Japanese do not put to use the talents of women.

The prevalence of hierarchical relationships among the Japanese is contrasted with the American view by two of the Japanese respondents, who found that Americans tend to favor *casual relationships* that are less formal and more relaxed. This tendency posed a problem for Japanese bosses in that the Japanese orientation assumes respect for superiors, while the American predisposition toward familiarity and informality often seems disrespectful. One Japanese mentioned that he has difficulty interacting with American subordinates because, in his view, Americans do not follow instructions very well, make excuses, and often *lack a sense of responsibility.*

The Japanese emphasis on group accomplishment presents problems, according to one American participant, because the Japanese are more *reluctant to recognize individual accomplishments.* This reluctance is also seen as leading to unclear criteria in the promotion of individual employees. One American interviewee remarked that it is difficult to deal with the implicit expectations among the Japanese because they expect Americans to think in long-term goals and to think like a Japanese manager: "A Japanese boss will quite often . . . expect you to think in long-term goals, think like a manager, even though it's not your job. I've heard that a million times—'Think like a manager.' And I want to say, 'Pay me to be a manager, and I'll think like one.' "

Another topic of concern mentioned by one American participant deals with *unclear job descriptions and responsibilities,* as well as differences in the corporate backgrounds of managers, which have lead to a massive turnover rate among the American managers. Additional sources of communication difficulties identified by American interviewees include the limited focus of Japanese managers, their different views of job functions, and their inability to understand the needs of personnel. Further remarks were made regarding the fact that Japanese bosses are less understanding, give minimal feedback and little praise, and avoid admitting their own mistakes.

Decision making. One prevalent feeling among the American interviewees was that the Japanese have a predisposition toward a *lengthy decision-making process.* One American interviewee described the decision-making process as involving "what they [the Japanese] call the preservation of harmony within the group. . . . It takes a while, quite a while, for a decision to be made. There has to be consensus within the group. But then, once the decision is made, the execution is carried out quickly, and nobody argues." To most of the American interviewees, this lengthy consensus-building process is often seen as undesirable and unnecessary because it requires many meetings that appear to be time-consuming, repetitive, and extraneous. One American interviewee commented: "[The Japanese] are very frustrating to deal with sometimes because of their lack of decisiveness. Sometimes, I feel that their attention is not focused directly on the heart of the problem . . . [but] on things that I consider . . . insignificant. And then something that is very significant they tend not to be worried about."

Four American participants emphasized the Japanese managers' need for a great deal of *background information* before they can voice their opinions or make decisions, which makes it difficult for other employees to make minor decisions. Along these same lines, two other American interviewees noted that the Japanese want to be *involved in every decision,* from small organizational matters to top-level decisions, which results in more work than is necessary and again prevents Americans from making any decisions. One American interviewee observed: "In general, I would say that the Japanese management here does not totally trust American employees or other American managers. . . . It's frustrating, and kind of frightening. . . . So the Japanese management get involved in very, very low-level decisions, which is something that I think Americans are not used to."

These management issues that the majority of the American interviewees found seriously troublesome were given less attention by our Japanese interviewees. Although two Japanese interviewees acknowledged that their decision-making process is slower, they countered that Americans tend to *draw conclusions too quickly* and that the Japanese way to review things over and over may indeed be an advantage. They also commented that Americans believe that problems can be solved with meetings, while the Japanese tend to talk to all of the personnel involved, engaging in *nemawashi,* and then to consult with their superiors before meetings take place. Two other Japanese respondents, in this regard, remarked that the Americans do not perceive things from a *long-term, company perspective* and, therefore, tend to focus only on day-to-day activities.

One issue, the relationship of the company to vendors or subcontractors, surfaced in the remarks made by both groups of interviewees. This issue crystallized the divergent views on management orientation between the two groups. According to two Japanese interviewees, the Japanese perceive that vendors should be humble and serve the buyer, or the company, and that they should maintain a hierarchical, subservient relationship to the company as is prevalent in Japan. Yet, according to two American interviewees, most companies in the United States have more of a cooperative relationship with vendors and work together in a combined effort for the sake of time and efficiency. The difference in these two types of management orientations as perceived by managers from both groups tends to put Americans in a predicament regarding the vendors. As one American interviewee put it: "The Japanese have the attitude that the vendor must provide everything, and they are not as willing to cooperate with [the vendors] . . . the Japanese managers tell us we are too easy on the vendors."

COPING STRATEGIES

As the interviewees addressed the significant intercultural challenges in the areas of language/communication behavior, work style/orientation, and management style/orientation, they also informed us about the various ways they individually had tried to deal with and manage such challenges. The methods employed to analyze the coping strategies involved listing all of the specific comments made in the raw data and calculating the frequencies of their appearance. Although many of these strategies were drawn from the question dealing with specific problematic incidents and the methods used to cope with those incidents, the entire interview itself was reviewed for pertinent information presented by the interviewees in response to other open-ended questions. In the final stages of analysis, the categories of cognitive, affective, and behavioral strategies emerged, as summarized in Table 7.3.

Cognitive Strategies

For both groups, the primary cognitive strategy for dealing with out-group members emerged with the *increased understanding of those cultural differences* that have been identified previously as being problematic. Both groups further noted that the *more intercultural experience* they gain, the better they become in dealing with intercultural challenges. Here, the intercultural experience includes not only the amount of interactions with out-group members at the company over time but also the knowledge gained from any kind of previous intercultural experience elsewhere and overseas.

Particularly for the American interviewees, understanding the Japanese culture in work and management styles and orientations ranks at the top of the list, followed by the learning of language and communication behavioral characteristics. Such an understanding alone was viewed by the Americans as being helpful in their coping with difficult situations. The areas of the Japanese cultural patterns cited by the American interviewees as important range from the Japanese emphasis on status and position, their work style/orientation such as group consciousness, their attention to detailed formats, mentor relationships, *nemawashi* practice (or negotiating under the table), and their verbal and nonverbal behavioral characteristics, as well as their cultural mindsets. Some American interviewees reported that they have tried to *learn how to understand each Japanese individual differently*. As one of these interviewees put it: "You have to develop how you talk to each Japanese

TABLE 7.3 Coping Strategies

Reported by Americans	Reported by Japanese
I. Cognitive Strategies	
*Learn/understand cultural differences Learn about each J's uniqueness	*Learn/understand cultural differences Improve English language Acquire many conversational topics Use active imagination to understand A
II. Affective Strategies	
*Be patient *Be open-minded Be adaptable/flexible Be willing to compromise Be diplomatic Be sensitive to situations Use perspective taking Keep a sense of humor Forget previous bad experiences	*Be patient *Be open-minded
III-a. Behavioral Strategies: Accommodation	
*Listen attentively *Discuss problems together Use simpler words/sentences Speak slowly Enunciate clearly Repeat messages Use written forms of communication Minimize communication distractions Adjust own work styles to J styles	*Listen attentively *Discuss problems together Improve English skills
III-b. Behavioral Strategies: Divergence	
*Avoid problematic situations/persons *Ignore problems Protest indirectly to superiors Protest directly File formal complaint	*Avoid problematic situations/persons *Ignore problems

NOTE: *Reported by both Japanese and American interviewees

person. Each one you talk to differently. . . . You learn how to say it so that the specific person will understand."

To the Japanese interviewees, on the other hand, improving their *English skill* was viewed as the primary strategy for dealing more effectively with Americans. Other coping strategies mentioned by Japanese interviewees include acquiring *a broad range of topics* on which they can draw to converse with Americans and using *active imagination and guessing* in trying to understand American employees and what they are trying to say.

Affective Strategies

In addition to cultural and language learning, both groups of interviewees presented many insightful ideas about how attitudinal and motivational qualities help them deal with out-group members. A significant convergence between Japanese and American interviewees is seen in emphasizing *patience* as an important virtue in this type of work environment. Another area of agreement is the need for *open-mindedness* as a helpful strategy to cope with difficult intercultural situations.

Several American interviewees emphasized that they try to be *adaptable* and *flexible,* rather than rigid and ethnocentric. They found these personal qualities essential to alleviating many of the intercultural difficulties. Relatedly, the *willingness to compromise, diplomacy, sensitivity to situational cues,* and some amount of *perspective taking* were pointed out by American interviewees as useful ways to overcome challenging situations. A good *sense of humor* also was suggested by some as helpful to quelling some of the impending difficulties. Others emphasized the need for a *"short-term memory"* to help forget the bad experiences that have occurred. One American interviewee made a special point that it is important for American employees to be more responsible for their own actions. Additional coping strategies were noted by a number of Japanese interviewees who emphasized *friendliness, frankness,* and *becoming more extraverted* in communicating with others.

Behavioral Strategies

We are able to group the varied behavioral strategies reported by interviewees into what Giles and his associates (Giles, Mulac, Bradac, & Johnson, 1987) referred to as "accommodation" and "divergence." These two categories serve as the basic behavioral responses that the American and Japanese employees have used in their individual efforts to try to avoid or manage the intercultural difficulties they have experienced.

Accommodation. Of the two types of behavioral strategies, accommodating strategies are cited more frequently by American interviewees. Much agreement is seen between the Japanese and the Americans in their emphasis on *listening* closely to each other and engaging in *private, face-to-face discussion.* Both groups thought that a combination of these two strategies is of the utmost importance to enhancing the quality of their intercultural communication, solving problems to their mutual satisfaction, and creating shared goals. One Japanese interviewee reflected that "miscommunication occurs when people don't listen to the other person and don't make sure that the other person understands what is said. We need to listen to each other and make sure they understand." An American interviewee particularly emphasized the importance of having personal discussions when having difficulty with Japanese co-workers: "I had a Japanese boss that used to yell at me, and scold me in front of others. . . . I knew that I couldn't disagree with him, or it would be disrespectful. So I finally started talking to him alone, and I ended up closing the door to his office. That showed him respect and allowed me to voice my opinions." Several other American interviewees reported the usefulness of having direct, private discussions with their Japanese counterparts when in disagreement or having a misunderstanding, so that compromises and other necessary adjustments can be worked out.

In addition to the importance of listening and discussing as coping strategies for both the Japanese and the Americans, other accommodating behaviors and activities were emphasized by both groups as crucial to effectively communicating without group members. In this regard, the strategies mentioned by Japanese interviewees were to *improve their English language skills* and to *solicit American superiors' help as mediators* in various conflict situations. One Japanese interviewee, having served as a mediator several times in quarrels between American and Japanese co-workers, pointed out the importance of maintaining a neutral stance to be effective in his role as mediator. He stated: "At those times, if I ever thought that I was superior to them, I would not have been able to solve the problem."

The American interviewees, in particular, presented a variety of other accommodating strategies for effective communication with their Japanese colleagues. Many American interviewees mentioned the importance of *adjusting their own speaking habits* to compensate for the linguistic constraints their Japanese co-workers are faced with by using simpler words and sentences, speaking slowly, enunciating clearly, and repeating some messages, as well as avoiding key words that may be misinterpreted by the Japanese counterpart. Also, using *the written channel of communication* was stressed by some American interviewees as helpful, including writing memos and letters to clarify or confirm previous conversations and using drawings, graphs, and pictures to help clarify what they are trying to say. One American interviewee stated:

"I always carry around a pencil and a piece of paper, and I've learned to draw pictures, a lot of block diagrams and just pictures." Relatedly, the importance of *using nonverbal expressions,* particularly hand gestures, was emphasized by a number of American interviewees, along with the idea of *minimizing distractions* when talking with the Japanese. As one American observed: "The more people speaking English at one time, or, for that matter, any outside distractions such as a television or radio, could confuse the Japanese staff with an onslaught of incoming information."

Additional behavioral strategies by Americans involved *making adjustments in their own work habits* in order to make themselves become more compatible with the Japanese work/management style and orientation. Specifically, they found it helpful to understand and follow the company chain of command. Three American interviewees also suggested that Americans should "*allow time* for the Japanese to make decisions and should not be in such a hurry." *Admitting one's mistakes* and *apologizing* for them, providing sufficient facts and explanations, and justifying decisions or disagreements to the Japanese co-worker's satisfaction are some of the other coping strategies mentioned by the American interviewees.

Divergence. To a lesser extent, some American interviewees reported the coping strategies that reflect a posture of not accommodating to the out-group's cultural and communication practices but, instead, increase the in-group-out-group psychological distance. Divergent strategies reported by a few American interviewees include altogether *avoiding* or "giving up on" certain Japanese staff members, particularly those whom they perceive to be rude or offensive or not interested in the cultural diversity at the company. One American interviewee noted: "After so many years of difficulties, many times I just throw up my hands and say, 'Whatever you want. I don't care. It's not my problem.' " Another American interviewee reported to have used the strategy of *ignoring* certain conflicts or problematic situations. This interviewee indicated that, in one case of conflict with a Japanese co-worker for which no clear solutions could be identified, he pretended as though no conflict existed until a later date when he was able to discuss the problem. During this discussion, the interviewee reported that he and his Japanese counterpart were able to agree to disagree.

In addition, some American interviewees reported to have resorted to *filing formal complaints* to the Human Resources Department and even *making outright protest moves* such as offering a resignation and *complaining to their superior.* No Japanese interviewees revealed that they used any divergent strategies, except one who mentioned his experience of difficulties with an American staff member who does not seem to listen to what he has to say. This interviewee reported having tried to avoid the American until he had no choice but to have to point out this problem.

DISCUSSION

The present analysis has explored the cultural differences as they are experienced and handled by Japanese and American co-workers striving to meet the daily necessities involved in working together. Our findings on the cultural differences between Japanese and Americans support many of the findings of prior research. The importance of a language difference, for instance, was emphasized clearly by both the American and Japanese interviewees, as was reported by Condon (1984), Nishida (1985), and Thayer and Weiss (1987). The inherent problems in dealing with a second language was demonstrated in the work of Gumperz (1982). The notion of culturally programmed differences in the amount of implicit and explicit information required in communication was well documented and theorized by Hall (1976) in terms of the contexting behavior in different cultures. Others such as Barnlund (1974), Ishii and Bruneau (1988), Masao (1973), and Kim (1991b) described Asian cultural and communication styles—from status consciousness, in-group loyalty, verbal indirection, verbal ambiguity, and facework, to emphasis on verbal modesty and interpersonal sensitivity. Regarding work and management styles of Japanese organizations, many of our results reinforce the previous findings by Cathcart and Cathcart (1988), Condon (1984), Nakane (1970), and L. Stewart (1988), to name only a few.

The primary contribution of the present study lies in the insights it provides into the various specific ways the cultural differences are played out in the course of the daily life of American and Japanese co-workers. As such, we are better able to locate the concrete points of disagreement and contention between the two groups' perceptions and interpretations of the difficulties they experience, as well as some of the areas in which the two groups do converge in mutual agreement and appreciation. In addition, the study identified the types of explicit cognitive, affective, and behavioral strategies that the American and Japanese co-workers have employed and found useful in coping with difficult situations. The cognitive, affective, and behavioral strategies they employ to make personal adjustments help us provide specific, real-life examples of the ideas of accommodation and divergence in the speech accommodation theory (Giles et al., 1987) and adaptation (Kim, 1988) fundamental to intercultural communication competence (Kim, 1991a).

Methodologically, we have described a qualitative analytic process that has enabled us to ascertain and elaborate on the feelings and views of the American and Japanese co-workers. The small sample size of this study, together with the fact that this study was carried out in only one Japanese subsidiary, poses limitations in the generalizability and comprehensiveness of the findings. Yet, we are encouraged by the fact that our interviewees have provided us with their rich and often intense intercultural experiences, allowing us to develop an in-depth understanding of their reality. From their experiences, we are able to conclude that the many difficulties reported in this work help explain the relatively low employee morale at the company in question—as was suggested by the American interviewees themselves. The difficulties stemming from a language barrier, differences in verbal and nonverbal style, as well as different work and management style clearly have contributed to the turnover rate that one representative of the Human Resources Department characterized as "higher than most American companies." According to this representative, a number of American managers, supervisors, and office personnel working directly with or under Japanese counterparts have left the company because of an inability to cope with the many intercultural challenges. Even those Americans who remain in the company sometimes find it futile to try to communicate with their Japanese counterparts and make a positive difference in the practices of the company, according to some American informants. Some of the Americans even have tried forming coalitions of small groups with common complaints about specific managers or policies they considered to be particularly ineffective and have brought their appeals to the Human Resources Department with little success.

The Japanese, on the other hand, were relatively reticent in expressing their frustrations throughout our interviews. Their answers to many of our open-ended questions were noticeably brief, compared with the frequently elaborate manner in which many of their American counterparts expressed themselves. Yet, it is not difficult to discern the intense frustrations the Japanese must be experiencing from the various episodes of intercultural challenges they reported during the interviews. Our American informants concurred with this observation as they noted that the difficulties the Japanese experience may be at least partly responsible for the minimal interaction they have with Americans during lunch hours and other informal social situations such as company parties.

We find it unfortunate that the many problems stemming from the differences between the two groups of employees have not been addressed seriously by the company leadership. Despite requests by several American workers for training programs designed to help ease the intercultural communication problems, the task of finding solutions has been left largely to each worker's individual efforts of trial and error. We believe that, with organizational leadership and willingness on the part of individual workers, many of the intercultural challenges can be met successfully once they are recognized as such. Overcoming cultural barriers is critical to the health and success of an intercultural company and to the morale of all workers, both American and Japanese.

Indeed, observations of the situations in a number of other Japanese-owned and managed companies in the United States suggest that much of the intercultural strain can be reduced through effective language and cultural instructions (Filipczak, 1992). In this regard, comparative replication studies of two or more companies will enable us to trace the extent that organizational leadership and commitment to intercultural education and training may help facilitate the quality of work life of individual workers. These studies can illuminate further the influence of differing sociocultural milieu on individual workers' intercultural expectations and practices. To this end, this chapter provides an initial research framework and database.

8

Co-Cultural Communication Within the Organization

DEVORAH A. LIEBERMAN • *Portland State University*
ELLENE GURTOV • *Portland State University*

A human resource manager in a Pacific Northwest organization recently stated:

> Some of the more interesting issues that we have [in the organization] are conflicts within a particular ethnic group but that are from diverse backgrounds. We had a situation not very long ago where there were two Vietnamese people on the same work team, who could not get along. And, you know, to most Americans, you would say, "They are both Vietnamese, they are going to love each other!" But, they did not. One was Buddhist. One was Catholic. One was from an urban area. One was from a rural area. One was highly educated. The other was uneducated. Yet, they performed the same tasks, so it caused a lot of conflict. (personal communication, March 18, 1993)

Scholars in the field of communication, studying diversity within organizational settings, have concentrated primarily on individuals from culturally disparate backgrounds (Chikudate, Barnett, & McFarland, 1990; Cox & Cooper, 1985; Goldhaber, 1993; Howard & Teramoto, 1981; Hudiburg, 1991; Nakanishi, 1984; Ouchi, 1981; Pascale, 1978; Rehder, 1981). Most of these studies investigated intercultural interactions among organizational employees who are from different countries and speak different first languages. If we limit ourselves to investigations that focus primarily on interactants from cultures with differences in language and region, we forfeit the opportunity of addressing culture and communication issues that surround us on a daily basis. Because organizations are becoming more diverse internally, composed of ethnic groups and races that may share the same national culture, it is important to examine co-cultural issues in multinational companies.

Little current research investigates interactions between and among employees from different *co-cultures* (cultures having coexisted in the

AUTHORS' NOTE: We thank I. Lieberman, O. Lieberman, Patricia Hamilton, and Joan McMahon for their help in preparing this chapter.

141

same mainstream culture for a length of time) working in an organization. The opening quotation of this chapter by a human resource manager is an example of conflict between individuals from co-cultures from the same (hemophilus) mainstream culture. The question arises, Why a chapter that addresses co-culture communication within an organization? It is assumed often that individuals who grow up in the same mainstream culture understand the instrumental, moral, competence, and terminal values of that culture (Samovar & Porter, 1988). This assumption leads interactants to the greatest pitfall: assumed similarity (Barna, 1991). Individuals existing within the same mainstream culture, but raised within different co-cultures or cultural.communities, bring many value and behavioral differences to a communication interaction. In this chapter we address these differences.

CO-CULTURAL COMMUNICATION

Shuter (1990a) asserted that intracultural communication theory is essential for developing a framework to "provide a conceptual basis for making intercultural communication comparisons between dissimilar societies" (p. 243). Yet, a review of literature reveals the lack of studies addressing co-culture interactions within organizations. Some theorists offer alarming figures regarding the increasing influx of diversity within the U.S. workforce and predict that we must suggest tools for coping with conflict that arises among the ever-increasing number of co-cultures (Waters, 1992). Other theorists suggest that scholars address the needs of particular ethnic groups within an organization as they interact with others from the same mainstream culture (Cushman & King, 1985; Shuter, 1985c, 1989). These theorists claim that we should not assume that individuals in organizations have similar values, attitudes, and behavioral styles because they grew up within the same mainstream culture. Rather, we need to address the differences that exist among co-cultures interacting within the same organization. We propose that an individual within an organization may exhibit more tolerance regarding value and behavioral differences for a fellow employee who was raised in a different mainstream culture than for a fellow employee from a different co-culture or community who was raised in the same mainstream culture. Because of assumed similarity, an individual may expect someone raised in the same mainstream culture to operate from the same value orientation as he or she operates. Schwartz (1989), in particular, speaks of issues regarding Hispanic gangs in the educational organization. He claims that Hispanic youth raised in the White middle-class culture embody values very different from those of students who participate in the same school system. Bell (1990) highlights women and African Americans as specific microcultures (or co-cultures) within organizations exhibiting particular communication styles endemic to those groups. Bell claims that these microcultures existing within the same mainstream culture are expected to exhibit behaviors in accordance with the mainstream culture and the organizational culture.

Throughout this chapter, we refer to the models depicted below. Model I (Figure 8.1) illustrates relationships between and among co-cultures as they interact within the organizational system, which in turn exists and is influenced by the co-cultures' mainstream culture. Model II (Figure 8.2) represents the implicit and explicit variables impinging on the individuals' interactions. Each level (Level C = the mainstream culture; Level B = the organizational culture; Level A = the individual within co-cultures) contains implicit and explicit values and communication styles. The values addressed in this model are based on Hofstede's four value dimension continua: power distance, collectivism/individualism, masculine/feminine, and uncertainty avoidance. It is significant to note that these values that exist at Levels A, B, and C each carry implicit and explicit assumptions and expectations. Accompanying these values are communication styles that are encouraged or discouraged (by those who create and/or control the symbols) at each level. These communication styles affect problem solving, reasoning, verbal behaviors, and nonverbal behaviors. Once again, implicit and explicit assumptions and expectations are embodied at each level.

MAINSTREAM CULTURE/CO-CULTURE/ CULTURAL COMMUNITY

Although the notion of culture often is associated with exotic, distant peoples and places, it is the overriding concept that perpetuates and reconfigures the rules by which all levels of society exist. What are the components of culture? We suggest that the grounding of culture (Brislin, 1993) stresses the "shoulds" that serve as a collective guide for individuals. Thus, Gregory (1983) claims that the shoulds are actually "learned ways of coping with experience" (p. 364) within differing contexts and situations. The shoulds, guides, and coping strategies make up the frame of reference that is a deposit of an individual's

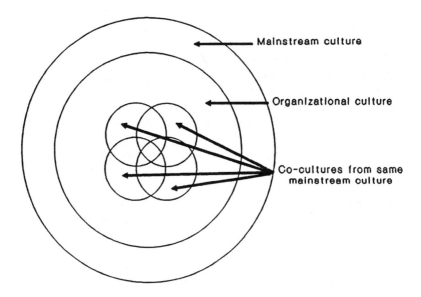

Figure 8.1. Co-Culture Organizational Model I

values, attitudes, and communication styles and "knowledge, experiences
. . . meanings, hierarchies, religion, timing, roles, spatial relations, concepts of the universe and material objects and possessions" (Samovar, Porter, & Jain, 1981, p. 24).

Even though these are basic constructs of culture, no single mainstream culture aligns itself with only one set of values or ideas (Long, 1990). The mainstream or umbrella culture within a society, however, is "the meaning and structures promulgated by the dominant culture, still dominant sociocultural order" (p. 4). Thus, the mainstream culture embodies and encourages a wide range of values, beliefs, and attitudes, while discouraging those outside this range.

The expression "common sense" is actually another way of saying that a person is exhibiting behaviors or values within the sanctioned range. A lack of common sense implies that behaviors exhibited or values expressed are outside the range of cultural appropriateness (Lieberman, Kosokoff, & Kosokoff, 1988). Thus, what is common sense in a co-culture may not be common sense throughout the mainstream culture, or vice versa.

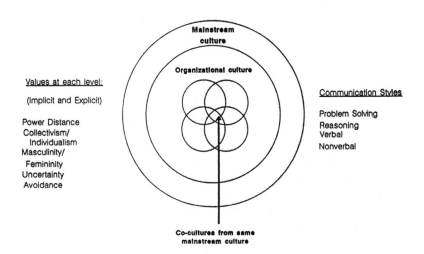

Figure 8.2. Co-Culture Organizational Model II

ORGANIZATIONAL CULTURE/ ORGANIZATIONAL CLIMATE

An *organization* is an agreed-on structure created by a group of individuals working cooperatively toward a common goal under an established authority and leadership (Scott, 1967). Although numerous theorists present various elements that comprise an organization (Goldhaber, 1993; Healey, 1956; Herzberg, 1968; Jablin, 1987a; Katz & Kahn, 1966; McPhee, 1985), each maintains that the common denominator is the group of individuals focused on a particular outcome (see Figure 8.1). From this organizational group, formal and informal communication systems evolve, comprising channels of upward, downward, and lateral communication networks that each have significant influence on the attitudes, feelings, perceptions, and motivation of the organizational members (Jain, Kanungo, & Goldhaber, 1980).

Some theorists describe organizational culture as synonymous with organizational climate. In fact, the two are very different. An *organizational climate* is a reflection of the attitudes and perceptions the members of the organization share at any particular time about elements of the organization. *Climate* may be considered as a reading of employees' attitudes at a specific time, whereas *culture* addresses identifiable symbols and values that permeate throughout an organization. The *organizational culture* represents a deeper, historical aspect of the organization. This culture evolves as implicit and explicit values and norms among the organization's members. These beliefs, attitudes, and values may be ascertained through studying members' interactions. Hofstede, Neuijen, and Ohayu (1990) maintain that the culture of an organization contains the following characteristics. It is (a) holistic, (b) historically determined, (c) related to anthropological concepts, (d) socially constructed, (e) soft, and (f) difficult to change. The element that distinguishes organizational culture is that it supposes "features of organizational units, not of individuals" (p. 297).

Developing a model (see Figure 8.2) to examine co-cultural communication within an organization assumes that individuals interacting within the organization and the corporate culture are from co-cultures subsumed within a mainstream culture. Co-cultures have been termed by other theorists as subcultures, microcultures, and tributary cultures. However, the prefix *co* (from *co-culture*) implies groups coexisting within the mainstream culture. For example, many co-cultures exist within the U.S. mainstream culture (e.g., African American, Italian American, Polish American, Jewish American). Thus, the term *co-culture* is adopted for this model. *Mainstream culture* is the group that creates the symbols and values that permeate society. Communities are groups that exist within the mainstream culture and share views or values that have not necessarily been passed from generation to generation. Examples of communities are rural community, urban community, gay community, timber community, and environmental community. It is important to note that even though one group of individuals may be labeled a co-culture and another group labeled a community, both still embody particular values, verbal and nonverbal behaviors that are exclusive to that group.

Both Models I and II (see Figures 8.1 and 8.2) depict values, rules, and modes of reasoning encouraged by the mainstream culture, organizational culture, and co-cultural levels. During an interaction, when any of these variables are in conflict with the expectations of individuals representing either the mainstream culture, the organizational culture, or a co-culture, the communication event is ripe for negative evaluation. The value dimension and patterns of reasoning encouraged by either mainstream culture, organizational culture, or co-culture are expanded below.

VALUES

An individual's values strongly influence personal choices, worldview, and behaviors. Although values may develop throughout our lives, deeply rooted unconscious values are acquired during our youth and are taught to us by those we hold as authority figures (see Figure 8.3). Our first authority figures are part of the nuclear family, extended family, and members of co-cultures and cultural communities. Thus, these base values are prescribed by our co-culture(s). At school and preschool age, children are exposed to authority figures who begin to introduce values and encourage behaviors espoused by the mainstream culture. Hofstede (1991) claims that "by the time a child is ten, most of his or her basic values are probably programmed into his or her mind" (p. 312). He continues that the bulk of our values are firmly in place by the time we become employed by an organization. Consequently, an organizational employee brings with him or her core values learned as a child within the co-culture and additional or modified values learned from mainstream culture authority figures. At this point, the employee is faced with values that are grounded in this particular corporate culture. Figure 8.3 depicts an individual's value system as layers of values learned throughout a lifetime. There are values held in common by the co-culture, the mainstream culture, and the corporate culture. The individual who exhibits behaviors consistent with the values of the organization usually is perceived as a team player. Also, some values may be contradictory between the three levels (or similarly aligned in any two layers). If so, the individual may feel dissonance about exhibiting a particular behavior or aligning with a particular corporate philosophy or career path.

Values may be explicit or implicit. *Explicit values* are those that are verbalized or written. *Explicit values* are taught to us as ways we should behave or should view the world. For example, on the one hand, some co-culture authority figures may say to a child, "You should never trust anyone but your family." On the other hand, other co-cultures teach, "You should trust people until they prove to you that they cannot be trusted, because everyone is basically good." Values that were stated explicitly to a child may become implicit when the person becomes an adult. Thus, as adults, some people assume that someone is innocent until proven guilty, while others assume that someone is guilty until proven innocent. It is when someone's behavior contradicts either an implicit or explicit value that one often is evaluated negatively or

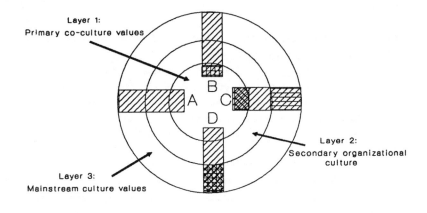

Layer 1:
Primary co-culture values

Layer 2:
Secondary organizational culture

Layer 3:
Mainstream culture values

Note:

A=similar values all layers
B=similar values layers 2 and 3
C=dissimilar values all layers
D=similar values layers 1 and 2

Figure 8.3. Layers of Values in One Individual

evaluates others negatively. This evaluation is in relation to the implicit or explicit value that is dominant within the context and the situation. For purposes of this chapter, the context, situation, and setting would be within the organization. The explicit values that guide an organization may be stated in the organization's by-laws, mission statement, and/or job descriptions. These also are seen in the formal communication networks.

Implicit values in an organization are the extensions or by-products of those values explicitly stated in the documents or formal communication networks. The implicit values are unspoken and are assumed to be understood by all (assumed common sense). This assumption, however, is not the actual case, and that is where misunderstanding most often occurs. The organizational rules and values often are learned in the informal communication networks (gossiping, socializing, meeting for breaks). An example of implicit value may be seen in the mission statement of the State of Oregon Employment Division. The mission is "to promote employment of Oregonians through development of a diversified, multi-skilled work force, while providing support during periods of unemployment" (1993). The explicitly stated values center around diversity, multiskilled, and support. An example of confusion over implicit values may be regarding the word *support*. Support for some may be monetary; for others, it may be emotional. The response may vary, dependent on the definition and value for the concept support promoted by the organizational culture, the individuals within the organization, and the individuals outside the organization (who need to interact with the organization).

Hofstede (1991) identified four value dimension continua by which co-culture, mainstream culture, and organizational culture values can be determined. Hofstede's original value dimension research was based on data from employees internationally in divisions of IBM corporation. The four values are (a) power distance, (b) uncertainty avoidance, (c) masculinity/femininity, and (d) individualism/collectivism.

The *power distance* value dimension refers to the amount of differentiation reinforced between individuals of perceived status levels. The larger the power distance between individuals in a mainstream culture, a co-culture, or an organizational culture, the more emphasis on respect, obedience, deference, reverence, veneration, age, family name, existential inequality, centralized power, and benevolent autocracy (Hofstede, 1991, pp. 35-36).

The *uncertainty avoidance* value dimension refers to concern about uncertainty of consequences of action and uncertainty about the future. Different societies have varying numbers of rules, laws, and norms that deal with uncertainty and become an accepted part of their culture. Feelings of anxiety are learned culturally in relation to degree of uncertainty in a given situation. Furthermore, coping strategies to reduce the uncertainty also are acquired. Hofstede (1991) claimed that technology, religion, and law are avenues employed to reduce uncertainty. Hofstede concluded, "If in a [culture] more people feel under stress at work, in the same [culture] more people want rules to be respected, and more people want to have a long-term career" (1991, p. 111). In cultures wherein uncertainty avoidance is more prevalent, Hofstede states:

> The organizations have many formal laws and/or informal rules controlling the rights and duties of employers and employees. There are also many internal rules and regulations controlling the work process. The exercise of discretionary power by superiors replaces, to some extent, the need for

internal rules. The need for rules in a [culture] with strong uncertainty avoidance is emotional. People—members of governments, civil servants, employers and employees—have been programmed since their early childhood to feel comfortable in structured environments. As little as possible should be left to chance. (pp. 120-121).

The *masculinity/femininity* value dimension refers to work goals identified as desirable by employees within organizations from particular cultures. Characteristics desired by employees that are high on masculinity include job recognition, challenging work, and opportunities for high earnings and advancement. Characteristics desired by employees that are high on femininity include good relationship with superior, work with people who cooperate well with each other, live in a desirable location, and job security. Hofstede (1991, pp. 82-83) found:

Masculinity pertains to [cultures] in which social gender roles are clearly distinct (i.e., men are supposed to be assertive, tough, and focused on material success whereas women are supposed to be more modest, tender, and concerned with the quality of life); femininity pertains to societies in which social gender roles overlap (both men and women are supposed to be models, tender and concerned with the quality of life).

Among Hofstede's organizational studies, occupations could be divided into six groups from the most masculine to the most feminine: (a) sales (professional and nonprofessional), (b) professional workers (engineers/scientists), (c) skilled workers/technicians, (d) managers of all categories, (e) unskilled and semiskilled workers, and (f) office workers.

The *individualism/collectivism* value dimension pertains to the degree to which ties between individuals are loose or tight (within the culture). The more individualistic people are, the more they are expected to look after themselves and their immediate families. The more collectivistic, the more cohesive the in-groups (from birth onward) and the more these groups serve to protect the individual in exchange for unwavering loyalty. Organizations within more collectivistically oriented cultures encourage loyalty to the team, self-effacement, subordination to the group, and a preference for personal relationships over tasks. Organizations within more individualistically oriented cultures encourage identity based on the individual and individual task completion, low-context communication, promotion based on skills, and preference of task over relationship (Hofstede, 1991, p. 67).

PATTERNS OF REASONING ENCOURAGED

Although scholars agree that intercultural communication theory is grounded in the concept that participants in any interaction bring with them a "system of symbols and meanings" (Reid, 1987) that shape their perceptions of shared phenomenon, few have addressed specific differences among cultures in their approaches to solving problems. Each co-culture teaches, trains, and molds those within its system to exhibit what is considered to be the most appropriate range of problem-solving methods (Lieberman, 1991, 1993).

Cultures tend to encourage more field-dependent or more field-independent approaches, as well as more global or more linear approaches to problem solving (Reid, 1987). It should be noted that a particular culture does not necessarily encourage either/or reasoning styles; rather, it reinforces and rewards one style more than another. Lieberman observed (1993) that teachers from various cultures tended to encourage students to develop particular reasoning styles by using aspects of the following patterns: field independent/field dependent, collectivistic/individualistic, high context/low context, and global reasoning/ linear reasoning. Sackmann (1992, p. 141) noted:

> At the individual level, sense making is an activity in which individuals use their cognitive structure and structuring devices to perceive situations and to interpret their perceptions . . . what differentiates collective sense making or cultural cognitions from individual ones is that the former are commonly held by a group of people in a given organization, even though members of the same cultural group may not be aware in their activities of what they hold in common.

Therefore, when mutually addressing a shared problem, they may initially problem-solve quite differently. However, the different approaches may not be understood on a cognitive level and be evaluated by others as lacking common sense.

CONCLUSION

The primary purpose of this chapter is to address the limitations faced if we focus intercultural/organizational communication research on studying interactants from heterophilous mainstream cultures. This chapter makes the case and presents a model for greater consideration and examination of heterophilous co-cultures within an organization from the same mainstream culture. Further research needs to be undertaken examining the notion that one assumes similarity of core values with another because of similar mainstream culture background. Also, researchers need to address behaviors exhibited by interactants when there is assumed similarity by interactants within co-cultures or between co-cultures. Questions addressing this avenue of research will lead the study of intercultural communication on a path that further expands the field.

9

Cultural Diversity and Intercultural Training in Multinational Organizations

ROSITA DASKAL ALBERT • *University of Minnesota, Minneapolis*

The thesis of this chapter is that intercultural training is the major avenue for creating an organization that is effective in dealing with cultural diversity, whether domestically or internationally, and that this type of training has been neglected and underused. *Intercultural training* is conceptualized broadly as encompassing all activities designed to facilitate effective interactions between culturally different persons. In this chapter I focus on the need for intercultural training in multinational organizations (MNOs), the reasons for the lack of intercultural training, and ways to increase knowledge of culture and cultural differences, detailing approaches for increasing cultural understanding, handling resistance, and correcting mistaken beliefs about intercultural training in MNOs.

THE NEED FOR CULTURAL DIVERSITY TRAINING

Organizations have to consider training for cultural diversity both domestically and internationally to a much greater extent than ever before. There are several important reasons:

Demographic Trends

More organizations are operating in the global arena, with people, goods, and services coming from and going to many different countries. This trend is on the increase. In 1985, estimates indicated 280 million

AUTHOR'S NOTE: An earlier version of this chapter was presented at the International Communication Association meeting in Miami, 1992. I am indebted to Richard Wiseman and two anonymous reviewers for valuable comments on an earlier draft, and to Harry Triandis for stimulating ideas and providing encouragement.

international travelers a year, of which only 30% are tourists (Copeland & Griggs, 1985).

Even organizations that operate only in one country have become increasingly diverse. By the year 2000, demographic trends in the United States indicate that the 85% of new entrants into the labor force will be minorities and women. Minority populations in urban areas of the United States have increased dramatically during the last decade: African Americans increased by 13.2%, American Indians and Aleuts by 37.9%, Asian Americans or Pacific Islanders by 107.8%, Hispanic Americans by 53%, and other races by 45.1% (U.S. Bureau of the Census, 1991). It is expected that an increasing proportion of those entering both educational institutions and the labor force will be from nondominant cultures.

The Cost of Not Having Intercultural Training

Intercultural interactions in international assignments have often been problematic: It has been estimated that between 20% and 50% of personnel sent overseas by U.S.-based multinational corporations return early (Mendenhall, Dunbar, & Oddou, 1987); more than half of U.S. multinational corporations had failure rates of 10% and 20%, and about 5% had failure rates of 30% (Tung, 1987). These data contrast unfavorably with the recall rates for 29 West European and 35 Japanese multinational corporations: 59% of the West European and 76% of the Japanese firms had failure rates under 5%, 38% of the Europeans and 10% of the Japanese had failure in the 6-10% range, and only 3% of the Europeans and 14% of the Japanese had failure rates between 11% and 19% (Tung, 1987, 1990).

The costs of these failed sojourns are considerable. Edwards (1978) estimated almost a quarter of a million dollars per expatriate failure when the cost of unrealized business is included. The costs of failed negotiations between businesspeople of different cultures is difficult to estimate, but it is also likely to be high.

On the domestic front, the cost in lost productivity in both schools and jobs can be characterized as enormous: In general, minorities have had high drop-out rates, reaching up to 70% for certain groups (Lucas, 1971). The financial costs to corporations stemming from failures to deal adequately with diversity have also been great (Hayles, 1992). Many of these costs could be prevented by proper use of intercultural training and related supportive measures, such as better selection and follow-up for overseas assignments, more attention to the needs of cultural minorities, and greater integration of intercultural training and intercultural perspectives into the organizational modus operandi.

Variety and Complexity
of Intercultural Contacts

Situations involving intercultural contact include (a) a manager from a multinational organization based in the Netherlands going to head a subsidiary in Brazil, (b) an African-American manager in a U.S. company having Euro-American subordinates, (c) a group of Chinese workers in mainland China working for a Japanese manager in a Hong Kong multinational organization (MNO), and (d) a Hispanic teacher in a U.S. school working with Anglo-American, African-American, and Korean pupils. The types, frequency, and number of such intercultural contacts in organizations are increasing greatly.

At work in each case is a national culture, an organizational culture, and the cultural background of the particular individual(s). In some cases, the three cultural levels—national, organizational, individual— will be the same. Increasingly, however, one or more of the cultures involved will be different. In cases with a degree of cultural divergence, there is likely to be a need for intercultural training. This need becomes apparent when one examines the miscommunications that can, and often do, occur in such situations (see Albert, 1983b, 1992a; Albert & Triandis, 1979, for examples of Hispanic/Anglo miscommunications; and Shuter, 1992, for examples of what Shuter calls Swedish/American "cultural collisions" in organizations).

An organization will often mirror the dominant culture of the country where it was founded and is headquartered (Hofstede, 1985). Foreign subsidiaries of corporations may develop subsidiary cultures that are "hybrids between the international organizational culture and local national cultures" (Hofstede, 1985, p. 351).

As organizations become increasingly diverse, many kinds of intercultural interactions—from majority-minority (a common form) to minority-minority interactions—will take place. Thus, one may have interactions between a "mainstream person" and a "cultural-minority person"; between two "cultural minority" persons; between an expatriate manager and a group of local persons; or between headquarters in one country and subsidiaries in other countries.

REASONS FOR THE LACK
OF INTERCULTURAL TRAINING IN MNOs

It would seem that all of these factors present persuasive evidence for the need for intercultural training in organizations. Why, then, is training rarely employed at all, and other times only used minimally? Lee (1983) reported that less than 10%, and Tung (1981) that only 33%, of U.S. multinational corporations offered any type of training for expatriates. This finding contrasts with the fact that 69% of European and 57% of Japanese multinational corporations had training programs to prepare employees for foreign assignments (Tung, 1984, 1987, 1988). The training programs offered by U.S.-based MNOs are seldom comprehensive, emphasizing only language, environmental briefing, and elementary knowledge of the culture. Only 20% of the multinational corporations include spouses in the programs, and none include the children. The majority of these programs last only one week or less. Basically, there are three reasons for the woefully inadequate use of intercultural training by U.S. multinational organizations:

Lack of Awareness of the Effect
of Cultural Differences

Often many individuals in an organization have little awareness about the fact that a person's behaviors, perceptions, feelings, values, and characteristic ways of doing things will be influenced heavily by societal culture. Perhaps even more important, is there little realization that organizational norms, rules, and procedures also reflect the societal culture in which they were established.

I encountered this frequently among school personnel when I conducted a large-scale program of research on cultural differences between Hispanic-American pupils and Anglo-American teachers (Albert, 1983b, 1986a, 1992a). This lack of awareness is more likely to be present among mainstream persons, because they may never have had reason to learn about cultural differences.

Intercultural training is important for those with little or no experience in interacting with culturally different others. However, simply having some intercultural experience does not guarantee an understanding of the perspectives of members from another culture (Triandis, 1991); unfortunately, it is quite common for persons who do interact with culturally different others to have little knowledge or understanding of the target culture.

Lack of Understanding of the Experience of the Cultural Minority Person

In many instances, cultural minority persons enter settings in which their supervisors, co-workers, or subordinates have limited knowledge about their cultural background. In addition to cultural differences in behaviors, perceptions, and values, the cultural minority person has experiences in the organization that may differ qualitatively from those of cultural mainstream persons. These two types of differences, cultural and experiential, if not acknowledged and understood, may create a variety of problems and have deleterious consequences for the MNO. In educational settings the ensuing problems may range from misunderstandings, to lack of learning, hostility, absenteeism, and conflict. Similarly, in work settings the problems may include lower productivity, higher absenteeism and turnover, equal opportunity lawsuits, poor performance, and unwise personnel decisions. This is a major reason for the necessity of intercultural training.

Lack of Knowledge About Intercultural Training

The most prevalent reason cited by business organizations for the low use of intercultural training is their belief that such training is not effective (Black & Mendenhall, 1990). Often, top management sees no need for this type of training (Runzheimer Executive Report, 1984, cited in Black & Mendenhall, 1990), are unwilling to support it, and use the employee's domestic track record as the primary criterion for selection for oversees assignments (Miller, 1973). Similarly, in educational settings there have been objections to intercultural education on the basis of cost and the view that this constitutes "coddling" of minorities (Albert & Triandis, 1985). These misperceptions about the nature and impact of intercultural training often undermine the motivation for implementing such training in MNOs.

INCREASING KNOWLEDGE OF INTERCULTURAL FACTORS

Cultural Differences and Organizational Research

Despite a growing realization of the effects of culture following Hofstede's (1980, 1991, 1992) seminal work and subsequent international research (e.g., Adler, 1986), awareness is still not as great as it should be among researchers and practitioners. In 1983, Adler wrote a scathing review of the lack of international research in organizational behavior, and although the situation has improved since that time, there is still plenty of room for work in this area.

Albert (1988) identified seven factors that have contributed to the neglect of research on cultural variables and that may contribute to ignorance about culture and resistance to intercultural training: (a) focus on the individual, rather than on normative patterns, (b) difficulty of obtaining funds, (c) methodological complexities in cross-cultural research, (d) lack of direct experience with other cultures on the part of researchers and practitioners, (e) fear of creating or reinforcing stereotypes, (f) historical goal of assimilation in the United States, and (g) ethnocentric tendencies. Research concerning ways to overcome the neglect and resistance engendered by these factors is a high priority.

Albert (1992c) proposed a new field, "polycultural organizational communication," to address "theory and research involving organizations in both international and domestic settings in which cultural differences operate" (p. 75). Albert offered theoretical and practical reasons for the new field, which will bring together two important strands in communication scholarship: organizational and intercultural research. Polycultural communication will encompass theory, research, and practice in both the cross-cultural (sometimes called comparative) and the intercultural domains. Within each of these domains, research may take place either internationally or domestically, thereby yielding four domains for inquiry. Triandis and Albert (1987) reviewed studies in both the comparative (studies or practices occurring in different countries or cultures) and the intercultural (studies or practices occurring when persons from different cultures interact) domains and underscored the importance of the intercultural domain for organizations (see also, Shuter, 1989).

In the human resource management field, Steers (1989) made an impassioned plea that researchers and practitioners consider the "cultural imperative." Arvey, Bhagat, and Salas (1991), in a thoughtful review of cross-cultural human resources management, noted that the greatest amount of research had occurred in the area of organizational behavior and theory (for reviews of work in this area, see Barrett & Bass, 1976; Bhagat, Kedia, Crawford, & Kaplan, 1990; Bhagat & McQuaid, 1982; Roberts, 1970). They called for more theoretically driven research, more descriptive research across a wide range of nationalities, more emphasis on the interconnectedness of the various human resources practices (e.g., selection and training) and more comparative and cross-cultural research. Frost and Cyr (1990) concured on the great need for more intercultural work: "Few studies provided an intercultural focus, . . . an increasingly important research area to explore, especially as organizations seek to incorporate multicultural dimensions of the workforce within firms" (p. 4).

How can theoretical, empirical, and practical work move forward? Triandis and Albert (1987) proposed dimensions of cultural difference that are particularly relevant to work in organizational settings and suggested numerous ideas for future research in both cross-cultural and intercultural organizational communication (see also, Arvey et al., 1991; Shuter, 1989). The need now is for solid polycultural theoretical and empirical work on organizations, work that addresses the issue of cultural differences in a manner that is useful for the development of intercultural training.

The Experience of the Cultural Minority Person

It is often difficult to characterize the organizational climate and the resultant feelings of persons who are culturally different from the dominant cultural pattern embedded in the organization; yet, if the perspective of cultural minority persons is to be understood adequately, it is necessary for researchers, as well as organizational leaders and practitioners, to obtain an accurate account of the experiences of these persons in organizations. Focusing on the experiences of cultural minority members does not mean that they should be viewed as constituting "the problem" (Shuter's [1992] proposal to call cultural minority members "co-culture" members is helpful in this regard). On the contrary, the need is for MNOs to become more sensitive to the cultural bases for their ways of doing things, their norms and values, and to the impact these may have on culturally different persons. To achieve greater sensitivity, it is especially important for organizations to consciously learn about the experiences of cultural minority persons in organizations, precisely because organizational leaders normally will be less familiar with these experiences than with those of majority members. It is necessary, therefore, to train both cultural majority and cultural minority members to understand cultural differences in behaviors, attitudes, values, perceptions, and interpretations of behavior.

Because organizations often will have a dominant organizational culture reflecting the national culture of its leaders, cultural minority members may find themselves in a situation that might be characterized as one of greater discomfort with the organizational modus operandi than is experienced by a cultural majority member. This is due, in part, to the different subjective cultures (Triandis, 1972) of the two groups, because subjective cultures affect not only actions but also perceptions and interpretations of organizational events. The experiences of a cultural minority or co-culture person in a MNO may include the following:

Encountering behaviors and being treated in a way that often goes counter to the norms of one's own culture. Cultures differ in a number of important dimensions (Triandis & Albert, 1987); one of these dimensions is the degree of power distance (Hofstede, 1980, 1991, 1992) that exists between individuals. As Hofstede pointed out, in high-power-distance cultures such as in Latin America, Korea, and Japan, people see a great distance between subordinates and their superiors and expect a subordinate to express deferential behavior and to take orders from superiors. Suppose a Latin American professor is hired by an American university where students call professors by their first name. This professor may feel uncomfortable being called "Jose" by his pupils. He also may feel uncomfortable calling his dean by her first name. Yet, his American pupils would not know that they are, in terms of his culture, insulting him every time they call him Jose—not understanding that he comes from a high-power-distance culture, these students may see his insistence that they call him by his title as "snobbish" or "elitist."

There are myriad such events in everyday organizational functioning that can create negative feelings on one or both sides of the cultural divide. An important function of intercultural training is to elucidate these differences so that persons receiving the training will better understand how others view the situation.

Having no place to bring up matters related to how one is treated and how this affects one's ability to do the job. Large organizations in the United States often have offices to deal with affirmative action or sexual harassment, but it is likely that many cultural minority persons who have unpleasant experiences in the organization do not use these resources. Some members of co-cultures may be reticent to seek redress because they have learned that, historically, persons who have sought redress have placed their jobs or their advancement in jeopardy. Others come from cultures wherein it would be considered to be disloyal or wrong to complain about superiors; still others may feel that such an office is too impersonal. It is likely that many minority members will feel uncomfortable even raising the issue. Studies assessing the proportion of cultural minority persons who do use these offices, and under what conditions, would be useful.

A culturally different person may feel that an unwelcome climate exists in the organization, but it may be difficult for this person to point to specific discriminatory acts. Such a situation may be especially true for those in the upper echelons of management, because they may see such an affirmative action office as serving primarily the needs of lower echelon employees. This observation is illustrated by a *New York Times* article reporting that a brain surgeon quit her tenured professorship after 25 years at the Stanford Medical School, saying she was "the long-time object of demeaning comments and unwelcome advances" ("Stanford surgeon," 1991, p. A22). One can only infer what her experience must have been like for her to resign and address the issue through the press! Despite being an American, in a country where to discriminate against someone on the basis of gender is against the law, and despite the likely presence of an official place to go with such a complaint, she obviously did not believe she had somewhere to go to get her concerns really dealt with!

Providing intercultural training may offer an opportunity for both mainstream and nonmainstream employees to become sensitized to the issues before they become serious problems. Thus, intercultural sensitization can serve an important preventive function.

Having feelings of vulnerability. The experience of being a minority may well include having feelings of vulnerability. This observation is based, in part, on the dependence of cultural minorities on the good will of the majority. It is well know that co-culture members of an organization are the last hired and the first fired. But even in situations where firing is not likely, cultural minorities still feel vulnerable to lack of promotion, lack of acceptance, rejection, and other punitive treatment. They often do not feel that they can, or want to, "rock the boat" (Wilson cited in Deutch, 1991).

Being perceived as a threat to the system. Cultural minorities may, at times, be perceived as a threat to the system because they may, directly or indirectly, question the status quo, since the modus operandi of the majority culture often does not address minority concerns. Some minorities may believe that "the system" either overtly or covertly thwarts their efforts, and, in some instances, even affronts their dignity.

Being perceived as different and, often, as inferior to mainstream persons. Both objective characteristics and subjective culture characteristics can contribute to the minority person being viewed as inferior. Among the objective characteristics are gender, race, and physical characteristics that are obvious and cannot be denied by cultural-minority persons. Subjective culture characteristics (Triandis, 1972) encompass behavior, norms, expectations, values, and characteristic ways of responding to the environment that stem from having had a different history and different life experiences from those typically encountered by mainstream persons. Given that a large body of research has shown that people are more attracted to similar others (Byrne, 1961, 1971), this evidence may well pose a problem for the minority person who is different.

In some instances, being seen as no different from everybody else. This experience may impose on cultural-minority persons the burden to "fit in": For women, to be "one of the boys"; for Jews in U.S. organizations, to be assimilated and not require days off on Jewish holidays. A double-bind situation is produced wherein the co-culture persons feel "dammed if they do, and damned if they don't" behave like the cultural majority.

How do organizations either facilitate or impede the integration of minorities into the organization? How do co-culture persons negotiate these difficulties and dilemmas? What are the generic challenges for organizations in dealing with cultural minority persons? What problems or issues are specific to certain organizational settings? Are there generic experiences of cultural minorities? What are the specific experiences of different groups of minorities in different types of organizational settings? What types of organizational programs are successful in integrating minorities and majorities? How do cultural majority members act vis-à-vis members of cultural minorities in the organization? How do stereotypes affect the expectations of both parties to the interaction? What do organizations need to do to facilitate and promote the development and integration of all persons in the organization?

The above is merely a rough sketch of issues related to the experience of cultural minorities that need to be addressed by organizational researchers, leaders, and training providers. Training that sensitizes persons at every level of the organization is the key to creating greater understanding of the role of culture in *everyone's* actions and perceptions, and of the differences in experience and in reactions of cultural minorities and majorities.

Knowledge of Intercultural Training

Much can be done to increase the degree of knowledge and sophistication that organizations have concerning intercultural training. That is not to say that research in this area is no longer needed; many aspects of intercultural training in organizations could be addressed profitably by researchers. However, intercultural training in organizations is one area where some research already exists, but it is either not known or ignored by many MNOs. Knowledgeable and enlightened MNOs do exist, of course, and with the growing realization of domestic diversity in the United States, their numbers may be increasing. There is also variation in the degree and depth of knowledge that MNOs possess. To foster greater knowledge of intercultural training in MNOs, both organizations and researchers have a role to play.

What organizations need to do. Organizations need to consider the method and amount of intercultural training to be provided for each employee. Organizations also need to familiarize themselves with the various training approaches that have been developed and tested, such as the didactic approach, the attribution training approach (which uses the intercultural sensitizer or culture assimilator; see Albert, 1983a, 1986b, in press; Brislin, 1986; Fiedler, Mitchell, & Triandis, 1971), the cultural self-awareness approach (Kraemer, 1973, 1978), the behavior modification approach (David, 1972), and the experiential approach and the interaction approach (Gudykunst, Hammer, & Wiseman, 1977). Extensive discussions of intercultural training are provided in Albert, 1986b, in press; Bennett, 1986; Brislin, 1986, 1989; Fowler & Mumford, in press; Gudykunst & Hammer, 1983; Landis & Brislin, 1983; Martin, 1986; Triandis, 1991.

It is important that organizations carefully consider who will provide this training (Paige, 1986). With the awareness of cultural diversity growing, many untrained providers are offering "quick fixes" to the issue of managing diversity, often without any background in intercultural communication. Theoreticians and researchers must insist that intercultural training be of the highest caliber and supported by theory and research. This is a growing challenge and one that deserves our earnest attention and concern.

Organizations also need to consider the goals of the training, the timing and location of the training, and fundamental issues that all training programs should address (Albert, 1986b). They need to consider thoroughly the ethical issues associated with intercultural training, both in terms of the quality and adequacy of the training, and in terms of the purpose to which the training will be put (Paige & Martin, 1983). In addition, they need to consider the integration of training with the organizational modus operandi, the articulation of training with selection, development, compensation, and other related policies, and the incorporation of diversity perspectives throughout the organization (Albert, 1992b, Arvey et al., 1991, Mumford, 1983, Ronen, 1989).

Above all, MNOs need to understand that a growing body of research on intercultural training has shown certain types of training, especially attribution training, to be effective. Again, many MNOs do not use training because they believe it to be ineffective. Other MNOs resist providing training out of fear of creating problems where they believe that none currently exists. Yet, this is one area where the evidence suggests that intercultural training is effective for sensitizing trainees to cultural issues and assisting them to be more interpersonally effective in intercultural encounters.

The documentation for this claim comes from 16 studies on the intercultural sensitizer reviewed by Albert (1983a), 29 studies reviewed by Black and Mendenhall (1990), and 3 additional studies on the intercultural sensitizer by Pollard (1989), Broaddus (1986), and Cushner (1989). These studies span many different groups of trainees, different methodologies, different types of training, and different target cultures. Together, they suggest that intercultural training may facilitate interpersonal relations between persons from different cultures, ease adjustment to a different culture, improve feelings of well-being and self-confidence, and even facilitate task performance.

Finally, organizations can help advance the knowledge base in this area by collaborating with and providing access to qualified researchers and by becoming more knowledgeable consumers of intercultural training.

What researchers need to do. As intercultural contact increases, work is needed to decrease ignorance of, and resistance to, intercultural training. To bring about this change, research findings need to be disseminated widely to MNOs. Furthermore, educational activities are needed to raise the level of understanding and sophistication about what constitutes quality intercultural training.

Also, there is a need to learn more about sources of resistance and how to deal with them. There are many forms of resistance: in my research (Albert, 1983a, 1986a; Albert & Nelson, 1993) some principals were reluctant to allow their schools to participate because they thought researchers would either discover or create problems. Others thought that "pupils are pupils," and they could not see any cultural differences. Still others resisted because of worries that illegal aliens would be reported to the immigration service or suspicions that we really were interested in the sexual behavior of pupils, and not in their cultural patterns.

To better understand the particular missions, circumstances, and organizational cultures of MNOs, there needs to be a willingness to engage in dialogue with MNOs, to learn from them, and to work with them in research on training. It is hoped that as organizations grapple with diversity on the domestic front, they will gain greater awareness and appreciation for the pervasiveness and importance of cultural issues, will be less likely to see it as a passing fad, and will be more open to intercultural training both domestically and internationally.

CONCLUDING REMARKS

In summary, the reasons organizations need intercultural training, why it has not been used more broadly, and the need for research and practice that includes the experience of cultural minorities in organizations have been reviewed. Much work needs to be done in describing the experience of culturally different members in organizations, in educating members of both the dominant and nondominant cultures about how cultural differences affect behavior in organizations, and in integrating changes that reflect increased cultural awareness throughout the organization. Although research on a number of aspects of training in organizations is needed, a body of research has already demonstrated the effectiveness of intercultural training in a variety of settings, including schools, military organizations, and business settings (Albert, 1983a; Black & Mendenhall, 1990).

Ronen (1989), after explaining the formidable task the international assignee (IA) faces, cogently concludes that although training does not solve all dilemmas or guarantee certain outcomes, it "does give the IA at least a fighting chance. The alternative is simply to search for individuals who, in addition to competence in functional areas and managerial skill, possess the patience of a diplomat, the zeal of a missionary, and the linguistic skill of a United Nations interpreter" (p. 447).

As Frost and Cyr (1990) stated: "Organizations are increasingly forced to consider new values, training systems, evaluation systems, and career-paths plans that remain relevant across national borders. Managing in a global environment means that old assumptions and practices require reconsideration" (p. 2). This reconsideration can best be achieved by those who recognize the critical role of intercultural training in forging the organization of the future.

References

Abboushi, S. (1990). The impact of individual variables on the work values of Palestinian Arabs. *International Studies of Management and Organization, 20*(3), 53-68.

Abe, H., & Wiseman, R. L. (1983). A cross-cultural confirmation of the dimensions of intercultural effectiveness. *International Journal of Intercultural Relations, 7,* 53-67.

Abramms-Mezhoff, B., & Johns, D. (1989). Success strategies—Dealing with diversity: Playing straight with a mixed deck. *Supervision, 50,* 14-16.

Acker, S. R., & Levitt, S. (1987). Designing videoconference facilities for improved eye contact. *Journal of Broadcasting and Electronic Media, 31,* 181-191.

Acker, S. R., & McCain, T. (1990, July). *Designers' and producers' values: Their social, technical, and economic influences on the success of videoconferencing.* Paper presented at the 4th Annual Visual Communication Conference, Lake Tahoe.

Adler, N. J. (1980). Cultural synergy: The management of cross-cultural organizations. In W. Burke & L. Goodstain (Eds.), *Trends and issues in OD: Current theory and practice* (pp. 163-184). San Diego: University Associates.

Adler, N. J. (1983). Cross-cultural management research: The ostrich and the trend. *Academy of Management Review, 8,* 226-232.

Adler, N. J. (1986). *International dimensions of organizational behavior.* Boston: Kent.

Adler, N. J. (1991). *International dimensions of organizational behavior* (2nd ed.). Boston: Kent.

Adler, N. J., Doktor, R., & Redding, S. (1989). From the Atlantic to the Pacific century: Cross-cultural management reviewed. In C. Osigweh (Ed.), *Organizational science abroad: Constraints and perspectives* (pp. 27-56). New York: Plenum.

Albert, R. D. (1983a). The intercultural sensitizer or culture assimilator: A cognitive approach. In D. Landis & R. Brislin (Eds.), *Handbook of intercultural training: Vol. 2. Issues in training methodology* (pp. 186-271). New York: Pergamon.

Albert, R. D. (1983b). Mexican-American children in educational settings: Research on children's and teachers' perceptions and interpretations of behavior. In E. E. Garcia (Ed.), *The Mexican-American child: Language, cognition, and social development* (pp. 183-194). Tempe: Arizona State University.

Albert, R. D. (1986a). Communication and attributional differences between Hispanics and Anglo-Americans. In Y. Y. Kim (Ed.), *Interethnic communication: Current research* (pp. 42-59). Newbury Park, CA: Sage.

Albert, R. D. (1986b). Conceptual framework for the development and evaluation of cross-cultural orientation programs. *International Journal of Intercultural Relations, 10,* 197-213.

Albert, R. D. (1988). The place of culture in modern psychology. In P. Bronstein & K. Quina (Eds.), *Teaching a psychology of people: Resources for gender and socio-cultural awareness* (pp. 12-18). Washington, DC: American Psychological Association.

Albert, R. D. (1992a). *Communicating across cultures.* Unpublished manuscript.

Albert, R. D. (1992b). *The design and implementation of intercultural training in MNOs: Issues and approaches.* Unpublished manuscript.

Albert, R. D. (1992c). Polycultural perspectives on organizational communication. *Management Communication Quarterly, 6,* 74-84.

Albert, R. D. (in press). The intercultural sensitizer or culture assimilator as a cross-cultural training method. In S. M. Fowler & M. Mumford (Eds.), *Intercultural sourcebook: Cross-cultural training methodologies.* Yarmouth, ME: Intercultural Press.

Albert, R. D., & Nelson, G. (1993). Hispanic/Anglo-American differences in attributions to paralinguistic behavior. *International Journal of Intercultural Relations, 17,* 19-40.

Albert, R. D., & Triandis, H. C. (1979). Cross-cultural training: A theoretical framework and some observations. In H. Trueba & C. Barnett-Mizrahi (Eds.), *Bilingual multicultural education and the professional: From theory to practice* (pp. 181-194). Rowley, MA: Newbury House.

Albert, R. D., & Triandis, H. C. (1985). Intercultural education for multicultural societies. *International Journal of Intercultural Relations, 9,* 319-337.

Albrecht, T., & Hall, B. (1991). Relational and content differences between elites and outsiders in innovation networks. *Human Communication Research, 17,* 535-561.

Amado, G., & Vinagre Brasil, H. (1991). Organizational behaviors and cultural context: The Brazilian "jeitinho." *International Studies of Management and Organization, 21,* 3, 38-61.

America the super-fit. (1993, February 13). *The Economist,* p. 67.

Arensberg, C. (1978). Theoretical contributions of industrial and development studies. In E. Eddy & W. Partridge (Eds.), *Applied anthropology in America* (pp. 49-78). New York: Columbia University Press.

Arvey, R. D., Bhagat, S. R., & Salas, E. (1991). Cross-cultural and cross-national issues in personnel and human resources management: Where do we go from here? *Research in Personnel and Human Resources Management, 9,* 367-407.

Asea-Brown-Boveri. (1988, May 28). *The Economist,* pp. 19-22.

Atiyahi, H. (1992). Research note: Research on Arab countries published in Arabic. *Organization Studies, 23,* 105-110.

Atwood, R. (1984). Critical perspectives on the state of intercultural communication research. In B. Dervin & M. Voigt (Eds.), *Progress in communication sciences* (Vol. 4, pp. 67-90). Norwood, NJ: Ablex.

Axtell, R. E. (1989). *The do's and taboos of international trade: A small business primer.* New York: John Wiley.

Ayman, R., & Chemers, M. M. (1991). The effect of leadership match on subordinate satisfaction in Mexican organizations: Some moderating influences of self-monitoring. *Applied Psychology, 40*(3), 299-314.

Bacharach, S. B., & Aiken, M. (1977). Communication in administrative bureaucracies. *Academy of Management Journal, 20,* 356-377.

Barna, L. (1991). Stumbling blocks in intercultural communication. In L. A. Samovar & R. E. Porter (Eds.), *Intercultural communication: A reader* (6th ed., pp. 345-353). Belmont, CA: Wadsworth.

Barnett, G. (1988). Communication and organizational culture. In G. Goldhaber & G. Barnett (Eds.), *Handbook of organizational communication* (pp. 101-130). Newbury Park, CA: Sage.

Barnett, R. J., & Muller, R. E. (1974). *Global reach: The power of the multinational corporations.* New York: Simon & Schuster.

Barnlund, D. (1974). The public and private self in Japan and the United States. In J. Condon & M. Saito (Eds.), *Intercultural encounters with Japan* (pp. 27-96). Tokyo: Simul.

Barnlund, D. (1975). *Public and private self in Japan and the United States.* Tokyo: Simul.

Barnlund, D. (1989). *Communicative styles of Japanese and Americans: Images and realities.* Belmont, CA: Wadsworth.

Barnlund, D., & Yoshioka, M. (1990). Apologies: Japanese and American styles. *International Journal of Intercultural Relations, 14,* 193-206.

Barrett, R., & Bass, B. (1976). Cross-cultural issues in industrial and organizational psychology. In M. D. Dunnette (Ed.), *Handbook of industrial and organizational psychology* (pp. 1639-1686). Chicago: Rand McNally.

Barsoux, J., & Lawrence, P. (1991). The making of a French manager. *Harvard Business Review, 6,* 43-52.

Bass, B., Burger, P., Doktor, R., & Barrett, G. (1979). *Assessment of managers: An international comparison.* New York: Free Press.

Beatty, J., McCune, J., & Beatty, R. (1988). A policy-capturing approach to the study of United States and Japanese managers' compensation decisions. *Journal of Management, 14*(3), 465-474.

Bechtold, C. H. (1984, April 9). Foreign finance risks: Inflation, devaluation, and exchange controls wreak havoc on foreign insurance programs. *Business Insurance, 18,* 33.

Becker, C. (1988). Reason for the lack of argumentation and debate in the Far East. In L. A. Samovar & R. E. Porter (Eds.), *Intercultural communication: A reader* (5th ed., pp. 243-252). Belmont, CA: Wadsworth.

Becker, S. (1976). Directions for intercultural communication research. In L. A. Samovar & R. E. Porter (Eds.), *Intercultural communication: A reader* (2nd ed., pp. 346-356). Belmont, CA: Wadsworth.

Bell, E. L. (1990). The bicultural life experience of career-oriented black women. *Journal of Organizational Behavior, 3,* 459-477.

BenDasan, I. (1970). *Japanese and Jews.* Tokyo: Yamamoto Shoten.

Benedict, R. (1946). *The chrysanthemum and the sword.* Boston: Houghton-Mifflin.

Bennett, J. M. (1986). Modes of cross-cultural training: Conceptualizing cross-cultural training as education. *International Journal of Intercultural Relations, 10,* 117-134.

Berger, C. J., & Cummings, L. L. (1979). Organizational structure, attitudes, and behaviors. In B. M. Staw (Ed.), *Research in organizational behavior* (Vol. 1, pp. 169-208). Greenwich, CT: JAI.

Berger, P., & Luckman, T. (1967). *The social construction of reality: A treatise in the sociology of knowledge.* Garden City, NY: Anchor.

Berman, S., & Hellweg, S. (1989). Perceived supervisor communication competence and supervisor satisfaction as a function of quality circle participation. *Journal of Business Communication, 26,* 103-119.

Berry, J. (1980). Introduction to methodology. In H. Triandis & J. Berry (Eds.), *Handbook of cross-cultural psychology* (Vol. 2, pp. 1-28). Boston: Allyn & Bacon.

Bhagat, R. S., Kedia, B. L., Crawford, S. E., & Kaplan, M. R. (1990). Cross-cultural issues in organizational psychology: Emergent trends and directions for research in the 1990s. In C. L. Cooper & I. R. Robertson (Eds.), *International review of industrial and organizational psychology* (Vol. 5, pp. 59-99). New York: John Wiley.

Bhagat, R. S., & McQuaid, S. J. (1982). Role of subjective culture in organizations: A review and directions for future research. *Journal of Applied Psychology, 67,* 653-685.

Bird, A., & Dunbar, R. (1991). Getting the job done over there: Improving expatriate productivity. *National Productivity Review, 10,* 145-156.

Black, S. J., & Mendenhall, M. (1990). Cross-cultural training effectiveness: A review and a theoretical framework for future research. *Academy of Management Review, 15,* 113-136.

Bond, M. (1988). Finding universal dimensions of individual variation in multicultural studies of values: The Rokeach and Chinese value surveys. *Journal of Personality and Social Psychology, 55,* 1009-1015.

Borsack, S. (1987). Choosing to do business through a foreign branch or a foreign subsidiary: A tax analysis. *Case Western Reserve Journal of International Law, 19,* 393-419.

Brandt, W. K., & Hulbert, J. (1976). Patterns of communications in the multinational corporation: An empirical study. *Journal of International Business Studies, 7*(1), 57-64.

Bretz, R., & Schmidbauer, M. (1983). *Media for interactive communication.* Beverly Hills, CA: Sage.

Brislin, R. W. (1986). A culture general assimilator: Preparation for various types of sojourns. *International Journal of Intercultural Relations, 10,* 215-234.

Brislin, R. W. (1989). Intercultural communication training. In K. M. Asante & W. B. Gudykunst (Eds.), *Handbook of international and intercultural communication* (pp. 441-457). Newbury Park, CA: Sage.

Brislin, R. W. (1993). *Understanding culture's influence on behavior.* Fort Worth, TX: Harcourt Brace Jovanovich.

Brislin, R. W., Cushner, K., Cherrie, C., & Yong, M. (1986). *Intercultural interactions: A practical guide.* Newbury Park, CA: Sage.

Broaddus, D. (1986). *Use of a culture-general assimilator in intercultural training.* Unpublished doctoral dissertation, Indiana State University, Terre Haute.

Brooke, M., & Remmers, H. (1970). *The strategy for multinational enterprise.* New York: American Elsevier.

Brown, E., & Sechrest, L. (1980). Experiments in cross-cultural research. In H. Triandis & J. Berry (Eds.), *Handbook of cross-cultural psychology* (Vol. 2, pp. 297-318). Boston: Allyn & Bacon.

Brown, P., & Ford, M. (1964). Address in American English. In D. Hymes (Ed.), *Language in culture and society* (pp. 234-244). New York: Harper & Row.

Brown, P., & Levinson, S. (1978). Universals in language usage: Politeness phenomena. In E. Goody (Ed.), *Questions and politeness* (pp. 256-289). New York: Cambridge University Press.

Buckley, A. (1987). Financing overseas subsidiaries. *Accountancy, 100,* 73-75.

Burgoon, M., & Miller, G. (1990). Paths. *Communication Monographs, 57,* 152-160.

Burke, K. (1968). *A rhetoric of motives.* Berkeley: University of California Press.

Burns, T., & Stalker, G. (1961). *The management of innovation.* London: Tavistock.

Byrne, D. (1961). Interpersonal attraction and attitude similarity. *Journal of Personality and Social Psychology, 62,* 713-715.

Byrne, D. (1971). *The attraction paradigm.* New York: Academic Press.

Carbaugh, D. (1988). Cultural terms and tensions in the speech at a television station. *Western Journal of Speech Communication, 52,* 216-237.

Casmir, F. (1978). A multicultural perspective of human communication. In F. Casmir (Ed.), *Intercultural and international communication* (pp. 241-260). Washington, DC: University Press of America.

Cathcart, D., & Cathcart, R. (1988). Japanese social experiences and concept of groups. In L. A. Samovar & R. E. Porter (Eds.), *Intercultural communication: A reader* (5th ed., pp. 186-192). Belmont, CA: Wadsworth.

Chan, L. (1980). A presentation of multinational advertising objectives, strategies, and creative execution by Singapore airlines. *Media Asia, 7,* 186-188.

Chao, Y. (1956). Chinese terms of address. *Language, 32,* 217-241.

Chemers, M. M., & Ayman, R. (1985). Leadership orientation as a moderator of the relationship between job performance and job satisfaction of Mexican managers. *Personality and Social Psychology Bulletin, 11,* 359-367.

Chikudate, N., Barnett, G., & McFarland, S. (1990, June). *A cross-cultural examination of organizational culture: A comparison of Japan and the United States.* Paper presented at the Annual Conference of the International Communication Association, Dublin, Ireland.

Chinese Culture Connection. (1987). Chinese values and the search for culture-free dimensions of culture. *Journal of Cross-Cultural Psychology, 18,* 143-164.

Choi, F. D., & Czechowicz, J. (1983). Assessing foreign subsidiary performance: A multinational comparison. *Management International Review, 23,* 14-27.

Christie, B. (1985). *Human factors of information in the office.* New York: John Wiley.

Clark, R. (1979). *The Japanese company.* New Haven, CT: Yale University Press.

Cohen, R. (1992, March 2). The very model of efficiency. *New York Times,* pp. D1-D8.

Condon, J. (1978). Intercultural communication from a speech communication perspective. In F. L. Casmir (Ed.), *Intercultural and international communication* (pp. 108-137). Washington, DC: University Press of America.

Condon, J. (1984). *With respect to the Japanese: A guide for Americans.* Yarmouth, ME: Intercultural Press.

Copeland, L., & Griggs, L. (1985). *Going international.* New York: Random House.

Costigan, D. (1971). *FAX: The principles and practice of facsimile communication.* Philadelphia: Chilton.

Cousins, S. (1989). Culture and self-perception and the United States. *Journal of Personality and Social Psychology, 56,* 124-131.

Cox, C. J., & Cooper, C. (1985). The irrelevance of American organizational sciences to the U.K. and Europe. *Journal of General Management, 11*(2), 27-34.

Cox, T., & Nkomo, S. M. (1990). Invisible men and women: A status report on race as a variable in organization behavior research. *Journal of Organizational Behavior, 11,* 419-433.

Crawford, A. B., Jr. (1982). Corporate electronic mail: A communication-intensive application of information technology. *MIS Quarterly, 6*(3), 1-13.

Cray, D. (1984). Control and coordination in multinational corporations. *Journal of International Business Studies, 15*(3), 85-98.

Culnan, M. J., & Markus, M. L. (1987). Information technologies. In F. M. Jablin, L. L. Putnam, K. H. Roberts, & L. W. Porter (Eds.), *Handbook of organizational communication: An interdisciplinary perspective* (pp. 420-443). Newbury Park, CA: Sage.

Cupach, W., & Imahori, I. (1991, November). *Managing social predicaments II: A comparison of Japanese and American facework.* Paper presented at the Annual Convention of the Speech Communication Association, Atlanta, GA.

Cushman, D., & King, S. (1985). National and organizational cultures in conflict resolution: Japan, the U.S., and Yugoslavia. In W. Gudykunst, L. Stewart, & S. Ting-Toomey (Eds.), *Communication, culture, and organizational processes* (pp. 115-133). Beverly Hills, CA: Sage.

Cushman, D., & King, S. (1993). High-speed management: A revolution in organizational communication in the 1990s. In S. A. Deetz (Ed.), *Communication yearbook 16* (pp. 209-236). Newbury Park, CA: Sage.

Cushman, D., & King, S. (1994). *High-speed management and organizational communication in the 1990s: A reader.* Albany: State University of New York Press.

Cushner, K. (1989). Assessing the impact of a culture-general assimilator. *International Journal of Intercultural Relations, 13*, 125-146.

Cusumano, M. (1988). Manufacturing innovation: Lesson from the Japanese auto industry. *Sloan Management Review, 30*(1), 29-39.

Dallinger, J. (1987). An analysis of men's and women's networks. In L. Nadler & W. Todd-Mancillas (Eds.), *Advances in gender and communication research* (pp. 13-21). Lanham, MD: University Press of America.

Dalton, D., Todor, W., Spendolini, M., Fielding, G., & Porter, L. (1980). Organizational structure and performance: A critical review. *Academy of Management Review, 5*, 49-64.

Darling, J. (1986). Managing up in the multinational firm. *Leadership and Organization Development Journal, 7*, 21-26.

David, K. (1972). Intercultural adjustment and applications of reinforcement theory to problems of "culture." *Trends, 4*, 1-64.

Davis, K. (1972). *Human behavior at work.* New York: McGraw-Hill.

Davis, S. M. (1971a). Authority and control in Mexican enterprise. In S. M. Davis (Ed.), *Comparative management: Organizational and cultural perspectives* (pp. 174-187). Englewood Cliffs, NJ: Prentice Hall.

Davis, S. M. (1971b). Politics and organizational underdevelopment in Chile. In S. M. Davis (Ed.), *Comparative management: Organizational and cultural perspectives* (pp. 188-209). Englewood Cliffs, NJ: Prentice Hall.

De Barry, W. (1959). Some common tendencies in neo-Confucianism. In D. S. Nivison & A. Wright (Eds.), *Confucianism in action* (pp. 25-49). Stanford, CA: Stanford University Press.

Dei, S. (1989, November). *The international rhetoric of Yashuhiro Nakasone.* Paper presented at the Annual Meeting of the Speech Communication Association, San Francisco.

Deutch, C. (1991, September 1). Pairing up for better understanding. *New York Times,* p. 23.

Dicle, U., Dicle, I. A., & Alie, R. E. (1988). Human resources management practices in Japanese organizations in the United States. *Public Personnel Management, 17,* 331-340.

Dodd, C. (1977). *Cross-cultural communication.* Dubuque, IA: Kendall/Hunt.

Doi, T. (1963). Some thoughts on helplessness and the desire to be loved. *Psychiatry, 26,* 266-272.

Doi, T. (1973). The Japanese patterns of communication and the concept of *amae. Quarterly Journal of Speech, 59,* 180-185.

Doi, T. (1989). *The anatomy of dependence.* Tokyo: Kodansha International.

Doktor, R., Lie, J., & Pillon, C. (1991). A systems theoretic perspective upon international organizational behavior: Some preliminary observations and hypotheses. *Management International Review, 31,* 125-133.

Donaldson, L. (1986). Size and bureaucracy in East and West: A preliminary meta-analysis. In S. R. Clegg, D. Dunphy, & S. Redding (Eds.), *The enterprise and management in East Asia* (pp. 22-31). Hong Kong: Center for Asian Studies.

Doz, Y., & Prahalad, C. K. (1981). Headquarter's influence and strategic control in MNCs. *Sloan Management Review, 23,* 15-29.

Dubin, R. (1978). *Theory building.* New York: Free Press.

Edstrom, W. G., & Galbraith, J. (1977). Transfer of managers and a coordination and control strategy in multinational organizations. *Administrative Science Quarterly, 22,* 248-263.

Edwards, L. (1978). Present shock, and how to avoid it abroad. *Across the Board, 15*(2), 36-43.

Ellis, D., & DelValle, C. (1993, April 19). Tall order for small businesses. *Business Week*, pp. 114-118.

Engelhoff, W. (1984). Patterns of control in U.S., U.K., and European multinational corporations. *Journal of International Business Studies, 15*, 73-83.

Estafen, B. D. (no date). *The comparative management of firms in Chile.* Bloomington: Indiana University Graduate School of Business.

Explaining the mystery. (1992, January 4). *The Economist*, pp. 15-18.

Eze, N. (1984). Sources of motivation among Nigerian managers. *Journal of Social Psychology, 25*, 53-68.

Faltermayer, E. (1993, April 19). The Fortune 500. *Fortune*, pp. 183-184.

Fayerweather, J. (1982). *International business strategy and administration.* Cambridge, MA: Ballinger.

Feigenbaum, A. (1961). *Total quality control: Engineering and management.* New York: McGraw-Hill.

Fiedler, F. (1967). *Theory of leadership effectiveness.* New York: McGraw-Hill.

Fiedler, F., Mitchell, T., & Triandis, H. (1971). The culture assimilator: An approach to cross-cultural training. *Journal of Applied Psychology, 55*, 95-102.

Filipczak, B. (1992). Working for the Japanese. *Training, 29*(12), 23-29.

Fishman, J. (1982). Whorfianism and the third kind: Ethnolinguistic diversity as a worldwide societal asset. *Language in Society, 11*, 1-14.

Fitch, K. L. (1994). Culture, communication, and interpersonal ideology. In S. Deetz (Ed.), *Communication yearbook 17* (pp. 104-135). Thousand Oaks, CA: Sage.

The Forbes 500s. (1993, April 26). *Forbes*, pp. 198-242.

Forbes, D. (1984). Insuring foreign subsidiaries presents a potpourri of pitfalls and promises for U.S. multinationals operating overseas. *Risk Management, 31*(1), 59-60.

Foster, L. W., & Flynn, D. M. (1984). Management information technology: Its effects on organizational form and function. *MIS Quarterly, 8*, 229-236.

Fowler, S. M., & Mumford, M. (in press). *Intercultural sourcebook: Cross-cultural training methodologies.* Yarmouth, ME: Intercultural Press.

Fraker, S. (1984, March 5). High-speed management for the high tech age. *Fortune*, pp. 62-68.

Friday, R. A. (1989). Contrasts in discussion behaviors of German and American managers. *International Journal of Intercultural Relations, 13*, 429-446.

Frost, P. J., & Cyr, D. J. (1990). Selective frames, findings, and futures: A review of the Second Conference on International Personnel and Human Resources Management. *Research in Personnel and Human Resources Management, 2*(Suppl.), 1-20.

Fukuzawa, Y. (1969). *Fukuzawa Yukichi zenshu [Collected works of Yukichi Fukuzawa].* Tokyo: Iwanami Shoten.

Fulk, J., & Boyd, R. (1991). Emerging theories of communication in organizations. *Journal of Management, 17*, 407-446.

Furnham, A., & Bochner, S. (1986). *Culture shock: Psychological reactions to unfamiliar environments.* New York: Methuen.

Garfein, R. T. (1989). Cross-cultural perspectives on the dynamics of prestige. *Journal of Services Marketing, 3*(3), 17-24.

Gates, S. R., & Egelhoff, W. G. (1986). Centralization in headquarters-subsidiary relationships. *Journal of International Business Studies, 17*(2), 71-92.

Giles, H., Mulac, A., Bradac, J., & Johnson, P. (1987). Speech accommodation theory: The first decade and beyond. In M. McLaughlin (Ed.), *Communication yearbook 10* (pp. 13-48). Newbury Park, CA: Sage.

Giles, H., & Pearson, H. (1990). Asian Pacific language and communication: Foundations, issues, and directions. *Journal of Asian Pacific Communication, 1,* 1-24.

Gillin, J. P. (1971). The middle segments and their values. In S. M. Davis (Ed.), *Comparative management: Organizational and cultural perspectives* (pp. 130-144). Englewood Cliffs, NJ: Prentice Hall.

Glenn, E. (1981). *Man and mankind.* Norwood, NJ: Ablex.

Goldenberg, S. (1988). *Hands across the ocean.* Boston: Harvard Business School Press.

Goldhaber, G. M. (1993). *Organizational communication* (6th ed.). Madison, WI: Brown & Benchmark.

Goldman, A. (1988). *For Japanese only: Intercultural communication with Americans.* Tokyo: Japan Times.

Goldman, A. (1989a). *Intercultural communication between Japanese and Americans.* Tokyo: Kirihara Shoten.

Goldman, A. (1989b, November). *Toward an intercultural/organizational interface in U.S.-Japanese communication: A, J, & Z communication in Japanese production line management.* Paper presented at a meeting of the Speech Communication Association, San Francisco.

Goldman, A. (1990a). Cultural abyss at the negotiating table: An examination of Japanese-U.S. communicative styles. *Human Communication Studies, 18,* 101-113.

Goldman, A. (1990b). Preparing for negotiations with Japanese organizations: A briefing for North American and European multinationals. *Multinational Employer, 7,* 16-17.

Goldman, A. (1990c, June). *Toward a Z-theory of communication: Negotiating an intercultural approach to Japanese-U.S. negotiating.* Paper presented at a meeting of the Communication Association of Japan, Tokyo.

Goldman, A. (1991). Negotiating protocol in Japan: A cross-cultural perspective. *International Journal of Management, 8,* 808-813.

Goldman, A. (1992a). A bicultural approach to public speaking: Facilitating Japanese-U.S. communication. *Human Communication Studies, 20,* 67-81.

Goldman, A. (1992b, November). *The centrality of ningensei to Japanese negotiating and interpersonal relations: Implications for U.S.-Japanese communication.* Paper presented at a meeting of the Speech Communication Association, Chicago.

Goldman, A. (1992c). Intercultural training of Japanese for U.S.-Japanese interorganizational communication. *International Journal of Intercultural Relations, 16,* 195-216.

Goldman, A. (1992d). Japanese managerial psychology: An analysis of cultural and organizational features of total quality control. *Journal of Managerial Psychology, 7,* 17-20.

Goldman, A. (1992e, November). *Strategic arenas of interaction with Japanese multinationals: Organizational, negotiating, proxemic, and performance protocols.* Paper presented at a meeting of the Speech Communication Association, Chicago.

Goldman, A. (1993a, November). *Keiretsus and Zaibatsus: A framework for Japanese organizational communication.* Paper presented at a meeting of the Speech Communication Association, Miami.

Goldman, A. (1993b). Implications of Japanese total quality control for Western organizations: Dimensions of an intercultural hybrid. *Journal of Business Communication, 30,* 29-48.

Goldman, A. (1993c). *Japanese-U.S. business communication.* Tokyo: Kirihara Shoten.

Goldman, A. (1993d). *Nippon Inc. vs. Raleigh Ltd.* Unpublished manuscript.

Goldman, A. (1993e). The centrality of culture and communication in international business. *Arizona Communication Association Journal, 19,* 9-18.

Goldman, A. (1994). *Doing business with the Japanese: A guide to successful communication, management, and diplomacy.* New York: State University of New York Press.

Goodenough, W. (1978). Multiculturalism as the normal human experience. In E. Eddy & W. Partridge (Eds.), *Applied anthropology in America* (pp. 79-87). New York: Columbia University Press.

Gregory, K. L. (1983). Native-view paradigms: Multiple cultures and culture conflicts in organizations. *Administrative Science Quarterly, 28,* 359-376.

Grunwald, W., & Bernthal, W. (1983). Controversy in German management. *Academy of Management Review, 8,* 233-241.

Gudykunst, W. (1983). Theorizing in intercultural communication. In W. Gudykunst (Ed.), *Intercultural communication theory: Current perspectives* (pp. 13-20). Beverly Hills, CA: Sage.

Gudykunst, W. (1985). Intercultural communication: Current status and proposed directions. In B. Dervin & M. Voigt (Eds.), *Progress in communication sciences* (Vol. 6, pp. 1-46). Norwood, NJ: Ablex.

Gudykunst, W. B., & Hammer, M. R. (1983). Basic training design: Approaches to intercultural training. In D. Landis & R. W. Brislin (Eds.), *Handbook of intercultural training: Vol. 1. Issues in theory and design* (pp. 118-154). New York: Pergamon.

Gudykunst, W. B., Hammer, M. R., & Wiseman, R. L. (1977). Analysis of an integrated approach to cross-cultural training. *International Journal of Intercultural Relations, 1*(2), 99-110.

Gudykunst, W. B., & Kim, Y. (1984). *Communicating with strangers: An approach to intercultural communication.* New York: Random House.

Gudykunst, W. B., & Nishida, T. (1984). Individual and cultural influences on uncertainty reduction. *Communication Monographs, 51,* 23-36.

Gudykunst, W. B., Yang, S., & Nishida, T. (1985). A cross-cultural test of uncertainty reduction theory: Comparisons of acquaintances, friends, and dating relationships in Japan, Korea, and the United States. *Human Communication Research, 11,* 407-455.

Gumperz, J. (1982). *Discourse strategies.* London: Cambridge University Press.

Hage, J., Aiken, M., & Marrett, C. B. (1971). Organization structure and communications. *American Sociological Review, 36,* 860-871.

Haglund, E. (1988). Japan: Cultural considerations. In L. A. Samovar & R. E. Porter (Eds.), *Intercultural communication: A reader* (5th ed., pp. 84-94). Belmont, CA: Wadsworth.

Hall, E. (1973). *The silent language.* Garden City, NY: Doubleday.

Hall, E. (1976). *Beyond culture.* Garden City, NY: Doubleday.

Hall, E. (1983). *The dance of life.* New York: Anchor.

Hall, E., & Hall, M. (1987). *Hidden differences: Doing business with the Japanese.* New York: Anchor.

Hall, J. (1959). The Confucian teacher in Tokugawa, Japan. In D. Nivison & A. Wright (Eds.), *Confucianism in action* (pp. 268-301). Stanford, CA: Stanford University Press.

Hall, P. (1986). The etic-emic distinction: Its observational foundation. In B. Dervin & M. Voigt (Eds.), *Progress in communication sciences* (Vol. 6, pp. 123-152). Norwood, NJ: Ablex.

Hamabata, M. (1990). *Crested kimono: Power and love in the Japanese business family.* Ithaca, NY: Cornell University Press.

Harris, P. R., & Moran, R. T. (1987). *Managing cultural differences* (2nd ed.). Houston: Gulf.

Harris, P. R., & Moran, R. T. (1991). *Managing cultural differences: High-performance strategies for a new world of business* (3rd ed.). Houston: Gulf.

Hayashi, S. (1988). *Culture and management in Japan* (F. Baldwin, Trans.). Tokyo: University of Tokyo Press.

Hayles, V. R. (1992, August). *Cultural diversity in a global perspective: Opportunities and challenges.* Paper presented at the Academy of Management Meeting, Las Vegas, NV.

Healey, J. H. (1956). *Executive coordination and control.* Columbus, OH: Ohio State University, Bureau of Business Research.

Hedlund, G. (1981). Autonomy of subsidiaries and formalization of headquarters subsidiary relationships in Swedish MNCs. In L. Otterbeck (Ed.), *The management of headquarters-subsidiary relationships in MNCs* (pp. 25-78). New York: St. Martin's.

Heenan, D. A. (1975). *Multinational management of human resources: A system approach.* Austin: University of Texas, Bureau of Business Research.

Heenan, D. A., & Perlmutter, H. V. (1979). *Management in the industrial world.* New York: McGraw-Hill.

Heimstra, G. (1982). Teleconferencing, concern for face, and organizational culture. In R. Bostrom (Ed.), *Communication yearbook 6* (pp. 874-904). Beverly Hills, CA: Sage.

Hellweg, S. (1987). Organizational grapevines. In B. Dervin & M. Voigt (Eds.), *Progress in communication sciences* (Vol. 8, pp. 213-230). Norwood, NJ: Ablex.

Hersey, P., & Blanchard, K. (1982). *Management of organizational behavior: Utilizing human resources* (4th ed.). Englewood Cliffs, NJ: Prentice Hall.

Herzberg, F. (1968). One more time: How do you motivate employees? *Harvard Business Review, 46,* 53-62.

Hickson, D., Hinings, C., McMillan, C., & Schwitter, J. (1974). The culture-free context of organization structure: A tri-national comparison. *Sociology, 8,* 59-80.

Hildebrandt, N., & Giles, H. (1983). The Japanese as a subordinate group: Ethnolinguistic identity theory in a foreign language context. *Anthropological Linguistics, 25,* 436-466.

Hiltz, S. R., & Turoff, M. (1978). *The network nation: Human communication via computer.* Reading, MA: Addison-Wesley.

Hirokawa, R. (1981). Improving intra-organizational communication: A lesson from Japanese management. *Communication Quarterly, 30,* 35-40.

Hirokawa, R., & Miyahara, A. (1986). A comparison of influence strategies utilized by managers in American and Japanese organizations. *Communication Quarterly, 34,* 250-265.

Hoffman, M. S. (1993). *The world almanac and book of facts.* New York: Scripps Howard.

Hofstede, G. (1980). *Culture's consequences: International differences in work-related values.* Beverly Hills, CA: Sage.

Hofstede, G. (1984). *Culture's consequences: International differences in work-related values* (abridged ed.). Beverly Hills, CA: Sage.

Hofstede, G. (1985). The interaction between national and organizational value systems. *Journal of Management Studies, 22*(4), 347-357.

Hofstede, G. (1991). *Cultures and organizations: Software of the mind.* New York: McGraw-Hill.

Hofstede, G. (1992, August). *Cultural constraints in management theories.* Paper presented at a meeting of the Academy of Management, Las Vegas, NV.

Hofstede, G., Neuijen, B., & Ohayu, D. D. (1990). Measuring organizational cultures: A qualitative and quantitative study across twenty cases. *Administrative Science Quarterly, 35,* 286-316.

Hou, W. (1986). Japanese management: American egg, oriental bird? *Singapore Management Review, 8,* 1-23.

Howard, N., & Teramoto, Y. (1981). The really important difference between Japanese and Western management. *Management International Review, 3,* 19-30.

Howe, R. (1971). A path goal theory of leader effectiveness. *Administrative Science Quarterly, 16,* 321-338.

Hsu, F. (1985). The self in cross-cultural perspective. In A. Marvella, G. DeVos, & F. Hsu (Eds.), *Culture and self* (pp. 24-55). Honolulu: University of Hawaii Press.

Huber, G., & Daft, R. (1987). The information environments of organizations. In F. M. Jablin, L. L. Putnam, K. H. Roberts, & L. W. Porter (Eds.), *Handbook of organizational communication: An interdisciplinary perspective* (pp. 130-164). Newbury Park, CA: Sage.

Hudiburg, J. (1991). Competing for Japan's deming prize. In B. H. Peters & J. L. Peters (Eds.), *Total quality management* (pp. 33-35). New York: Conference Board.

Hui, C., & Triandis, H. (1984). Quantitative methods in cross-cultural research: Multidimensional scaling and item response theory. In R. Diaz-Guerrero (Ed.), *Cross-cultural and national studies in social psychology* (Vol. 2, pp. 69-79). New York: Elsevier.

Hulbert, J., & Brandt, W. (1980). *Managing the multinational subsidiary.* New York: Holt, Rinehart & Winston.

Hymes, D. (1972). Models of the interaction of language and social life. In J. J. Gumperz & D. Hymes (Eds.), *Directions in sociolinguistics: The ethnography of communication* (pp. 35-71). New York: Holt, Rinehart & Winston.

Irvine, S., & Carroll, W. (1980). Testing and assessment across cultures: Issues in methodology and theory. In H. Triandis & J. Berry (Eds.), *Handbook of cross-cultural psychology* (Vol. 2, pp. 181-244). Boston: Allyn & Bacon.

Ishida, H. (1986). Transferability of Japanese human resource management abroad. *Human Resource Management, 25,* 103-120.

Ishihara, S. (1990). *The Japan who can say no.* New York: Simon & Schuster.

Ishii, S., & Bruneau, T. (1988). Silence and silences in cross-cultural perspective: Japan and the United States. In L. A. Samovar & R. E. Porter (Eds.), *Intercultural communication: A reader* (5th ed., pp. 310-315). Belmont, CA: Wadsworth.

Jablin, F. M. (1987a). Formal organization structure. In F. M. Jablin, L. L. Putnam, K. H. Roberts, & L. W. Porter (Eds.), *Handbook of organizational communication: An interdisciplinary perspective* (pp. 389-419). Newbury Park, CA: Sage.

Jablin, F. M. (1987b). Organizational entry, assimilation, and exit. In F. M. Jablin, L. L. Putnam, K. H. Roberts, & L. W. Porter (Eds.), *Handbook of organizational communication: An interdisciplinary perspective* (pp. 679-740). Newbury Park, CA: Sage.

Jaeger, A. M. (1983). The transfer of organizational cultures overseas: An approach to control in the multinational corporation. *Journal of International Business Studies, 14,* 91-114.

Jahoda, G. (1988). J'accuse. In M. Bond (Ed.), *The cross-cultural challenge to social psychology* (pp. 86-95). Newbury Park, CA: Sage.

Jain, H., Kanungo, R. N., & Goldhaber, G. (1980). Attitudes toward a communication system: A comparison of anglophone and francophone hospital employees. *Human Communication Research, 6,* 178-184.

Jamieson, K. (1988). *Eloquence in an electronic age: The transformation of political speechmaking.* New York: Oxford University Press.

Japan refuses to get down to nitty-gritty: U.S rejects sending negotiator to trade talks. (1985, February 27). *Japan Times,* p. 1.

Javetski, B., Toy, S., Templeton, J., Melcher, R., & Rossant, J. (1993, February 15). Europe's economies: What must be done. *Business Week,* pp. 22-26.

Jeannet, J. P. (1985). Volkswagen's tough choices in Brazil's crash effort to switch from petrol to alcohol fuel. *International Management, 40*(10), 130-138.

Jones, K. (1984). Everywhere abroad and nowhere at home: The global corporation and the international state. *International Journal of the Sociology of Law, 12,* 85-103.

Joynt, P. (1985). Preface. In P. Joynt & M. Warner (Eds.), *Managing in different cultures* (pp. 6-8). New York: Columbia University Press.

Kameoka, V. (1984). Construct validation of psychological measures in cross-cultural research: Analysis of linear structural relationships. In R. Diaz-Guerrero (Ed.), *Cross-cultural and national studies in social psychology* (Vol. 2, pp. 57-68). New York: Elsevier.

Katz, D., & Kahn, R. (1966). *The social psychology of organizations.* New York: John Wiley.

Kawashima, T. (1949). *Nippon shakai no kazoku-teki kosei* [*The family-modeled view/construction of Japanese society*]. Tokyo: Gakuseishobo.

Kiesler, S., Siegel, J., & McGuire, T. W. (1984). Social psychological aspects of computer-mediated communication. *American Psychologist, 39,* 1123-1134.

Kim, Y. Y. (1988). *Communication and cross-cultural adaptation: An integrative theory.* Clevedon, UK: Multilingual Matters.

Kim, Y. Y. (1991a). Intercultural communication competence: A systems-theoretic view. In S. Ting-Toomey & F. Korzenny (Eds.), *Cross-cultural interpersonal communication* (pp. 259-275). Newbury Park, CA: Sage.

Kim, Y. Y. (1991b). Intercultural personhood: An integration of Eastern and Western perspectives. In L. A. Samovar & R. E. Porter (Eds.), *Intercultural communication: A reader* (6th ed., pp. 401-411). Belmont, CA: Wadsworth.

King, Y. Y., & Bond, M. (1985). The Confucian paradigm of man: A sociological view. In W. Teng & D. Wu (Eds.), *Chinese culture and mental health: An overview* (pp. 29-46). New York: Academic Press.

Kleinberg, J. (1989). Cultural clash between managers: America's Japanese firms. *Advances in International Comparative Management, 4,* 221-243.

Kraemer, A. J. (1973). *Development of a cultural self-awareness approach to instruction in intercultural communication.* Alexandria, VA: Human Resources.

Kraemer, A. J. (1978). *Teacher training workshop in intercultural communication: Instructor's guide.* Alexandria, VA: Human Resources.

Kras, E. S. (1989). *Management in two cultures: Bridging the gap between U.S. and Mexican managers.* Yarmouth, ME: Intercultural Press.

Krueger, G. P. (1976). *Teleconferencing in three communication modes as a function of the number of conferees.* Unpublished doctoral dissertation, Johns Hopkins University, Baltimore.

Kujawa, D. (1983). Technology strategy and industrial relations: Case studies of Japanese multinationals in the United States. *Journal of International Business Studies, 14,* 9-22.

Kumara, U., Hara, Y., & Yano, N. (1991). On understanding behavior characteristics of Japanese manufacturing workers: An analysis of job climate. *International Journal of Intercultural Relations, 15,* 129-148.

Kume, T. (1985). Managerial attitudes toward decision-making: North America and Japan. In W. Gudykunst, L. Stewart, & S. Ting-Toomey (Eds.), *Communication, culture, and organizational processes* (pp. 231-251). Beverly Hills, CA: Sage.

Lagmay, A. (1984). Western psychology in the Philippines: Impact and response. *International Journal of Psychology, 19,* 31-44.

Laidlaw, K. A. (1977). The industrial community in Peru: An experiment in worker participation. *International Review of Modern Sociology, 7,* 1-11.

Landis, D., & Brislin, R. W. (Eds.). (1983). *Handbook of intercultural training.* New York: Pergamon.

Larkin, T. J., & Larkin, S. (1993). *Communicating change.* New York: McGraw-Hill.

Lauterbach, A. (1966). *Enterprise in Latin America: Business attitudes in a developing economy*. Ithaca, NY: Cornell University Press.

Lawrence, P., & Lorsch, J. (1967). *Organization and environment: Managing differentiation and integration*. Cambridge, MA: Harvard University Press.

Leak, J., & Smith, R. (1984). Factoring receivables: Tax considerations of investing accumulated foreign earnings. *Tax Executive, 36,* 197-209.

Lebra, T. (1976). *Japanese patterns of behavior*. Honolulu: University of Hawaii Press.

Lebra, T. (1992). *Japanese social organization*. Honolulu: University of Hawaii Press.

Lee, C. (1983, July). Cross-cultural training: Don't leave home without it. *Training,* pp. 20-25.

Lee, Y., & Larwood, L. (1983). The socialization of expatriate managers in multinational firms. *Academy of Management Journal, 26,* 657-665.

Leitko, T., & Kowalewski, D. (1985). Industry structure and organizational deviance: Multinational corporations and questionable foreign payments. *Contemporary Crises, 9,* 127-147.

Lieberman, D. A. (1991). Ethnocognitivism and problem solving. In L. A. Samovar & R. E. Porter (Eds.), *Intercultural communication: A reader* (6th ed., pp. 229-234). Belmont, CA: Wadsworth.

Lieberman, D. A. (1993). Ethnocognitivism, problem solving, and hemisphericity. In L. A. Samovar & R. E. Porter (Eds.), *Intercultural communication: A reader* (7th ed., pp. 178-193). Belmont, CA: Wadsworth.

Lieberman, D. A., Kosokoff, S., & Kosokoff, J. (1988). What's common about common sense? *ORTESOL, 10,* 13-27.

Likert, R. (1961). *New patterns of management*. New York: McGraw-Hill.

Lincoln, J., Hanada, M., & McBride, K. (1986). Organizational structures in Japanese and U.S. manufacturing. *Administrative Science Quarterly, 31,* 338-364.

Lincoln, J., & Kalleberg, A. (1990). *Culture, control, and commitment: A study of work organization and work attitudes in the United States and Japan*. Cambridge, UK: Cambridge University Press.

Lincoln, J., Olson, J., & Hanada, M. (1978). Cultural effects on organizational structure: The case of Japanese firms in the United States. *American Sociological Review, 43,* 829-847.

Liu, S., & Allinson, R. (Eds.). (1988). *Harmony and strife: Contemporary perspectives, East and West*. Hong Kong: Chinese University Press.

Long, C. M. (1990). Persistence of subcultural organizations: An analysis surrounding the process of subcultural change. *Communication Quarterly, 38,* 1-12.

Lou, C., & Borden, G. (1989). Management communication in a multicultural corporation: The U.S. and Taiwan. *Howard Journal of Communications, 1*(4), 219-231.

Lucas, I. (1971). *Puerto Rican dropouts in Chicago: Numbers and motivation*. Chicago: Council on Urban Education.

Luenemann, U., & Knutson, T. (1993). Intercultural communication training: A call for continued interdisciplinary research. *Arizona Communication Association Journal, 19,* 122-148.

Maguire, M., & Pascale, R. (1978). Communication, decision making, and implementation among managers in Japanese and American managed companies in the United States. *Sociology and Social Research, 63,* 1-23.

Malabre, A. (1992, January 27). The outlook. *Wall Street Journal,* p. A1.

March, J., & Simon, H. (1958). *Organizations*. New York: John Wiley.

March, R. (1990). *The Japanese negotiator: Subtlety and strategy beyond Western logic*. Tokyo: Kodansha.

Marked change in communication patterns of Japanese participants at Fifth Annual Japanese-U.S. Shomoda Conference. (1981, September 4). *Asahi Shimbun* (Evening ed.), p. 3.

Martin, J. N. (Ed.). (1986). Theories and methods in cross-cultural orientation [Special issue]. *International Journal of Intercultural Relations, 10*(2).

Martin, S. (1964). Speech levels in Japan and Korea. In D. Hymes (Ed.), *Language in culture and society* (pp. 407-415). New York: Harper & Row.

Masao, K. (1973). Indigenous barriers to communication. *The Japan Interpreter, 8*(3), 96-108.

Mascarenhas, B. (1982). Coping with uncertainty in international business. *Journal of International Business Studies, 12*(2), 87-98.

Maslow, A. (1970). *Motivation and personality* (2nd ed.). New York: Harper & Row.

Mathis, G. (1986). How to plan a satellite videoconference. *Public Relations Journal, 33*(2), 36-37.

Matsumoto, M. (1988). *The unspoken way*—Hargei: *Silence in Japanese business society.* New York: Kodansha International.

McBrian, C. (1978). Language and social stratification: The case of Confucian society. *Anthropological Linguistics, 2,* 320-326.

McIntire, M. (1972). Terms of address in an academic setting. *Anthropological Linguistics, 14,* 286-291.

McNaughton, W. (1974). *The Confucian vision.* Ann Arbor: University of Michigan Press.

McPhee, R. D. (1985). Formal structure and organizational communication. In R. D. McPhee & P. K. Tompkins (Eds.), *Organizational communication: Traditional themes and new directions* (pp. 149-178). Beverly Hills, CA: Sage.

Mendenhall, M. E., Dunbar, E., & Oddou, G. R. (1987). Expatriate selection, training, and career-pathing: A review and critique. *Human Resource Management, 26,* 331-345.

Meyer, D. (1986). Taxation of intellectual property: Foreign aspects. *Tax Executive, 38,* 127-138.

Miller, E. (1973). The international selection decision: A study of managerial behavior in the selection decision process. *Academy of Management Journal, 16,* 234-252.

Miller, V. (1989, May). *A quasi-experimental study of newcomers' information-seeking behaviors during organizational entry.* Paper presented at the Annual Meeting of the International Communication Association, San Francisco.

Misumi, J., & Peterson, M. F. (1985). The performance-maintenance (PM) theory of leadership: Review of a Japanese research program. *Administrative Science Quarterly, 30,* 198-223.

Moran, R. T., & Harris, P. R. (1982). *Managing cultural synergy.* Houston: Gulf.

Morrow, L. (1992, February 10). Japan in the mind of America. *Time,* pp. 16-21.

Moseley, R. (1992, November 29). On brink of unity Europe fracturing. *Chicago Tribune,* p. 1.

Mumford, S. J. (1983). The cross-cultural experience: The program manager's perspective. In D. Landis & R. Brislin (Eds.), *Handbook of intercultural training: Vol. 2. Issues in training methodology* (pp. 83-99). New York: Pergamon.

Murakami, Y., Kumon, S., & Sato, S. (1979). *Bunmei to shite no ie shakai [The Ie society as a civilization].* Tokyo: Chuokoronsha.

Nakane, C. (1967). *Tateshakai no ningen kankei [Human relations in a vertical society].* Tokyo: Kodansha International.

Nakane, C. (1970). *Japanese society.* Berkeley: University of California Press.

Nakanishi, M. (1984, May). *The nature of the Japanese productivity system: Its implications to organizational communication.* Paper presented at a meeting of the International Communication Association, San Francisco.

Nakanishi, M. (1986). Perceptions of self-disclosure in initial interaction: A Japanese sample. *Human Communication Research, 13,* 167-190.

Neustupny, J. (1987). *Communicating with the Japanese.* Tokyo: Japan Times.

Nishida, H. (1985). Japanese intercultural communication competence and cross-cultural adjustment. *International Journal of Intercultural Relations, 9*(3), 277-289.

Nivison, D., & Wright, A. (Eds.). (1959). *Confucianism in action.* Stanford, CA: Stanford University Press.

Nomura, N., & Barnlund, D. (1983). Patterns of interpersonal criticism in Japan and the United States. *International Journal of Intercultural Relations, 7*(1), 1-18.

Nonaka, I. (1990). Redundant, overlapping organization: A Japanese approach to managing the innovation process. *California Management Review, 32,* 27-38.

Northrop, F. (1966). *The meeting of the East and the West.* New York: Collier. (Original work published 1946)

Nystrom, P. (1990). Vertical exchanges and organizational commitments of American business managers. *Group and Organizational Studies, 15,* 296-312.

Ogino, T., Misono, Y., & Fukushima, C. (1985). Diversity of honorific usage in Tokyo: A sociolinguistic approach based on a field survey. *International Journal of Sociology of Language, 55,* 23-29.

Okabe, R. (1973). Yukichi Fukuzawa: A promulgator of Western rhetoric. *Quarterly Journal of Speech, 59,* 186-195.

Okabe, R. (1983). Cultural assumptions of East and West: Japan and the United States. In W. Gudykunst (Ed.), *Intercultural communication theory: Current perspectives* (pp. 21-44). Beverly Hills, CA: Sage.

Okabe, R. (1987). Cultural assumptions of East and West: Japan and the United States. In W. Gudykunst (Ed.), *Intercultural communication theory* (pp. 21-44). Newbury Park, CA: Sage.

Okabe, R. (1989, November). Unpublished statements as a responder to a panel of papers presented in the Intercultural Rhetoric Division, at a meeting of the Speech Communication Association, San Francisco.

Olaniran, B. (1993). Japanese managerial communication processes: Implications for U.S. organizations. *Arizona Communication Association Journal, 19,* 166-185.

Oliver, R. (1962). *Culture and communication: The problem of penetrating national and cultural boundaries.* Springfield, IL: Charles C Thomas.

O'Reilly, B. (1992, October 19). How to keep exports on a roll. *Fortune,* pp. 68-72.

Ostrom, D. (1991, February 1). SII follow-up talks focus on antimonopoly action. *Japan Economic Institute Report, 4*(B), 5-7.

Ouchi, W. (1981). *Theory Z: How American business can meet the Japanese challenge.* Reading, MA: Addison-Wesley.

Page, N. R., & Wiseman, R. L. (1993). Supervisory behavior and worker satisfaction in the United States, Mexico, and Spain. *Journal of Business Communication, 30,* 161-180.

Paige, R. M. (1986). Trainer competencies: The missing conceptual link in orientation. *International Journal of Intercultural Relations, 10,* 135-158.

Paige, R. M., & Martin, J. N. (1983). Ethical issues and ethics in cross-cultural training. In D. Landis & R. W. Brislin (Eds.), *Handbook of intercultural training: Vol. 1. Issues in theory and design* (pp. 36-60). New York: Pergamon.

Pareek, U., & Rao, T. (1980). Cross-cultural surveys and interviewing. In H. Triandis & J. Berry (Eds.), *Handbook of cross-cultural psychology* (Vol. 2, pp. 127-180). Boston: Allyn & Bacon.

Pascale, R. (1978). Communication decision making across cultures: Japanese and American comparisons. *Administrative Science Quarterly, 23,* 91-109.

Pascale, R. T., & Athos, A. G. (1981). *The art of Japanese management: Applications for American executives.* New York: Warner.

Pegels, C. (1984). *Japan vs. the West: Implications for management.* Boston: Kluwer-Nijhoff.

Pennington, D. (1985). Intercultural communication. In L. A. Samovar & R. E. Porter (Eds.), *Intercultural communication: A reader* (4th ed., pp. 30-39). Belmont, CA: Wadsworth.

Perez Perdomo, R. (1990). Corruption and business in present-day Venezuela. *Journal of Business Ethics, 9,* 555-566.

Perlmutter, H. V. (1969). The tortuous evolution of the multinational corporation. *Columbia Journal of World Business, 4,* 9-18.

Perlmutter, H. V., & Heenan, D. A. (1983). How multinational should your top managers be? In D. N. Dickson (Ed.), *Managing effectively in the world workplace* (pp. 69-87). New York: John Wiley.

Philips, A. F. (1983). Computer conferences: Success or failure. In R. Bostrom (Ed.), *Communication yearbook 7* (pp. 837-856). Beverly Hills, CA: Sage.

Philipsen, G. (1987). The prospect for cultural communication. In L. E. Kincaid (Ed.), *Communication theory from Eastern and Western perspectives* (pp. 245-254). New York: Academic Press.

Pollard, W. R. (1989). Gender stereotypes and gender roles in cross-cultural education: The cultural assimilator. *International Journal of Intercultural Relations, 13,* 57-72.

Porter, R. (1972). An overview of intercultural communication. In L. A. Samovar & R. E. Porter (Eds.), *Intercultural communication: A reader* (pp. 4-23). Belmont, CA: Wadsworth.

Poynter, T. (1986). Managing government intervention: A strategy for defending the subsidiary. *Columbia Journal of World Business, 21*(4), 55-65.

Prosser, R. (1989). *The cultural dialogue.* Washington, DC: SIETAR.

Putnam, L. L., & Cheney, G. C. (1983). A critical review of research traditions in organizational communication. In M. Mandler (Ed.), *Communications in transition* (pp. 206-224). New York: Praeger.

Rapoport, C. (1992, June 29). The torch Swede invades the U.S. *Fortune,* pp. 76-79.

Rauch, J. (1992). *The outnation: A search for the soul of Japan.* Boston: Harvard Business School Press.

Redding, S. G., & Pugh, P. (1986). The formal and informal: Japanese and Chinese organization structures. In S. R. Clegg, D. Dunphy, & S. Redding (Eds.), *The enterprise and management in East Asia* (pp. 54-65). Hong Kong: Center for Asian Studies.

Rehder, R. R. (1968). *Latin American management: Development and performance.* Reading, MA: Addison-Wesley.

Rehder, R. R. (1981). What American and Japanese managers are learning from each other. *Business Horizons, 24,* 63-70.

Rehder, R. R. (1988). Japanese transplants: A new model for Detroit. *Business Horizons, 31,* 52-61.

Reid, J. (1987). The learning style preferences of ESL students. *TESOL Quarterly, 21,* 87-111.

Reischauer, E. (1977). *The Japanese.* Cambridge, MA: Harvard University Press.

Remembering the unthinkable. (1992, November 7). *The Economist,* p. 17.

Rice, R. E. (1984). Mediated group communication. In R. E. Rice (Ed.), *The new media: Communication, research, and technology* (pp. 129-154). Beverly Hills, CA: Sage.

Rice, R. E., & Richards, W. D., Jr. (1985). An overview of network analysis methods and programs. In B. Dervin & M. Voigt (Eds.), *Progress in communication sciences* (Vol. 7, pp. 105-165). Norwood, NJ: Ablex.

Riquelme Perez, J. (1968). Managerial resource development in Chile. In R. R. Rehder (Ed.), *Latin American management: Development and performance* (pp. 119-134). Reading, MA: Addison-Wesley.

Roberts, K. (1970). On looking at an elephant: An evaluation of cross-cultural research related to organizations. *Psychological Bulletin, 74,* 327-350.

Ronen, S. (1989). Training the international assignee. In R. A. Katzell (Ed.), *Training and development in organizations* (pp. 417-453). San Francisco: Jossey-Bass.

Rosch, M., & Segler, K. (1987). Communication with Japanese. *Management International Review, 27,* 56-67.

Rosenzweig, P., & Singh, J. (1991). Organizational environments and the multinational enterprise. *Academy of Management Review, 16,* 340-361.

Rossi, A., & Todd-Mancillas, W. (1987). Machismo as a factor affecting the use of power and communication in the managing of personal disputes: Brazilian versus American male managers. *Journal of Social Behavior and Personality, 2*(1), 93-101.

Rowland, D. (1985). *Japanese business etiquette: A practical guide to success with the Japanese.* New York: Warner.

Ruben, B. D. (1977). Human communication and cross-cultural effectiveness. *International and Intercultural Communication Annual, 4,* 98-105.

Ruffner, E., & Ettkin, L. (1987). When a circle is not a circle. *Advanced Management Journal, 52,* 9-15.

Sackmann, S. A. (1992). Culture and subcultures. *Administrative Science Quarterly, 37,* 140-161.

Saeed, S. M. (1986). *Managerial challenge in the Third World.* New York: Praeger.

Samovar, L. A., & Porter, R. E. (Eds.). (1988). *Intercultural communication: A reader* (5th ed.). Belmont, CA: Wadsworth.

Samovar, L. A., Porter, R. E., & Jain, N. C. (1981). *Understanding intercultural communication.* Belmont, CA: Wadsworth.

Sarros, J. (1992). What leaders say they do: An Australian example. *Leadership and Organizational Development Journal, 13,* 21-27.

Saville-Troike, M. (1982). *The ethnography of communication: An introduction.* New York: Basil Blackwell.

Schneiderman, B. (1987). *Designing the user interface.* Reading, MA: Addison-Wesley.

Schollhammer, H. (1971). Organizational structures of MNCs. *Academy of Management Journal, 14,* 345-365.

Schonberger, R. (1982). *Japanese manufacturing techniques: Nine hidden lessons in simplicity.* New York: Free Press.

Schonberger, R. (1986). *World class manufacturing.* New York: Free Press.

Schonberger, R. (1987). *World class manufacturing casebook: Implementing JIT and TQC.* New York: Free Press.

Schwartz, A. J. (1989). Middle-class educational values among Latino gang members in East Los Angeles County high schools. *Urban Education, 24*(3), 323-342.

Schwartz, B. (1959). Some polarities in Confucian thought. In D. Nivison & A. Wright (Eds.), *Confucianism in action* (pp. 50-62). Stanford, CA: Stanford University Press.

Schwartzman, H. B. (1993). *Ethnography in organizations*. London: Sage.

Scott, W. G. (1967). *Organizational theory*. Homewood, IL: Irwin.

Seddon, J. (1987). Assumptions, culture, and performance appraisal. *Journal of Management Development, 6*(3), 47-54.

Seror, A. (1988). Cross-cultural organizational analysis: Research methods and the Aston Program. *International Studies of Management and Organization, 18,* 31-43.

Sethi, S. P. (1987). The multinational challenge. *New Management, 4,* 53-55.

Shively, D. (1959). Motoda Eifu: Confucian lecturer to the Meiji emperor. In D. Nivison & A. Wright (Eds.), *Confucianism in action* (pp. 302-334). Stanford, CA: Stanford University Press.

Shuter, R. (1984, September 2). Know the local rules of the game. *New York Times,* pp. 86-87.

Shuter, R. (1985a). Assignment America: Foreign managers beware. *International Management, 40*(6), 83-87.

Shuter, R. (1985b, November). *Intercultural organizational communication.* Paper presented at the Annual Meeting of the Speech Communication Association, Denver.

Shuter, R. (1985c, November 22). When the manager is a stranger in a familiar land. *Wall Street Journal,* p. 55.

Shuter, R. (1989). The international marketplace. In M. K. Asante & W. B. Gudykunst (Eds.), *Handbook of international and intercultural communication* (pp. 392-406). Newbury Park, CA: Sage.

Shuter, R. (1990a). The centrality of culture. *Southern Journal of Communication, 55,* 237-249.

Shuter, R. (1990b). When the boss is a stranger in a familiar land. In D. Asman (Ed.), *Wall Street Journal on managing* (pp. 213-219). Garden City, NY: Doubleday.

Shuter, R. (1992, May). *Confessions of an intercultural organizational consultant: An action research framework for conducting intercultural organizational investigations.* Paper presented at a meeting of the International Communication Association, Miami.

Siegel, G. B. (1984). Performance appraisal for development of human resources in the Democratic Republic of the Sudan. *Public Personnel Management, 13*(2), 147-156.

Siegle, L. (1993). Management differences between the German and French. *Guardian, 13,* 17-21.

Simon, J. (1978). *Basic research methods in the social sciences.* New York: Random House.

Slobin, D., Miller, S., & Porter, L. (1968). Forms of address and social relations in a business organization. *Journal of Personality and Social Psychology, 8,* 289-293.

Smircich, L., & Calas, M. (1987). Organizational culture: A critical assessment. In F. M. Jablin, L. L. Putnam, K. H. Roberts, & L. W. Porter (Eds.), *Handbook of organizational communication: An interdisciplinary perspective* (pp. 228-263). Newbury Park, CA: Sage.

Smith, A., & Tayeb, M. (1988). Organizational structures and processes. In M. Bond (Ed.), *The cross-cultural challenge to social psychology* (pp. 116-127). Newbury Park, CA: Sage.

Smith, P. (1992). Organizational behaviors and national cultures. *British Journal of Management, 3,* 39-51.

Smith, P., & Peterson, M. (1988). *Leadership, organizations, and culture.* Newbury Park, CA: Sage.

Sommer, R. (1969). *Personal space.* Englewood Cliffs, NJ: Prentice Hall.

Spradley, J. P. (1979). *The ethnographic interview.* New York: Holt, Rinehart & Winston.

Spradley, J. P. (1980). *Participant observation.* New York: Holt, Rinehart & Winston.

Sproull, L., & Kiesler, S. (1986). Reducing social context clues: Electronic mail in organizational communication. *Management Science, 32,* 1492-1512.

Stanford surgeon quits, citing sex harassment. (1991, June 4). *New York Times,* p. A22.

Starosta, W. (1993). Re-centering culture within communication studies. *Arizona Communication Association Journal, 19,* 19-26.

State of Oregon Employment Division. (1993). *Mission statement.* Salem: Author.

Stebbings, R. Y. (1987). Export controls: Extraterritorial conflict: The dilemma of the host country employee. *Case Western Reserve Journal of International Law, 19,* 303-341.

Steers, R. M. (1989). The cultural imperative in HRM research. *Research in Personnel and Human Resources Management, 1*(Suppl.), 23-32.

Stewart, E. (1972). *American cultural patterns: A cross-cultural perspective.* La Grange Park, IL: Intercultural Network.

Stewart, E. (1985). Culture and decision making. In W. Gudykunst, L. Stewart, & S. Ting-Toomey (Eds.), *Communication, culture, and organizational processes* (pp. 177-211). Beverly Hills, CA: Sage.

Stewart, L. (1988). Japanese and American management: Participative decision making. In L. A. Samovar & R. E. Porter (Eds.), *Intercultural communication: A reader* (5th ed., pp. 182-185). Belmont, CA: Wadsworth.

Stewart, T. A. (1991, August 12). GE keeps those ideas coming. *Fortune,* pp. 41-49.

Strauss, S. (1978). A social world perspective. *Studies in Symbolic Interaction, 1,* 119-126.

Stull, J. (1985). Demonstrating empathy for foreign-born employees through openness and acceptance: A quasi-experimental field study. *Journal of Business Communication, 23,* 31-40.

Sullivan, J. (1981). The relationship between conflict resolution approaches and trust: A cross-cultural study. *Academy of Management Journal, 24,* 803-815.

Sundaram, A., & Black, J. (1992). The environment and internal organization of multinational enterprises. *Academy of Management Review, 17,* 729-757.

Swierczak, F. (1991). Leadership and culture: Comparing Asian managers. *Leadership and Organization Development Journal, 12,* 3-10.

Tayeb, M. (1987). Contingency theory and culture: A study of matched English and Indian manufacturing firms. *Organization Studies, 8*(3), 241-261.

Taylor, W. (1991). The logic of global business: An interview with ABB's Percy Barnevick. *Harvard Business Review, 69*(2), 90-105.

Teagarden, M. B., & von Glinow, M. A. (1990). Contextual determinants of HRM effectiveness in cooperative alliances: Mexican evidence [Special issue]. *Management International Review, 30,* 23-36.

Thayer, N. B., & Weiss, S. E. (1987). The changing logic of a former minor power. In H. Binnendijk (Ed.), *National negotiating style* (pp. 45-74). Washington, DC: U.S. Department of State, Foreign Service Institute.

Thornton, S. (1990). Leadership traits that work worldwide. *Association Management, 42,* 22-34.

Ticehurst, W. (1992, May). *Getting to the bottom of cross-cultural measurement: Does it mean the same down under?* Paper presented at a meeting of the International Communication Association, Miami, FL.

Ting-Toomey, S. (1985). Toward a theory of conflict and culture. In W. Gudykunst, L. Stewart, & S. Ting-Toomey (Eds.), *Communication, culture, and organizational processes* (pp. 71-86). Beverly Hills, CA: Sage.

Ting-Toomey, S. (1988). Intercultural conflict styles: A face-negotiation theory. In Y. Kim & W. Gudykunst (Eds.), *Theories in intercultural communication* (pp. 213-235). Newbury Park, CA: Sage.

Toyne, B. (1976). Host country managers of multinational firms: An evaluation of variables affecting their managerial thinking patterns. *Journal of International Business Studies, 7*(1), 39-55.

Triandis, H. C. (1972). *The analysis of subjective culture.* New York: John Wiley.

Triandis, H. C. (1988). Collectivism vs. individualism: A reconceptualization of a basic concept in cross-cultural social psychology. In G. Verma & C. Bagley (Eds.), *Crosscultural studies of personality, attitudes, and cognition* (pp. 60-95). New York: Macmillan.

Triandis, H. C. (1991, August). *Training for diversity.* Paper presented at a meeting of the American Psychological Association, San Francisco.

Triandis, H. C., & Albert, R. (1987). Cross-cultural perspectives. In F. Jablin (Ed.), *Handbook of organizational communication* (pp. 264-295). Newbury Park, CA: Sage.

Triandis, H. C., Brislin, R., & Hui, C. (1988). Cross-cultural training across the individualism-collectivism divide. *International Journal of Intercultural Relations, 12*(3), 269-288.

Trimble, J. (1988). Putting the etic to work: Applying social psychological principles in cross-cultural settings. In M. Bond (Ed.), *The cross-cultural challenge to social psychology* (pp. 109-121). Newbury Park, CA: Sage.

Tung, R. L. (1981). Selection and training of personnel for overseas assignments. *Columbia Journal of World Business, 16,* 68-78.

Tung, R. L. (1984). *Key to Japan's economic strength: Human power.* Lexington, MA: Lexington.

Tung, R. L. (1987). Expatriate assignments: Enhancing success and minimizing failure. *Academy of Management Executive, 1*(2), 117-126.

Tung, R. L. (1988). Career issues in international assignments. *Academy of Management Executive, 2,* 241-244.

Tung, R. L. (1990). International human resource management policies and practices: A comparative analysis. *Research in Personnel and Human Resources Management, 2*(Suppl.), 171-186.

Uhlig, R. P., Farber, D. J., & Bair, J. H. (1979). *The office of the future: Communication and computers.* Amsterdam: North-Holland.

U.S. Bureau of the Census. (1991). *Statistical abstract of the United States: 1991.* Washington, DC: Government Printing Office.

Usunier, J. (1991). Business time perceptions and national cultures: A comparative survey. *Management International Review, 31,* 197-217.

Van Maanen, J. (1976). Breaking in: Socialization to work. In R. Dubin (Ed.), *Handbook of work, organization, and society* (pp. 67-120). Chicago: Rand McNally.

Van Maanen, J., & Barley, S. (1982). *Occupational communities: Culture and control in organizations* (TR-10 Technical Report). Cambridge, MA: Sloan School of Management.

Vineberg, G. (1985). Multinationals hedging against currency shifts. *Chain Store Age Executive, 61*(6), 15-17.

Vroom, V., & Yetton, P. (1973). *Leadership and decision making.* Pittsburgh: University of Pennsylvania Press.

Walton, E. (1961). How effective is the grapevine? *Personnel, 28,* 45-49.

Wanner, B. (1991, May 24). Faction leader's death sparks political maneuvering. *Japan Economic Institute Report, 20*(B), 1.

Waters, H. (1992). Race, culture, and interpersonal conflict. *International Journal of Intercultural Relations, 16,* 437-454.

Weihrich, H. (1990). Management practices in the United States, Japan, and the People's Republic of China. *Industrial Management, 32,* 3-7.

Welch, J. (1988, April 27). Managing for the nineties. *GE Speech Reprint.*

Welch, J. (1993, January 25). Jack Welch's lessons for success. *Fortune,* pp. 86-93.

Wetzel, P. (1988). Are powerless communication strategies the Japanese norm? *Language in Society, 17,* 555-564.

White, R., & Poynter, T. (1984). Strategies for foreign-owned subsidiaries in Canada. *Business Quarterly, 49*(1), 59-69.

Whitney, C. (1993, April 4). With Europe in flux, no more politics as usual. *New York Times,* p. A3.

Wiio, O. (1989, May). *Intercultural and international issues and variables in comparative studies in organizational communication.* Paper presented at a meeting of the International Communication Association, San Francisco.

Wilkes, M. V. (1990). Networks, e-mail, and fax. *Communications of the ACM, 33,* 631-633.

Wittenberg-Cox, A. (1991). Delivering global leaders: Top multinationals are putting high fliers through an exclusive management course. *International Management, 46*(1), 52-53.

Womack, D. (1982, November). *A model of negotiations in intercultural and organizational settings.* Paper presented at a meeting of the Speech Communication Association, Louisville, KY.

Woods, W. (1992, July 27). The global 500. *Fortune,* pp. 175-200.

Workout. (1991, September). *GE Silicones News* [Special issue], pp. 1-7.

World Bank. (1993). *World development report.* New York: Oxford University Press.

Yasin, M. M., & Stahl, M. J. (1990). An empirical investigation of managerial motivational effectiveness in the Arab culture. *International Studies of Management and Organization, 20*(3), 69-81.

Yuasa, Y. (1977). *Shintai: Toyoteki shinshinron no kokoromi [The body: An Asian view of mind and body].* Tokyo: Sobunsha.

Yum, Y. (1987a). Korean philosophy and communication. In D. Kincaid (Ed.), *Communication theory: Eastern and Western perspectives* (pp. 71-85). New York: Academic Press.

Yum, Y. (1987b). The practice of *uye-ri* in interpersonal relationships in Korea. In D. Kincaid (Ed.), *Communication theory: Eastern and Western perspectives* (pp. 87-100). New York: Academic Press.

Yum, Y. (1988). The impact of Confucianism of interpersonal relationships and communication patterns in East Asia. *Communication Monographs, 55,* 374-388.

Zeira, Y., & Shenkar, O. (1990). Interactive and specific parent characteristics: Implications for management and human resources international joint ventures. *Management International Review, 30,* 7-22.

Zhurvlev, A. L., & Shorokhova, E. V. (1984). Actual problems of applied sociology and social psychology. *Psikjologicheskii Zhurnal, 6*(3), 156-157.

Index

Accommodation, 9, 134-138
Adaptation, 9, 139
Address, forms of, 51, 53, 160
Africa, 6, 7, 79, 95
African Americans, 143, 146, 154-155
Amae, 48, 50, 52, 54-56, 63-64
Ambiguity, 125
American Indians, 154
American-Japanese communication, 9,
   117-140
Arabs, 6
Argentina, 82, 95, 97
Asea Brown Boveri (ABB), 95, 97,
   104-114
Asia, 6, 10, 11, 79, 99
Asian Americans, 154
Assimilation, 23, 25
Audioconference, 27-28
Autonomy, 18

Best Practice Program, 102-104
Brazil, 7, 82-83, 87
Britain, 4-5, 33, 35, 40, 47, 54, 62, 65,
   68, 74, 104

Canada, 4-7, 54
Centralization, 9, 15, 17-19, 81
Chile, 77, 82-83, 87
China, 5-7, 33, 70-71, 97
Classical economic theory, 95
Co-cultural communication, 141-152,
   159-160
Collectivism, 5, 15, 23-24, 4-7, 49-50,
   52, 54, 56-57, 62-63, 67-70, 73-74,
   82, 91, 118, 129, 143, 149-151
Colombia, 82-87, 93
Communication interaction patterns, 121

Compodrazgo, 79
Computers, 25-27
Confianza, 86-87
Confucian philosophy, 4-5, 48-51, 60,
   66-67, 70-71, 74
Connectionalism, 77
Contextuality, 15, 25, 77
Contingency theory, 4, 41
Continuous improvement process, 111-112
Convergence, 34-36, 40, 47, 72-73
Cross-Functional Teamwork Program,
   101-103, 111-112
Cultural diversity, 10, 20, 22-23, 25, 30,
   141, 153-165
Cultural minorities, 153-165
Culture-free hypothesis, 34
Culture-invariance, 30-31
Culture-variance, 30-32, 34-36

Decentralization, 17
Decisionmaking, 5, 13, 46, 53, 55, 57,
   59-61, 80-82, 90-91, 118-119, 125,
   131-132
Denmark, 6, 104
Distance, 5, 14-15, 19, 21
Divergence, 9, 34-35, 134-135, 137-138,
   155

Economic development in U.S. and
   Western Europe, 94-114
Electronic mail, 27
Emic approach, 5, 6, 10, 35, 48
Environmental complexity, 12, 13, 29
Equivalence:
   conceptual/linguistic, 39, 42
   functional, 39, 42
   metric, 39-40, 42

Ethnocentric, 13, 20-21, 45-46, 54, 57, 71-72
Ethnography, 88-89, 93
Ethos, 67-68
Etic approach, 5, 10, 35
Europe, 3, 5-7, 10-11, 16, 18, 45-46, 54, 60, 71-72, 79, 94-14, 154, 156
European Economic Community (EEC), 104-105
Expatriate, 5, 8, 19, 4-5, 47, 49-52, 61, 68, 74, 154, 155
Explicit values, 147-148

Facsimile (fax) communication, 26-27
Field independent/field dependent, 151
Formalization, 9, 15-16, 35, 76, 79, 91-92, 130
France, 6, 7, 32, 104, 107

Gaijin, 52, 54, 58, 66, 69
General Electric Corporation (GE), 95, 97-107, 111-114
Geocentric, 13-14, 20-21
Germany, 6-8, 62, 65, 68, 99, 104, 107, 109
Giri, 48, 54-56, 64
Greco-Roman rhetorical tradition, 67

Haragei, 48, 52, 54-56, 59-61, 65-69
Hierarchy, 124, 130-131
High-context, 15, 25, 27-28, 32, 52, 57, 118, 151
High-speed management, 112
Hispanics, 142-143, 154-156
Holland, 99
Hong Kong, 4, 71, 95-97
Honne, 45, 47-48, 52-56, 58, 61, 67-69, 71-72, 74
Horizontal complexity, 15, 17

Implicit values, 148-149
Individualism, 5, 15, 23-24, 49, 51, 54, 56, 58, 61, 63-65, 72, 81-83, 91, 118, 129, 131, 143, 149-151
Information transmission, 124, 128
In-group, 122

Internal benchmarking system, 106, 109-112

Japan, 3-7, 9-10, 21, 23-25, 32-33, 35, 45-74, 77, 96, 99, 103-104, 107, 117-139, 160
Japanese-Western communication, 45-74, 117-140
Jen, 49-54, 56-58, 60, 62-63, 67, 69, 71, 72
Jews, 162
Just-in-time production (JIT), 46, 62, 64, 72

Kaisha, 48, 66-67
Kao, 54
Keiretsu, 48, 50, 52-55, 73
Kimochi, 60
Kokoro, 48, 72
Korea, 23, 71, 97, 99, 155, 160

Language, 14, 20, 22, 26, 31-32, 41, 47, 51, 54, 60, 67, 89, 113, 118, 123-125, 133, 136, 138-156
Latin America, 6-7, 10-11, 75-93, 160
Leadership, 4, 5, 33, 53, 57, 111, 114, 140
Lesser developed nations (LDNs), 16
Li, 49-54, 56-58, 60, 63, 66-69, 71-72
Listening focus, 126
Low-context, 15, 25, 58, 61, 118, 150-151

Mainstream culture, 141-152, 156-157, 161-162
Malaysia, 97, 120
Management style/orientation, 6, 8, 34, 123-124, 130-133, 139
Marugakae, 48, 66, 68, 73
Masculinity-femininity, 5, 70, 118, 143, 149-150
Matomari, 53
Matrix management system, 106-113
Meishi, 50, 53-54
Message diffusion, 22
Mexico, 7, 47, 75, 77-78, 81-83, 87, 95, 97, 99
Motivation, 76, 90-91

NEGOPY, 22
Negotiated Linking Program, 100-101
Negotiating protocols, 45, 58-61, 69
Nemawashi, 53, 58, 125, 128, 132-133
Netherlands, 155
Network roles, 20
New communication technologies, 9, 15,
    19, 25-28
Nigeria, 7
Nihonjinron syndrome, 53
Ningensei, 45-74
Nomothetic model, 36-37
Nonverbal communication, 66, 68-69,
    123-126, 133, 137, 143

Omote, 71
Organizational assimilation, 9, 15, 19,
    22-23, 25
Organizational climate, 145, 159
Organizational culture, 146, 149, 155
Organizational protocols, 45, 54, 70, 117
Organizational universals, 4, 5, 7, 34-35
Ormoiyari, 60
Out-group, 122-123, 133
Overspecialization, 124, 127-128

Padrinazgo, 76, 87
Palanca, 76, 83-87, 93
Palestinian, 6
Parallel informal networks (PINs), 19-22
Patron, 79, 80, 83
Performance appraisal, 33, 34, 78
Performance protocols, 45, 64-70
Peru, 82
Polycentric, 13-14, 16, 20-21
Polycultural communication, 158
Portugal, 26, 79, 95, 97
Power-distance, 5, 15, 18-19, 21, 24, 27,
    70, 81-82, 90, 118, 143, 149, 160
Presentational protocols, 65-70
Proxemic protocols, 45, 48-49, 51,
    55-56, 61-64, 69, 71-72
Psychological profiles, 121
Public table negotiations, 48, 57-61

R&D programs, 102, 106, 107, 110-112

Reciprocity, 49-50, 52, 58-62, 67, 69, 79,
    87, 92
Regiocentric, 13-14, 20-21
Ringi, 58, 61

Sexual harassment, 160-161
Shoji, 61
Shu, 49-54, 56-60, 62-63, 69, 71-72
Singapore, 95-97
Socialization, 22-25
Soto, 48, 71
Soviet Union, 5
Spain, 6, 79, 95, 97
Speaking focus, 126
Speech accommodation theory, 9, 139
Speechmaking, 48-49, 64-70
Structuring processes, 9, 15, 16, 19
Sudan, 34, 40
Sweden, 6, 99, 104, 107, 155
Switzerland, 6, 104, 107
Systems theory, 4

Taiwan, 5, 71, 95-97, 99
Tatemae, 45, 47-48, 52-55, 58, 60-61,
    66, 69, 71, 74
Teleconferencing, 25-27
Thailand, 97
Theory-validation model, 36-37
Theory X, 56, 71
Theory Y, 56, 71
Theory Z, 64
Total quality management (TQM), 4-6,
    56-57, 62, 64, 70, 72
Town meeting format, 101
Training, 3, 9-10, 46, 75, 78, 89-90, 110,
    114, 140, 153-165
Tramitadores, 86
Transformational leadership, 111
Turn-taking styles, 28

U.S. Bureau of Economic Analysis, 12
Uchi, 48, 66, 67, 68, 71
Uncertainty-avoidance, 5, 15-16, 21,
    23-25, 81-82, 118, 143, 149
Uncertainty-reduction theory, 24, 118

United States, 3-6, 9-12, 16-18, 21,
  23-24, 26, 32-33, 35-36, 40, 46-47,
  51, 54, 57, 65, 71-83, 90, 92,
  94-114, 117-140, 153-165
Ura, 71

Validity, 9, 30, 34, 37, 39-41
Venezuela, 82-83, 87
Vertical complexity, 15-17
Videoconference, 28

Vietnamese, 141

WA, 48
Work performance, 124
Work style/orientation, 123-124,
  127-129, 133, 139

Z-communication, 73

About the Contributors

JEFFREY C. ADY is an Assistant Professor in the Department of Communication at the University of Hawaii, Manoa. He earned his PhD at the University of Kansas. His research interests include methodological analyses of cross-cultural studies, intercultural communication, and organizational processes.

ROSITA DASKAL ALBERT is an Associate Professor in the Department of Speech-Communication, University of Minnesota, Minneapolis. A native of Brazil, she received a PhD in social psychology from the University of Michigan. Her research has focused on Hispanic-Anglo interactions, on the development and evaluation of intercultural training, and on intercultural training in organizations. She proposed the field of "polycultural organizational communication" and is currently conducting research on French and American multinationals. Her research has appeared in the *Handbook of Intercultural Training, The Handbook of Organizational Communication,* the *International Journal of Intercultural Relations*, and *Management Communication Quarterly.* She is on the editorial board of the *International Journal of Intercultural Relations.*

LECIA ARCHER is a doctoral student in the Department of Communication at the University of Colorado, Boulder. She holds an MBA from San Diego State University. Her research interest is the impact of technology on organizational communication.

LING CHEN is an Assistant Professor of Communication at the University of Oklahoma, Norman. She received her PhD from the Communication Department at Ohio State University. Her major areas of interest are intercultural communication, interpersonal communication, and language and communication. Her work has been published in *Gazette* and the *Asian Journal of Communication.*

DONALD P. CUSHMAN is a Professor of Communication at the State University of New York, Albany. He coauthored (with Dudley Cahn) *Communication in Interpersonal Relations* and coedited (with Sarah Sanderson King) *High-Speed Management and Organizational Communication in the 1990s.* His work has appeared in all major journals in the field, and he has served as consultant to numerous organizations.

KRISTINE L. FITCH is an Assistant Professor in the Department of Communication at the University of Colorado, Boulder. She holds a PhD in communication from the University of Washington, Seattle. Her research interests are communication and culture. Her work has been published in *Communication Monographs, Communication Yearbook,* and *Journal of Research on Language and Social Interaction.*

LYNN M. FRITZ is a Customer Communication Director with Antolino and Associates, Inc., a financial services firm in Columbus, Ohio. She received her MA in communication from Ohio State University, Columbus. Her research interests include conflict management and decision making within organizations, and the impact of technology on these processes.

ALAN GOLDMAN is President of Goldman & Associates consulting group, with headquarters in Scottsdale, Arizona. He is a cross-cultural communication and management consultant. His research has appeared in a broad spectrum of communication, business, management, and psychology journals in the United States, Europe, and Japan. He has authored six books on human communication processes. While living in Tokyo, he consulted and conducted intercultural training for Japanese MNCs doing business with Western organizations. He has also served as Chief "Trade Around the World" writer for the Bush Administration and the U.S. Congress.

ELLENE GURTOV is a master's candidate in the Speech Communication Department at Portland State University in Oregon. Her interests are in issues related to communication in organizational settings.

YOUNG YUN KIM is a Professor of Communication at the University of Oklahoma, Norman. She received her PhD from Northwestern University, Evanston, Illinois. Her current research interests include the role of communication in cross-cultural adaptation of immigrants and sojourners, as well as in facilitating domestic interethnic relations. She has published extensively in academic journals and currently serves on several editorial boards, including *Human Communication Research, International Journal of Intercultural Relations,* and *Communication Theory.* Among her recently published books are *Communication and Cross-Cultural Adaptation, Theories in Intercultural Communication* (with W. Gudykunst), and *Communicating With Strangers* (with W. Gudykunst).

SARAH SANDERSON KING is Professor and former Chair of the Department of Communication at Central Connecticut State College, New Britain. Her five books include *Human Communication as a Field of Study, Political Communication: Engineering Visions of Order in the Socialist World,* and *High-Speed Management and Organizational Communication in the 1990s* the latter two coedited with Donald Cushman.

DEVORAH A. LIEBERMAN is an Associate Professor of Speech Communication at Portland State University in Oregon. Her research has focused on cultural diversity in the organization, ethnocognitivism, and intercultural education. She is actively involved in intercultural training and consulting. She coedited the international studies text: *Revealing the World: An Interdisciplinary Reader for International Studies.* Her work has appeared in speech communication and general semantics journals.

SHERYL PAULK is a doctoral candidate in the Department of Communication, University of Oklahoma, Norman, and works as the lead translator at an American-based Japanese firm. She received her BA at the University of Colorado, Boulder, and studied at Sophia University, Tokyo, for several years. Her research interests lie in the area of intercultural communication, with an emphasis on language and sociolinguistic interaction, particularly as they apply to the organizational setting.

ROBERT SHUTER is Professor and Chairperson of the Department of Communication and Rhetorical Studies at Marquette University, Milwaukee. He coined the term "intercultural organizational communication" in 1985 and has written numerous articles on the topic. His research has been published in such journals as *Journal of Social Psychology, Communication Monographs,* and *Journal of Communication,* as well as the *Wall Street Journal* and *New York Times.* He is currently on the editorial board of *Human Communication Research.*

JC. BRUNO TEBOUL is an Assistant Professor of Communication at DePaul University, Chicago. He received his PhD from the Communication Department at Ohio State University, Columbus. His research interests include organizational assimilation processes, small group communication, and communication in culturally diverse work settings. His work has appeared in *Communication Reports* and *Journal of Language and Social Psychology.*

RICHARD L. WISEMAN is a Professor of Speech Communication at California State University, Fullerton. His research interests include intercultural communication competence, interpersonal persuasion, and teaching effectiveness. He coedited *Intercultural Communication Competence* (with Jolene Koester) and has published work in *Communication Yearbook, Communication Monographs, Journal of Business Communication, Research in Higher Education,* and *International Journal of Intercultural Relations.* He has served as Chairperson to the Intercultural Communication Divisions of the Speech Communication Association and the Western States Communication Association.